SOUPS

SOUPS

Marguerite Patten

BLOOMSBURY

First published 1996 by Bloomsbury Publishing Plc,
2 Soho Square, London W1V 6HB

A copy of the CIP entry for this book is available
from the British Library

ISBN 0 7475 2736 9

10 9 8 7 6 5 4 3 2 1

Designed by Hugh Adams, AB3
Typeset by Hewer Text Composition Services, Edinburgh
Printed in Great Britain by Clays Ltd, St Ives plc

Contents

INTRODUCTION

Soup of the evening, beautiful soup!
Beautiful soup! who cares for fish,
Game, or any other dish?
Who would not give all else for two
Pennyworth only of beautiful soup?

Lewis Carroll (1832–98)

I do not entirely agree with the words spoken in *Alice in Wonderland* about the time to eat 'beautiful soup'. I welcome it in the middle of the day and late at night, as well as in the evening. Many soups are economical dishes, though the cost today may be a little more than two pennyworth. Soup is easy to digest and wonderfully soothing, so it is ideal when you are rather tired and unwilling to eat more solid foods. Hot soups are warming in cold weather and cold soups refreshing in the heat of summer.

Soup has been an important part of family and special occasion meals in many countries of the world for centuries. It is reported that the Ancient Greeks ate **black broth** (presumably a type of soup), but sadly I do not have a recipe for this. The Romans made soup, known as **polus**, and the historian **Apicus** records the impressive selection of vegetables, herbs and seasonings they used in cooking them.

The countries occupied by the Romans all have a great tradition of soup-making. Although the word **polus** is not used today, it was undoubtedly the origin of the French word **potage**. In England this became **'pottage'**, which has been used for centuries to describe some British soups.

The first chapter of this book gives information to help you make soups that have a perfect flavour and consistency. It includes recipes for various stocks – the secret of many good soups – although modern stock (bouillon) cubes can be used as an alternative when home-made stock is not available.

Our approach to stock has changed a great deal: no longer is there a large pot on the kitchen range into which liquid, leftover bones and other foods have to be boiled daily in an effort to stop the contents becoming rancid. Nowadays the stock is kept in the safety of the refrigerator or freezer, awaiting the time when it can be used. There is clear information about freezing stock in Chapter One and also at the end of recipes, for it is a great asset to have containers of soup waiting for you to heat as required.

Stock can be prepared in various ways: apart from in a saucepan, in the oven, in a microwave or in a pressure cooker (see page 11).

It is a mistake to think one needs a vast selection of ingredients to make a good soup – quite the contrary. If you make a **tomato soup**, or order it in a restaurant, you expect the soup to have a definite flavour of **tomatoes**. If, due to an over-long list of other ingredients, the **tomato** taste has been lost, it is *not* a good soup. Carefully chosen herbs, spices and other suitable ingredients must be chosen to enhance the flavour of the basic ingredient(s). You will find information about these in Chapter One.

Knowing how many keen cooks are short of time, Chapter Two is devoted to **quick soups**. Each of the varied recipes can be cooked within 30 minutes. The soups are based on vegetables, fish, meat, chicken, fruit and cheese.

Clear soups follow in Chapter Three. These will be enjoyed by people who appreciate the flavour of a classic consommé, and are ideal if you want to lose a little weight. There are many suggestions for giving a special touch to consommés, together with other clear soups, including those based on beer or wine. These retain an alcoholic flavour, but the alcohol content is destroyed during cooking.

Chapter Four includes vegetable soups from around the world, but all have one thing in common – I have kept the cooking times to a minimum to retain the flavour, colour and texture of the ingredients. This is a change from old-fashioned vegetable soups, where the cooking time was so long that the lovely fresh flavour of the vegetables was lost.

Obviously, this chapter will be of special appeal to vegetarians. Although some recipes suggest using chicken stock, this is a personal opinion and vegetarians can easily substitute vegetable stock (see page 15) or water with a vegetable stock cube.

Soups based on fish, meat, poultry and game fill Chapters Five, Six and Seven. Many of these soups are sufficiently satisfying to make a complete light meal, particularly the chowders, broths and intriguing sticky gumbo soups. A list of soups that make a one-dish meal appears just before the index (see page 337).

Hot soups far outnumber cold soups in this book, as hot ones are more popular. Sometimes, however, a hot soup can be turned into a cold one by adding a little extra liquid so that the consistency is perfect when the ingredients cool. As a lover of chilled, jellied and even iced soups, I am delighted to find that more and more people are discovering the virtues of cold soups on a warm day. You will find a good selection on pages 279 to 298.

In many countries soups based upon fruit are traditional favourites. We in Britain, alas, have not established that tradition. Fruit soups can be an appetizing and refreshing start to a meal at any time of the year, but they must be made with a subtle mixture of sweet and sharp or savoury flavours, so it does not appear you are serving a fruit dessert at the start of the meal.

I hope you will enjoy using this book and, like me, you will extol the virtues of good home-made soups at all times.

Marguerite Patten

MEASUREMENTS

All the recipes in this book give metric, imperial and American weights and measures. Note that American pints and tablespoons are smaller than the British equivalent.

Use measures from one column only – do not mix them.

All spoon measures are *level*.

Soups are not like cakes, where strict adherence to a recipe is important to maintain the balance of ingredients. In a soup the quantity of each ingredient is very much a matter of personal taste, but the recipes have been tested with the quantities given.

Choice of Ingredients

Where recipes give a choice of ingredients, such as butter or margarine, vegetable or chicken stock, the first-mentioned ingredient is my preferred choice.

Chapter One

PERFECT SOUPS

There is such a wide range of soups, based on an almost endless variety of ingredients and flavours, that it may sound difficult to give a few golden rules about making good ones. In fact, it is relatively simple to summarize these.

Flavour: Generally, soup is the first course of a meal, or the second course if served after an hors d'oeuvre: as such, the flavour must not be so pronounced that it will overwhelm the taste of the foods that are to follow; it should be interesting but not too strong. This point is emphasized in the introduction to the various chapters.

The soup should be well seasoned but never over-seasoned, so it is wise to add relatively little salt, pepper and other flavourings at the beginning of the cooking period. Taste the soup when it is cooked and adjust the seasoning just before serving.

If, by some unlucky chance, you over-salt the soup, see page 332.

Consistency: It is important to get this right. Purée soups, for example, should be rather like a thickish cream. The correct amount of liquid is given in the recipes but this is a guide only. If your saucepan lid does not fit as well as it should, you may lose more liquid than anticipated during the course of cooking. If a soup is kept heating gently for some time until ready to serve, the liquid will evaporate and the soup will become thicker. Check the consistency as well as the flavour at the last minute; too thick soups are not appealing.

If the soup is thinner than desired, there are various ways of correcting this (see page 8).

Additions: All the recipes in this book can be varied in many ways, so you can enjoy giving your own individual touch, but do not get carried away and add too many extra ingredients. The principal flavour in, say, a tomato soup should be tomatoes, not over-strong stock, herbs or spices. These ingredients should be included to bring out the taste of the tomatoes, not overwhelm them.

Appearance: The look of a soup is important, so choose garnishes that enhance the appearance, as well as the flavour, of the particular mixture of ingredients. Appropriate garnishes are suggested in the recipes, and there are additional suggestions in each chapter and on pages 299–331.

Temperature: Make sure soups are served at the right temperature. Hot soups should be piping hot, so warm the dishes before serving. Cold soups should be well chilled: a tepid soup is not appealing to most people.

Imagination: Be imaginative in your choice of soups. Nowadays we enjoy ingredients and dishes that come from many different countries, that is why I have included a number of soup recipes from around the world, as well as the much-loved familiar flavours. It is easy to obtain the ingredients in supermarkets or shops specializing in ethnic foods.

TO COOK SOUPS

The cooking time given in the recipes assumes the soup is being cooked in an ordinary saucepan. Choose a good heavy pan so there is no possibility of the ingredients burning, and make sure the lid fits as tightly as possible so that evaporation of the liquid is not more than it should be during the cooking process. If the lid on your pan is a poor fit, place a sheet of foil under it to ensure a tighter fit.

Other ways of cooking soups are outlined below. These may prove more convenient for you.

Oven cooking: If the oven is already being used, cooking soup in it too is a sensible way of saving fuel. It is also a good method if you want to leave the soup unattended for there is no possibility of it sticking to the pan. Make sure you use a covered casserole. I find oven cooking less suitable for vegetable soups because it is slow and therefore you lose the fresh flavour of the vegetables. It is, however, quite a good method for longer cooking fish and meat soups. Ideally, the ingredients should be brought to the boil on top of the cooker, then transferred to a casserole and covered tightly.

The initial cooking of onions and similar ingredients should be done in an ordinary pan, or in a casserole if made of suitable material, on top of the cooker.

Preheat the oven to 180°C/350°F/gas mark 4. Allow 50 per cent longer cooking time in the oven than when cooking in a saucepan.

Pressure cooking: This is an excellent way of cooking many soups because it saves time and results in an excellent flavour. Do not use the rack in the cooker. As explained in the chapter introductions, less liquid is needed for pressure cooking because the cooling time is shorter.

Use the pressure cooker, without a lid, as an ordinary pan to fry the onions or other ingredients at the beginning, and again at the end when adding egg yolks or cream.

Microwave cooking: This method of cooking soups does not save as much time as you might imagine because liquids are relatively slow to reach boiling point in a microwave. The introduction to each chapter includes specific hints on using a microwave for particular soups.

The initial frying of onions and suchlike can be done in the container in the microwave. Always chop the ingredients very evenly for this method of cooking.

When you add cream, eggs and other enriching ingredients, cook the soup slowly on a lower setting. Stir or whisk regularly and make sure the liquid does not boil.

Microwave soup in a large, microwave container with a lid, or cover it with cling film or kitchen paper during the cooking period. Use full power until the soup reaches boiling point, or is very hot (according to the instructions in the recipe), then set to defrost for the cooking time. If the soup seems to be cooking too quickly on this setting, turn to an even lower one.

Allow the soup to stand for at least 2 minutes before serving.

MICROWAVE TERMS

Various terms are used to describe the settings on a microwave. On the whole, I tend to use the words *full power*, but many manufacturers simply say *high*, which means exactly the same thing.

Defrost is a term used by most manufacturers of microwaves, and this gives half the full output.

If the recipe states 'turn to a low setting', I suggest you use *warm* or the lowest setting on your dial.

Just like cooking in an oven or a saucepan, you need to check cooking progress, for microwaves vary considerably in their output and therefore their speed of cooking.

As stated above, it is advisable to let microwaved soup stand for 2 minutes before serving because cooking continues during that time.

Safety first

Although microwave containers are specially manufactured, ovenproof glass bowls are ideal for making soup in a microwave; allow a sufficiently large container so there is no possibility of the soup boiling over. Reduce the setting if there is any danger of this happening.

Be very careful when removing hot containers from of the microwave. Use oven gloves to protect your hands. If the container is the type that could crack, place the bowl on a *dry* surface in the kitchen: a wooden board is ideal.

COMMON WAYS
TO THICKEN SOUPS

There are various ways of thickening soups to give the desired consistency. If you find the soup is thinner than you wish, this can be easily rectified by following steps 3, 4, 5 or 6 before serving.

1) **The ingredients** themselves help to thicken the mixture. Potatoes and other starchy root vegetables are excellent for this purpose, which is why vegetable soups are frequently made with no other thickening agent.

Similarly, when fish, meat, poultry and fruit soups are puréed, you will achieve just the right consistency without adding flour or any other thickener.

2) **Cereals**, particularly rice, are very popular additions to soup. Unless the recipe states to the contrary, you should use round-grain (pudding) rice or the Italian arborio (risotto) rice for thickening purposes, even though they do give a slightly cloudy appearance to the liquid. Long-grain rice gives a clearer liquid, but is not so effective at thickening.

Old-fashioned recipes use tapioca and sago instead of rice. If you would like to substitute these, use exactly the same quantity as stated for rice.

3) **Flour** is another very common thickening agent. Potato flour may be used instead of ordinary flour, and in exactly the same quantity. Cornflour (cornstarch) is another alternative. In this case you require exactly half the amount of cornflour as given for flour in the recipe because it has twice the thickening quality.

All these flours may be used at the last moment if the soup is too thin. Blend 2 tablespoons (2½ tablespoons) flour or 1 tablespoon (1¼ tablespoons) cornflour with a little cold water, stock or milk, depending upon the recipe. Add several ladles of the hot soup to the blended ingredients, return to the pan and whisk or stir briskly for several minutes as the soup boils and thickens. If the recipe advises gentle cooking because of egg, cream or wine content, cook slowly for at least 10 minutes. Always check the flavouring after this to make sure there is no taste of inadequately cooked flour or cornflour.

If the soup is only slightly too thin, reduce the quantities above.

4) **Beurre Manié** is a classic method used to thicken liquids. Mix equal amounts of butter and flour together, e.g. 115 g/4 oz (½ cup) butter and 115 g/4 oz (1 cup) flour.

To add Beurre Manié. Make sure the soup is very hot, then drop small amounts – the size of a large pea – into the soup. Wait until this is absorbed before adding any more. Continue like this until the soup is the right consistency. Store any left-over beurre manié in a covered container in the refrigerator for future use. The addition of butter adds a pleasing richness to the soups.

5) **Eggs** also thicken mixtures, although the yolks alone are better for this purpose. Whisk the eggs or yolks with a little cold water, milk, stock or wine (depending upon the recipe). Carefully spoon a little hot soup over the blended eggs or yolks then return to the pan, whisking over a low heat until the soup is adequately thickened.

6) **Double (heavy) cream** immediately adds a thicker consistency, as well as a richer taste, to soups. Thick yoghurt can also be used for the same purpose, as can fromage frais, but these are less rich in flavour. However, they are much lower in calories than cream.

Take great care the soup does not boil when adding dairy products to a soup that contains wine or acid ingredients like lemon juice. It must simmer gently.

7) **Longer heating** with the lid off the pan during cooking so the liquid evaporates and the soup becomes thicker. This is not an ideal method, as prolonged cooking can obliterate the fresh taste of the ingredients.

UNUSUAL WAYS TO THICKEN SOUPS

All soups can be sieved or liquidized, but if they are not suitable for making into a smooth purée, the following three ingredients will successfully thicken them.

1) **One or two peeled and diced old potatoes** can be added to the other ingredients during the cooking period. If the cooking time of the soup is short, peel and grate the potatoes so they will cook more quickly. Stir the soup briskly with a wooden spoon to ensure the potato has disintegrated.

2) **Oatmeal** is excellent for thickening soups and stews. A little imparts a pleasantly nutty flavour, but too much makes for a sticky and rather cloying texture.

If using very fine pinhead, fine or medium oatmeal (as opposed to rolled oats), mix with a little water, stock or milk (depending upon the recipe) and add halfway through the cooking period. Stir briskly until the soup reaches boiling point again and starts to thicken. Stir from time to time, as oatmeal or rolled oats tend to stick to the pan. (Sticking is not a problem if the soup is cooked in a microwave.)

If using quick-cooking rolled oats, follow the same procedure but add towards the end of the cooking time.

If using oats to replace flour in a recipe, use approximately half the amount of oatmeal or rolled oats as given for flour.

3) **Breadcrumbs** are excellent for thickening soups since they do not form lumps or stick to the pan. Add a few tablespoons of fine breadcrumbs to the

soup just before the end of the cooking time. Simmer for a few minutes, then stir briskly to blend the crumbs with the other ingredients.

TO PURÉE SOUPS

The ingredients in many soup recipes need to be made into a smooth purée. There are various ways of achieving this.

Sieving: This is the classic way of making sure you have a perfectly smooth mixture, entirely free from small pieces of skin, seeds or particles of meat, fish or vegetables. While a metal sieve can be used for many ingredients, it is advisable to choose a hair or nylon sieve where the ingredients include acid fruits, lemon juice, vinegar or tomatoes because metal can spoil the colour and give a slightly metallic flavour to the soup.

Place the sieve over a large bowl or clean saucepan and rub the ingredients firmly through the mesh with a wooden spoon. Always wash and dry the sieve with great care after use. Allow hair or nylon sieves or those with plastic rims to dry naturally at room temperature.

Liquidizing after cooking: This method of puréeing ingredients involves using a liquidizer (blender) or food processor. In most cases a liquidizer is better than a food processor for preparing a puréed soup since the goblet allows a large amount of liquid to be included with the solid ingredients.

Using a liquidizer: If the soup ingredients are very hot, warm a glass liquidizer goblet before filling it. This ensures it will not crack.

Never fill the goblet more than three-quarters full as the liquid rises dramatically when the machine is switched on. It is better to purée the soup in several batches.

Make sure the lid of the goblet is firmly in position and hold it down as you switch on so it cannot be forced off as the liquid and other ingredients rise in the goblet.

If you find that firm particles of meat are not completely puréed or that skin and pips remain, sieve the mixture after liquidizing it. These two processes are far less time-consuming than simply sieving the ingredients.

Liquidizing before cooking: Raw vegetables for soup can be liquidized to speed up the cooking process. Prepare them as necessary and cut into small chunks; place in the liquidizer with a small amount of water or stock and switch on. The result will be rather like grated vegetables.

The one vegetable I have never found completely satisfactory liquidized in this way is onions: they seem to retain rather a raw taste, even with prolonged cooking. Spring onions or shallots, however, work perfectly well because they have a milder taste.

Processing: While food processors are better than liquidizers at making smooth purées of solid ingredients, such as cooked meat, poultry and firm vegetables, the amount of liquid in most soup recipes means that it may well leak through the centre cavity where the cutting blades fit in the food processor bowl. The solution is to transfer the solid ingredients from the pan to the processor bowl using a perforated spoon, then add only a little of the liquid. The remaining soup can be poured through a strainer.

Never process the ingredients for too long or they become sticky, rather than a smooth purée.

Using a pestle and mortar: This is a traditional method, which involves pressing ingredients by hand to produce a smooth purée. As this method is very slow, it's suitable only if there are few solid ingredients in the soup.

Using a potato masher: If a soup contains potatoes or other root vegetables which have become really soft during cooking, the liquid can be strained into a bowl, and the vegetables mashed separately until smooth. Return the liquid to the purée in the pan and reheat.

Using a vegetable mill: A mouli-grater can be used for puréeing if you have no other utensils. Spoon a small amount of cooked vegetables into the grater cavity and turn the handle to push them through the holes. The purée will not be quite as smooth as when using the other methods described. Note that a mouli-grater is not strong enough to purée cooked meat.

MAKING STOCK

'Stock' is the culinary term given to the liquid produced when the bones, skin and other parts of animals or fish and/or vegetables are simmered in liquid. Do not imagine, however, that home-made stock is essential to successful soups. In some recipes water is perfectly adequate, for the other ingredients have sufficient flavour and the soup could be spoiled by the addition of stock. In other recipes, where stock is specifically mentioned, you would be well advised to give additional flavour to the soup by using stock as the liquid or by adding a commercial alternative (see page 13).

The basic way to make stock is to simmer the ingredients in a saucepan on top of the cooker (see approximate cooking times below). There are, however, alternative ways of preparing stock.

Oven cooking: Instead of using a saucepan, place the ingredients, plus the liquid, in a tightly covered casserole in the oven. This is a sensible idea if the oven is already being used to cook something else. The ideal temperature should be about 150°C/300°F/gas mark 2. Allow about 50 per cent **longer** cooking time than when using a saucepan. If the lid of the casserole fits very tightly, you may produce rather more stock than when a saucepan is used since the evaporation will be less.

Pressure cooking: This form of cooking is ideal for making stock and the cooking time considerably shorter than using a saucepan. As there is also less evaporation, you can be a little more sparing with the water. Use about 450 ml/¾ pint (scant 2 cups) instead of each 600 ml/1 pint (2½ cups) you would use in a saucepan or casserole.

Remove the trivet (rack) from the base of the cooker, then put in the water, vegetables, bones, etc. Never have the pan more than half-full. Fix the lid and bring up to high (maximum) pressure. Maintain this pressure for the time stipulated in the recipe for stock. Allow the pressure to drop steadily at room temperature. Strain the stock and store until needed.

Microwave cooking: This is an excellent way of making stock, although the saving of time is not as great as when using a pressure cooker. As water takes quite a long time to heat in a microwave, it is usually quicker to boil a kettle.

Place the ingredients for the stock in a large microwave bowl, add the recommended amount of water, then cover the bowl with a lid or plate.

Set the microwave to defrost and leave for 5–10 minutes. If at the end of that time the liquid is boiling rapidly, lower the setting slightly and continue cooking for the time stipulated in the recipe.

Be very careful when removing the hot stock from the microwave, especially if using a ceramic bowl. Place on a dry surface. Strain the stock, allow to cool and store until needed.

Removing Fat from Stock

As the stock cools and clears, the fat floats to the top of the liquid. If you are in a hurry to use the stock, you can spoon most of this off. It is, however, far better to allow the stock to become very cold. In the case of meat stocks, the fat will form a fairly solid layer which can be lifted from the liquid with a knife. The fat from poultry and game birds tends to be softer, so this should be spooned off.

Fat from stock can be used instead of the butter, margarine or oil in a soup recipe, provided it is suitable, i.e. use beef dripping in soups where beef stock is used and a strong, meaty flavour is required; use chicken fat in soups based on chicken. Do not use the fat from stock in delicately flavoured vegetable soups for it would give too pronounced a taste.

Storing Stock

Strain the stock carefully through a fine sieve into a bowl to remove all particles of bone, skin and vegetables. Allow to become quite cold, then cover the bowl and place in the refrigerator.

After some hours you may find that a layer of fat has formed on top of the liquid. It is a good idea to spoon or lift this away as it can cause stock to deteriorate. The fat can be used in various forms of cooking.

The stock can be stored for 3 days in the refrigerator. If you want to store it for up to a week, pour the chilled stock into a saucepan and bring to boiling point. Maintain at this temperature for several minutes, then cool again and replace in the refrigerator.

If you want to store stock for more than a week, even with re-boiling, then it is wise to freeze it (see below).

Freezing Stock

All stocks freeze well. Remove any fat from the top of the liquid, as this can become slightly rancid in freezing. Freeze the stock in small containers so you have a reasonable amount for making a particular soup. Mark the containers clearly as all stocks look alike when frozen.

If short of space in the freezer, it is wise to boil the strained stock vigorously in an uncovered pan to *reduce* the quantity but *increase* the flavour. One of the most practical ways to freeze stock is to boil it down until very concentrated then pour it into ice-making trays and freeze until firm. Transfer the cubes of stock to clearly marked boxes or bags. When needed, simply add 1 or 2 frozen stock cubes to the other ingredients in a soup. This very strong stock should be diluted with water.

Frozen stock should be used within 3 months.

Using Wines in Stock

As the stocks in this book are to be used for a wide variety of soups, I prefer to make them with water rather than wine. Water produces a stock that will not overwhelm the flavour of the other ingredients in a soup. It is very simple to add a little wine to the soup itself if you feel that it will improve the flavour; in fact, the addition of alcohol is suggested in a number of recipes.

Commercial Stocks

Home-made stock takes time and effort to prepare, so you might prefer to use ready-made stock cubes and flavourings. These are available in many varieties, but they often have a high salt content. Take care, therefore, when adding extra salt to soup: taste first and add judiciously.

It is also advisable to use rather less commercial flavouring than recommended on the packet in case your basic soup ingredients already have a strong flavour and require very little extra seasoning.

Beef Stock

Cooking time: about 3 hours
Makes about 1.2 litres/2 pints (5 cups)

In view of the fairly long time needed to make a good beef stock, it is sensible to prepare a reasonable quantity at one time. The recipe given below is ideal for most soups where a slightly delicate flavour of beef is required. The stock is not sufficiently strong to be termed a Beef Consommé (see page 68). Fresh bay leaves are used below; if substituting dried bay, use just one leaf.

Metric/Imperial	Ingredients	American
1 kg/2¼ lb	beef bones	2¼ lb
1 medium	onion	1 medium
2 medium	carrots	2 medium
2 or 3	celery sticks	2 or 3
2	bay leaves	2
2.4 litres/4 pints	water	10 cups
to taste	salt and freshly ground black pepper	to taste

It is a good idea to crack the bones, or ask the butcher to do this, as cracked bones yield more flavour. Peel and thickly slice the onion and carrots, and chop the celery into small pieces. Put all the ingredients into a large saucepan, bring to boiling point, then remove the scum that floats to the top. Cover the pan, lower the heat and simmer gently for 3 hours.

Strain and use or store as described on page 12.

VARIATIONS

● BACON OR HAM STOCK
Use the liquid from boiling a joint of bacon or ham. If the stock is lacking in flavour, boil it in an open pan until more concentrated in flavour. One or two rashers (slices) of bacon can be cooked in the stock to produce a stronger taste.

● CHICKEN STOCK
Use the carcass of a chicken instead of beef bones in the recipe above. If the carcass is rather small, cook a raw joint of chicken in the liquid.

This stock is not sufficiently strong to use as a **Chicken Consommé** (see page 71).

● GAME STOCK

The bones of game birds or venison make a very rich stock. Use them instead of beef bones in the recipe above. The recipe for **Game Consommé** is on page 72.

● BROWN STOCK

Use the bones of mutton or lamb instead of beef in the recipe above. The flavour is not quite as good, but it is an acceptable alternative.

● WHITE OR VEAL STOCK

Use veal bones in the recipe for Beef Stock to produce a really good stock. Failing this, use the carcass of a chicken, turkey or guinea fowl. The recipe for **Veal Consommé** is on page 69.

● VEGETABLE STOCK

Use the liquid from cooking vegetables, or make a special stock by peeling and chopping 1 or 2 onions, 2 carrots, a few celery sticks and 2 or 3 cauliflower florets, and simmer in approximately 1.2 litres/2 pints (5 cups) of water for 20 minutes. Season lightly during cooking. Strain and use or store (see pages 12–13).

FREEZING: See page 13.

QUICK TIP *Allow 45 minutes to 1 hour in a pressure cooker for the Beef Stock and other stocks based upon the same recipe. (For information about pressure cooking stock, see page 12.)*

Allow about 10 minutes in a pressure cooker for Vegetable Stock.

Allow 1 to 1¼ hours in a microwave for the Beef Stock and other stocks based upon the same recipe, and about 15 minutes for the Vegetable Stock. (For details on using a microwave oven to prepare stock, see page 12.)

Duck and Goose Stock

These stocks are made in the same way as Beef Stock (see page 14). Use the carcass of the birds to make a strongly flavoured liquid. As well as the bay leaves, 2 or 3 sage leaves can be added to the other ingredients.

Most present-day ducklings and ducks are much leaner than in the past, but they still have an appreciable amount of fat, and geese have considerably more. Much of this fat will have run out when cooking the bird, but the carcass may still have some fat adhering to it. Do not remove this or any particles of skin, for they both add flavour to the stock. It is important, though, to remove all the fat from the top of the cold stock for reasons explained on page 12, and to prevent any soup it is used in becoming over-greasy.

Any fat removed from these stocks should be used in cooking. Goose fat is particularly good for roasting vegetables.

Stock for Oriental Soups

Chicken stock is ideal for these soups. Follow the directions for making Beef Stock on page 14, but add 1 teaspoon finely grated root ginger to give a piquant flavour. Do not exceed this amount as the ginger should not be too pronounced. For a more interesting flavour, add 1 or 2 small pork bones to the chicken carcass.

Fish Stock

Cooking time: 30 to 40 minutes
Makes about 600 ml/1 pint (2½ cups)

A really rich fish stock gives body and flavour to fish soups. The stock is made from the head, skin, bones, tail and fins of the fish, or from the well-washed shells of lobster, prawns or shrimps. The quantity of bay leaves used is a matter of personal taste. The number given overleaf refers to fresh bay leaves; if using the dried variety, use only half the amount for they are very strong. When making stock for delicately flavoured bisques (see page 193), be sparing with the vegetables and herbs.

Metric/Imperial	Ingredients	American
900ml/1½ pints	water	3¾ cups
	fish head, skin, etc.	
1 medium	onion	1 medium
1 medium	carrot	1 medium
1	celery stick, optional	1
2 fresh	bay leaves	2 fresh
to taste	chervil, parsley or herbs, depending on recipe	to taste
to taste	salt and freshly ground white pepper	to taste
to taste	little lemon zest	to taste

Put the water into a saucepan and add the fish parts: the more you use, the stronger the flavour of the finished stock. Peel the onion and carrot, chop the celery and add to the water with all the other ingredients. Bring the liquid to simmering point, cover the pan and cook steadily for 30 to 40 minutes. Strain and use or store as instructed on pages 12–13.

VARIATION

● **SHELLFISH STOCK**

Follow the recipe above, but use the shells of lobster or other crustaceans. The shells produce a stock with an attractive pale pink colour. Strain and use or store as instructed on pages 12–13.

FREEZING: See page 18.

QUICK TIP *Allow 10 to 15 minutes in a pressure cooker. (For details on using a pressure cooker to make stock, see page 12.)*
Allow about 25 minutes in a microwave. (For details on using a microwave to make stock, see page 12.)

FREEZING SOUPS

It is extremely useful to have containers of home-made soup in the freezer, ready to defrost and heat quickly. Information about freezing is included in all recipes where it is satisfactory. If a recipe states 'Do not freeze', it is for a very good reason. Either I have found that the flavour of that particular soup deteriorates badly in freezing, or the firm texture of some of the ingredients is lost, or there is an ingredient in the soup that should not be frozen.

Clear soups freeze especially well. The information about storing stocks (see page 12) applies to clear soups too.

Puréed soups, such as the vegetable soups on pages 99 to 179, freeze well, with a few exceptions. When defrosted, you may find that a soup has separated, i.e. there is a layer of clear liquid and a layer of very thick purée. Whisk vigorously as you heat the soup and the original consistency should return. If it is still a little thin, simmering in an uncovered pan for some minutes should restore the original consistency.

Creamy soups, such as those on pages 110 and 193, can be problematic. Clear instructions about freezing these are given wherever it can be done successfully. When reheating a frozen soup that contains cream, eggs, wine or lemon juice, take great care that it does not boil and curdle (separate): simmer gently and whisk continually during the reheating process. Flour-thickened soups have a tendency to separate slightly when frozen. There are two solutions:

- Use cornflour (cornstarch), arrowroot or potato flour (fecule) instead of ordinary wheat flour for thickening the soup. All these ingredients are less likely to cause separation during freezing and defrosting.

  If you use cornflour or arrowroot instead of ordinary flour, allow exactly half the amount specified in the recipe as cornflour and arrowroot have twice the thickening ability of flour.

  If you use potato flour instead of ordinary flour, allow the same amount specified in the recipe.

- Prepare and cook the soup to the stage where it should be thickened, allow it to cool, then pack and freeze it. Make a note on the label about the amount of thickening and any extra ingredients needed when the soup is reheated.

A good 'safety measure' when freezing puréed, creamy and flour-thickened soups is to sprinkle 1 teaspoon cornflour on top of the soup when it is packed for freezing. When it is reheated, this cornflour can be stirred into the other ingredients and it will cook and add a little thickening as the soup heats.

Packing Soups for Freezing

Use freezer boxes and make sure they are well filled: the less air space, the better the results in freezing. On the other hand though, all soups contain a large amount of liquid and this will expand during freezing. If the box is completely filled the expanded mixture could force the lid right off. Allow about 1.25 cm/½ inch of space above the level of the soup. Label the box clearly with the type of soup and the date it was made.

If you have no suitable freezer boxes, put large, strong freezer bags into sugar cartons or similar containers. Pour the soup into the bag, which is well supported by the rigid container. Leave until the soup is frozen, then remove the filled bag from the container. You will have a neat package which fits well into the freezer. Seal the bag (allowing 1.25 cm/½ inch air space) and label.

To save room in the freezer, halve the amount of liquid in the recipes so you have a very concentrated soup. Make a note on the label of the amount of liquid that should be added when reheating the soup.

Storage Times

Clear soups, such as consommé, should be used within 3 months; soups containing eggs and cream within 2 months; vegetable soups within 4 months; meat, fish and poultry soups within 3 months.

INGREDIENT QUANTITIES

All the recipes in this book have the proportions of onion, garlic and other flavouring vegetables that I have found best enhance the flavour of the main ingredients in each particular soup.

The exact weight of main ingredients is given in each recipe, but in the case of flavouring vegetables, such as onions and carrots, I have generally stated 'a medium onion' and not specified the weight. This is to save the bother of weighing or measuring the amount, as this is obviously a matter of personal taste and you could use less or more of these ingredients.

To give an idea of the approximate weight I used when testing the recipes, I list on page 20 some of these usual ingredients and their weights (before peeling or other preparation).

In a few cases, no weight or measure is given because the amount used makes very little difference to the recipe.

VEGETABLE	small	medium	large
1 cabbage	550 g/1¼ lb	900 g/2 lb	1.25 kg/2¾ lb
small portion	100 to 125 g/ 4 to 5 oz		
1 carrot	50 g/2 oz	100 g/4 oz	200 g/7 oz
1 cauliflower, heavy old stalks removed	550 g/1¼ lb	900 g/2 lb	1.35 kg/3 lb
1 courgette (zucchini)	100 g/4 oz	175 g/6 oz	225 g/8 oz
1 cucumber	300 g/10 oz	400g/14 oz	550 to 675 g/ 1¼ to 1½ lb
1 garlic head	100 g/4 oz	175 g/6 oz	225 g/8 oz
1 leek	175 g/6 oz	275 g/9 oz	375 to 400 g/ 13 to 14 oz
1 mushroom	15 to 25 g/½ to 1 oz	50 g/2 oz	75 to 100 g/3 to 4 oz
1 onion	100 g/4 oz	175 to 200 g/ 6 to 7 oz	275 to 300 g/ 9 to 10 oz
1 red or green pepper	175 g/6 oz	275 g/9 oz	350 g/12 oz
1 potato	100 g/4 oz	275 g/9 oz	400 to 450 g/ 14 oz to 1 lb
1 shallot	50 g/2 oz	100 g/4 oz	150 to 175 g/ 5 to 6 oz
1 tomato	75 g/3 oz	150 to 175 g/ 5 to 6 oz	275 to 300 g/ 9 to 10 oz
1 turnip	175 g/6 oz	275 g/9 oz	300 to 350 g/ 10 to 12 oz
FRUIT			
1 avocado	225 g/8 oz	300 g/10 oz	350 g/12 oz
1 dessert apple	75 to 100 g/ 3 to 4 oz	175 g/6 oz	225 to 275 g/ 8 to 9 oz

HERBS IN SOUPS

Herbs are one of the ingredients which help to flavour soups. Use fresh rather than dried herbs whenever possible, as their flavour is better and more subtle. If you do not grow herbs, you can buy them from good supermarkets. As only a small amount is used in a soup, you can chop and freeze the surplus for future use. Herbs keep for several days in the salad drawer of the refrigerator.

When substituting dried herbs for fresh ones, always reduce the quantity in the recipe by half, or even less, for dried herbs have a much stronger flavour. Although the recipes suggest the herbs that I feel are ideal for particular soups, you may like to experiment by using others, as listed below.

Choosing Herbs for Soups

If doubtful as to whether you would like the flavour of a particular herb, add a small sprig to the soup at the beginning of the cooking period. Taste the soup after a short while and remove the herb if you feel it has given enough flavour or you do not like the taste. If you do like the herb, you could chop a few leaves and add these to the other ingredients, or use them for garnish.

Aragula (see Rocket).

Balm has a lemony flavour and, while it is rarely used in savoury dishes, you could add a small sprig as an alternative to lemon and remove it before serving the soup.

Basil is a herb associated with tomato dishes, and is excellent in many soups containing tomatoes. Do be sparing with the amount you use, for it has a very strong and pungent taste. **Lemon basil** is particularly good in tomato soups.

Bay leaves are used a great deal in cooking. The large green shiny leaves should be removed before puréeing or serving the soup. Fresh leaves have a delicate taste, but dried ones are very strong.

Borage, although generally associated with drinks, has small blue flowers which can be floated on fruit soups as a colourful garnish (see page 263).

Bouquet garni is a small bunch of fresh or dried herbs which can be removed before making a purée or serving the soup. Tiny sachets of dried bouquet garni can also be added to the soup and removed in the same way as the fresh herbs.

Burnet is a cucumber-flavoured herb and could be used in suitable soups to enhance the cucumber taste.

Chervil tastes like parsley but has a more delicate flavour. It can be used instead of parsley, and its delicate leaves make an attractive garnish.

Chives are an invaluable herb, whether as part of a **bouquet garni**, as a delicate flavouring on their own, or as garnish. Ordinary chives have a mild onion taste, while **garlic chives** give the taste of mild garlic.

Coriander leaves and seeds, which are used a great deal in Oriental cooking, also appear in some recipes in this book. The leaves have a distinctly bitter taste.

Dill has a slight aniseed flavour. Chopped dill is an excellent addition to fish, both in the soup and as a garnish. Use sparingly.

Fennel bulb makes a wonderful soup (see page 36) and the chopped feathery leaves look most attractive as a garnish. The aniseed taste blends well with some fish soups.

Garlic is an invaluable addition to many dishes, and soups are no exception. Use sparingly in delicately flavoured soups. One or two cloves (segments) from the complete head are generally sufficient. See the recipe for Garlic Soup on page 127.

Marjoram has a slightly sweet taste that blends well with tomato dishes, including soups. With **oregano** it makes an interesting alternative to **basil**.

Mint has a very distinctive taste, so use sparingly in soups. It is particularly good in certain chilled soups. There is a range of different mints you may like to try, including apple mint, eau de cologne mint and horse mint.

Oregano is the name given to wild marjoram; it has a slightly stronger flavour than marjoram, so should be used sparingly in soups.

Parsley is undoubtedly the most popular and widely used of all herbs. There are two types – the curly leaf and the flat leaf. The flat leaf parsley has the stronger taste. Do not use too much parsley in a soup. The stalks impart more flavour than the leaves, so tie a few stalks together, add these to the soup and remove them before puréeing or sieving.

Rocket is also known as aragula. The dark leaves are popular in salads, but a few can be floated on top of a soup as a garnish. They are particularly good with tomato and vegetable soups.

Rosemary has a strong aromatic taste. It can be used sparingly in meat and other soups. When dried, the flavour is very pronounced.

Sage leaves enhance some meat soups. When dried, the flavour is ultra strong, so use sparingly.

Savory, also called **summer savory**, is used too rarely. It is a good herb in bean soups. The flavour is not unlike that of thyme but rather more peppery.

Sorrel has a taste and appearance rather like spinach. There are recipes for sorrel soups on pages 155 and 156.

Tarragon blends well with many ingredients, particularly chicken, fish and tomatoes. It has a refreshing, aromatic taste.

Thyme is a strongly aromatic herb, available in many varieties. **Lemon thyme** is one of the best, but all kinds of thyme impart an interesting flavour to a range of soups. Do not be too generous with the amount you add as it can become overpowering.

SPICES IN SOUPS

Spices should be used sparingly in soups because their flavour becomes very pronounced when added to a mixture containing a high percentage of liquid.

If you want to extract the utmost flavour from a spice, heat it in a pan with the fat stipulated in the recipe, or with the onions and/or garlic (if these are used). Even if the recipe does not list a spice, you may care to add a little, following the guidelines below. Note that spices deteriorate in flavour with long-term storage.

Allspice, as the name suggests, has the flavour of a mixture of spices. A little combines well with vegetable soups, fruit soups and some meat soups.

Anise has a distinctly aniseed flavour and is not suitable for soups. The only occasion when it might be used is to enhance a soup containing fennel, which already has an aniseed flavour (see page 36).

Caraway is obtainable in the form of seeds. A small amount is excellent added to a cabbage soup.

Cardamom is obtainable both in powder and seed form. It is often used to make curries, so any soup with a curry flavour could have a very small amount of this spice added.

Cinnamon is obtainable in the form of ground spice or sticks. It is suitable in fruit soups and is sometimes used in home-made curry powder.

Chilli is obtained from dried chilli peppers. Use very sparingly in soups in place of cayenne pepper.

Cloves are available as a ground spice or whole dried flower-buds. The only soup which would be improved by a very small amount is the Apple Soup on page 264.

Coriander is obtainable as a ground spice, as seeds or as a fresh herb, and is often used in curry powder. The slightly bitter taste is good in Oriental soups, but use very sparingly.

Cumin, in the forms of powder or seeds, is a valuable ingredient in curry powder.

Curry powder and **Curry paste** are both used in certain soups. There is a wide variety on the market, so choose brands that will be the most useful for soup-making, generally those with a fairly mild flavour, as soups should not have an overpowering taste. The paste is easier to blend with other soup ingredients than the powder, and tends to give a more mellow flavour. A recipe for Home-made Curry Powder is on page 25.

Garam masala is another blending of spices, used a great deal in Arab dishes, including the Harira on page 218.

Ginger can be used in soups in the fresh root form or as a ground spice. It gives a pleasant bite to some vegetable soups.

Juniper is sold as dried berries. Use a teaspoonful in game soups, see page 260.

Mace is the outer skin of nutmeg and is obtainable as blades (pieces of skin) or ground. It can be used instead of nutmeg.

Nutmeg is obtainable as a whole dried nut or as a ground spice. A better flavour is achieved by grating the whole nut when required. The combination of a sweet and slightly bitter taste is quite pleasant in some vegetable soups, such as Corn Soup (see page 114).

Paprika is a ground spice made from peppers. There are various kinds, but the most popular has a sweetish flavour. Its attractive, deep orange-red colour enhances many soups. If stale, paprika develops a very musty taste.

Saffron, available as strands or a ground powder, comes from a special variety of crocus and is the most expensive of all spices. It is used to give a golden colour, as well as a delicate flavour, to many dishes, including the Harira on page 218.

Turmeric is a spice used a great deal in pickles. It is not of great value in soups unless you want to enhance the golden colour. It has a sweet-savoury taste.

To Extract the Flavour from Seeds

Many spices are obtainable in seed form, and these give a better flavour than ground spices. To obtain the very maximum of flavour from seeds, place them in a dry frying pan and heat gently over a low heat for about 2 minutes. The seeds will darken slightly and give off a definite smell. They are then ready to be used.

If you wish to grind the seeds after heating them, use a pestle and mortar or a spice mill. A coffee grinder could be used instead but this must be washed very thoroughly after use otherwise it will affect the flavour of the coffee.

Home-made Curry Powder

The following recipe has a good mixture of flavours and produces a moderately hot curry taste.

Blend together:

1 teaspoon cardamom seeds, removed from their pods

2 teaspoons cumin seeds

2 teaspoons coriander seeds

1 teaspoon mustard seeds

1 teaspoon black peppercorns

Put the mixture on a baking tray and place in a preheated oven set to 180°C/350°F/gas mark 4 for 9 minutes. Remove and leave until cold.

Add:

2 dried hot chilli peppers

½ teaspoon ground ginger

3 teaspoons ground turmeric

½ teaspoon ground cinnamon

¼ teaspoon grated or ground nutmeg

Place all the ingredients in a mortar, liquidizer or food processor and grind to a smooth powder. Store in a covered container and use as required.

VARIATION

- For a hotter flavour use more chilli peppers or a good pinch ground chilli powder and/or more ground ginger.

SEASONINGS IN SOUPS

Throughout this book you will find the words: to taste, salt and freshly ground black (or white) pepper. This means you add them gradually, tasting as you do so.

Never add too much seasoning at the beginning of the cooking period as the other ingredients will change the flavour as they cook. Vegetables, for example, contain appreciable amounts of mineral salts which contribute to the salt taste.

Freshly ground pepper has a far better taste than ready-ground pepper, which may have been stored for some considerable time and so developed a slightly musty taste. You need to buy black and/or white peppercorns and pepper mills.

Some recipes specify using **white pepper** which is less usual in cooking than **black pepper**, in order to preserve the colour of a soup. **White pepper** has a stronger flavour than **black pepper**, so use it sparingly.

Freshly ground **sea salt** or **kitchen salt** has a better taste than ready-prepared table salt.

In addition to ordinary salt, **celery salt** has a very pleasing flavour and can enhance the taste of many soups, especially those based on vegetables.
Mustard: English mustard can be obtained in powder form, or ready-mixed in tubes or pots. There are also various *herb-flavoured* and *wholegrain* English mustards, which have an exceptionally good flavour. If adding powdered mustard to soup towards the end of the cooking time, mix it with a little water first so that it blends more easily with the liquid.

There are also many **French** mustards, perhaps the most famous of which is **Dijon**. All can also be used to season soups.

SERVING SOUP

Check that the cups, bowls or soup plates you are using are well warmed if serving hot soups, or chilled in the refrigerator, if space permits, when serving chilled, jellied or iced soups.

Always taste the soup before serving it and add more seasoning if necessary (see page 25). If in doubt, allow people to season their own servings: this means that personal preferences can be more easily met.

If by some unhappy chance you over-salt the soup, read the suggestions under PUT IT RIGHT on page 332. (These would also help to overcome a too peppery taste.)

If you feel the soup is lacking in flavour, read the suggestions for rectifying this on page 332.

Check the consistency of the soup before serving it. If too thick, dilute it slightly. If too thin, read page 332 which gives ways of thickening it at the last minute.

If a soup containing cream, eggs or wine has curdled (separated), whisk briskly away from the heat. If that does not correct the appearance, see page 333.

Check that all garnishes are ready before ladling out the soup so that they can be added quickly and the soup served at the appropriate temperature – either piping hot or refreshingly cold.

Chapter Two

QUICK SOUPS FOR BUSY PEOPLE

Often I have heard people say, 'I love home-made soups but I have no time to make them.' This implies that all soups take a long time to prepare and cook, but in most cases that is not true. On the following pages you will find a selection of appetizing soups which are exceptionally quick and easy to make. They use a range of readily available ingredients.

Ideas about cooking have changed over the years. Once it was considered right to simmer soup for a long time to give the best result. Nowadays we find that in most instances a shorter cooking time is better for retaining the flavour of the ingredients. This is particularly true when cooking vegetable soups.

You may be surprised to see that this chapter starts with a recipe for a basic White Sauce, but this is often an important part of a soup recipe. The sauce can be used as an alternative to cream, but it is also an excellent basis for a number of quick, creamy and nutritious soups.

In order to save time preparing fresh stock, the recipes in this section use water and stock (bouillon) cubes. There is a good range of these on the market, but some are rather salty, so be careful when adding extra seasoning.

The first group of soups is based on vegetables, and you will find preparation hints on page 33. These are followed by interesting recipes based on fish, poultry, canned consommé and cheese.

A microwave is suitable for cooking many soups, particularly those made with young vegetables (see page 33) and fish. You do not save a great deal of time with this appliance when heating a fairly large amount of liquid, so I suggest you boil the required amount of water in a kettle then add this to the ingredients in the bowl in the microwave. There are brief hints on using the microwave for each group of soups in this chapter, and more information on page 12.

Use a microwave instead of a saucepan for making a White Sauce (see page 29). It is far easier to wash a bowl than a sticky pan.

Pressure cookers have gone rather out of fashion, but if you own one it is certainly useful for making soups, particularly when you are in a hurry (see pages 6, 33 and 42).

As you will find when you use the recipes that follow, home-made soups *can* be made in a very short time and you will be rewarded with excellent results.

White Sauce

Cooking time: 10 to 15 minutes
Serves 4 to 8, depending on the recipe

A white sauce is an important ingredient in quite a number of soup recipes. In most cases it should have a pouring consistency, as in the recipe below. The quantities given here will make 600 ml/1 pint (2½ cups) of sauce.

Metric/Imperial	Ingredients	American
25 g/1 oz	butter or margarine	2 tablespoons
25 g/1 oz	plain (all-purpose) flour	¼ cup
600 ml/1 pint	milk	2½ cups
to taste	salt and freshly ground black pepper	to taste

Heat the butter or margarine until just melted, then remove from the heat and stir in the flour. Return to a low heat and stir for 1 or 2 minutes. Gradually add the milk, stirring all the time, then allow the sauce to boil steadily for about 5 minutes. Reduce the heat and simmer gently for another 5 minutes. The longer cooking gives a better flavour. Season to taste.

VARIATIONS
- Omit 2 or 3 tablespoons (2½ to 3¾ tablespoons) milk and add this amount of single (light) cream to give a richer flavour.
- Instead of 25 g/1 oz (¼ cup) flour, use 15 g/½ oz (2 tablespoons) cornflour (cornstarch). This thickens the sauce very rapidly and ensures an ultra-smooth texture.

- To add extra flavour to the sauce, add a chopped onion, one or two chopped celery sticks and a small bunch of herbs (parsley, thyme and a little rosemary) to the milk. Bring the milk to boiling point, allow it to stand for as long as possible so that it absorbs the various flavours, then strain and use in the sauce.
- Vegetarians can use soya milk (see below) and non-dairy fat in the sauce.

FREEZING: The sauce is better freshly made, but it freezes well as part of a soup.

QUICK TIP *Blending method: put all the ingredients into a saucepan and whisk briskly as the sauce comes to the boil and thickens. Put all the ingredients into a suitable microwave bowl. Stir or whisk briskly, immediately before starting to cook on full power for approximately 2½ to 3 minutes. Stir or whisk every 30 seconds to ensure a smooth sauce.*

Soya Milk

Cooking time: 2 to 3 minutes
Makes: good 450 ml/¾ pint (2 cups)

Although you can buy ready-made soya milk, it is not difficult to make at home.

Metric/Imperial	Ingredients	American
450 ml/¾ pint	water	scant 2 cups
25 g/1 oz	soya flour	¼ cup
2 tablespoons	sunflower oil	2½ tablespoons
1 teaspoon	sugar	1 teaspoon

Liquidize the water, flour and oil. Pour into a saucepan, add the sugar and bring to the boil as quickly as possible. Liquidize again for perfect smoothness, allow to become cold, then chill thoroughly. Whisk well before using.

DO NOT FREEZE

VEGETABLE SOUPS
BASED ON WHITE SAUCE
Cooking time: about 20 minutes
Serves 4

One of the easiest and quickest ways to produce a home-made soup is to make a
White Sauce (see page 28), then add your chosen ingredients to it and heat for a
short time.

● ARTICHOKE (GLOBE) SOUP

Finely chop, sieve or liquidize 4 to 5 well-drained cooked or canned globe
artichoke hearts. Add to the hot White Sauce together with 3 or 4
tablespoons (3¾ or 5 tablespoons) artichoke liquid. Heat thoroughly.
Remove from the heat and stir in 1 tablespoon (1¼ tablespoons) lemon
juice, 150 ml/¼ pint (⅔ cup) single (light) cream, 2 tablespoons (2½
tablespoons) chopped chives, and 1 tablespoon (1¼ tablespoons) finely
chopped parsley.

● ARTICHOKE (JERUSALEM) SOUP

Make 300 ml/½ pint (1¼ cups) purée by sieving cooked Jerusalem
artichokes. Add to the White Sauce, together with 150 ml/¼ pint (⅔
cup) liquid from cooking the artichokes, 4 tablespoons (5 tablespoons)
finely chopped spring onions (scallions) or thinly sliced leeks. Heat
thoroughly, then flavour with a little seasoning, including celery salt.
Top the soup with cream or yoghurt and finely chopped red pepper or
paprika.

● ASPARAGUS SOUP

Open a 300 g/10 oz can asparagus spears. Drain but reserve the liquid
from the can. Cut off about 8 tips for garnish, then liquidize the spears
and reserved liquid. Heat the White Sauce and add the asparagus purée
with seasoning to taste. Serve topped with a little soured cream or
yoghurt and the asparagus tips. Garnish with heart-shaped croutons (see
page 305).

● BEETROOT CREAM SOUP

Peel and coarsely grate about 225 g/8 oz (½ lb) cooked beetroot (weight
when peeled and grated). (Use tiny summer beets if possible.) Make the
White Sauce, add the beetroot and stir gently over the heat. Pour in 150 ml/
¼ pint single (light) cream and 1½ tablespoons (2 tablespoons) lemon

juice. Heat gently without boiling. Serve topped with a thick layer of finely chopped parsley and chives.

Low-fat yoghurt could be used instead of cream.

● **BROCCOLI CREAM SOUP**
Use about 225 g/8 oz (½ lb) cooked broccoli (weight when cooked). Strain but save 150 ml/¼ pint (⅔ cup) of the cooking liquid. Cut off a few very small florets for garnish and sieve or liquidize the remainder to make a purée. Add the broccoli stock to the White Sauce, heat thoroughly, then stir in the vegetable purée with 25 g/1 oz (2 tablespoons) butter and a good pinch of grated or ground nutmeg. Heat thoroughly. Top the soup with finely chopped skinned tomatoes and the broccoli florets.

Cooked cauliflower can be used instead of broccoli.

● **CARROT CREAM SOUP**
Heat the White Sauce and add 300 ml/½ pint (1¼ cups) single (light) cream or extra milk. Peel and grate 225 g/8 oz (½ lb) carrots (weight when peeled and grated). Add to the hot mixture together with 2 tablespoons (2½ tablespoons) finely chopped spring onions (scallions), 1 teaspoon chopped savory or ½ teaspoon dried savory and seasoning to taste. (Use marjoram or oregano if savory is not available.) Heat well but do not overcook the soup, for in this recipe the grated carrots should remain firm. Garnish with chopped chives.

Instead of all carrots, use 225 g/8 oz (½ lb) mixed root vegetables such as grated carrots, swede (rutabaga), turnip and parsnip and/or celeriac.

● **SPEEDY CHESTNUT SOUP**
Heat the White Sauce, add 300 ml/½ pint (1¼ cups) vegetable, ham or chicken stock (see pages 14–15) and 350 g/12 oz (¾ lb) canned unsweetened chestnut purée. Stir until very hot and smooth then add a good pinch paprika and/or curry powder. Top with soured cream or yoghurt, or finely chopped crisp bacon.

● **SPEEDY LEEK SOUP**
Thinly slice and cook about 350 g/12 oz (¾ lb) leeks in just 150 ml/¼ pint (⅔ cup) of water with seasoning to taste. Make the White Sauce while the leeks are cooking. Blend with the leeks and liquid in the pan, and adjust the seasoning. Top with paprika and chopped parsley or finely chopped crisp bacon.

● **SPINACH CREAM SOUP**
Make the White Sauce. Use approximately 225 g/8 oz (½ lb) frozen chopped spinach. Add the block of frozen spinach to the sauce, heating

gently and stirring frequently as the spinach defrosts and blends with the sauce. When thoroughly heated, add 300 ml/½ pint (1¼ cups) single (light) cream or extra milk, a little grated or ground nutmeg and a shake of cayenne pepper. Heat and serve the soup topped with blanched flaked almonds.

Use approximately 350 g/12 oz (¾ lb) fresh or frozen leaf spinach, cook and sieve or liquidize to make a purée. Add to the White Sauce, then continue as above.

A purée of cooked young nettle leaves can be used instead of spinach (see page 135).

FREEZING: **Do not freeze** any of these soups: they are better freshly made.

FISH, MEAT AND POULTRY SOUPS BASED ON WHITE SAUCE
Cooking time: about 20 minutes
Serves 4

• SEAFOOD SOUP
Make the White Sauce, add 300 ml/½ pint (1¼ cups) Fish Stock (see page 16) or water plus a few drops of anchovy essence and heat thoroughly. Stir 100 g/4 oz (¼ lb) frozen shelled prawns (shrimps) into the hot sauce. Allow to stand for a short time, without cooking, so that they defrost. Add the same weight of flaked, cooked or canned salmon and of chopped smoked salmon or flaked crabmeat. Heat for a few minutes only. Top with chopped fennel leaves.

Use all prawns or all salmon instead of the mixture of fish.

Heat 2 or 3 tablespoons (2½ to 3¾ tablespoons) finely chopped fennel root with the sauce before adding the fish.

• CREAMY HAM AND MUSTARD SOUP
Make the White Sauce. Mix 300 ml/½ pint (⅔ cup) single (light) cream with 2 tablespoons French or ready-made English mustard and add to the sauce and heat. Finely dice or mince 225 g/8 oz (½ lb) cooked ham and add to the sauce with 1 tablespoon (1¼ tablespoons) finely chopped parsley. Heat for a few minutes only and season to taste.

• SPEEDY CHICKEN SOUP
Make the White Sauce and add 150 ml/¼ pint (⅔ cup) chicken stock (see page 14). Finely dice or mince 350 g/12 oz (¾ lb) cooked chicken and add

to the other ingredients with 1 teaspoon finely grated lemon zest, 1 teaspoon French or ready-made English mustard and 3 tablespoons (3¾ tablespoons) double (heavy) cream. Heat gently and serve topped with blanched flaked almonds.

FREEZING: **Do not freeze** any of these soups: they are better freshly made.

QUICK VEGETABLE SOUPS

Choose young vegetables whenever possible because they cook in a shorter time than older ones. Frozen vegetables, which have been partly cooked by blanching before freezing, make excellent alternatives to fresh vegetables, especially when time is limited or a particular fresh vegetable is not obtainable.

Microwave cooking is excellent for vegetable soups if the vegetables are young, but less efficient for cooking older vegetables, as they do not become really tender.

You will need to check cooking progress carefully the first time you use the microwave for a particular vegetable soup, but on the whole allow about 25 per cent less cooking time than on a conventional hob. Make sure all the vegetables are cut into small, even-sized pieces and reduce the amount of liquid in the recipe by 150 ml/¼ pint (⅔ cup).

There is more information about using microwaves on page 7.

Pressure cooking provides a good way of cooking vegetables for soup, even when the vegetables are older. Allow half the cooking time given in the recipe when the cooker reaches pressure, and reduce the amount of liquid in the recipe by 25 per cent.

Further information about pressure cookers appears on page 6.

Clear Mushroom Soup

Cooking time: 20 minutes
Serves 4 to 6

This quickly made soup is ideal for slimmers since it contains no fat. It has an excellent flavour, but can be made to look more enticing by topping each portion with a spoonful of lightly whipped cream. Large open mushrooms or chestnut mushrooms are ideal for this soup.

Metric/Imperial	Ingredients	American
550 g/1¼ lb	mushrooms	1¼ lb
1 small bunch	spring onions (scallions)	1 small bunch
2 tablespoons	finely chopped parsley	2 tablespoons
1 litre/1¾ pints	water	scant 4½ cups
1	beef, chicken or vegetable stock cube	1
to taste	salt and freshly ground black pepper	to taste

Wipe the mushrooms, cut and discard the ends of the stalks. Chop the mushrooms roughly. Prepare the spring onions, using only the white bulbs. Put the mushrooms, onions and parsley into a pan with the water and stock cube. Bring to the boil and simmer for 15 minutes. Sieve or liquidize and reheat.

VARIATION
- I often add a little yeast extract, rather than a stock cube, as this gives an excellent flavour to the liquid. Take care when adding other seasonings as yeast extract tends to be very salty.

FREEZING: This soup freezes very well.

Corn Soup

Cooking time: 25 minutes
Serves 4 to 6

This is a soup I first tasted in South Africa, where it is generally called Mealie
Soup. It is delicious and ready in minutes. Use fresh corn, if in season, as the
flavour is much better than canned or frozen corn.

Metric/Imperial	Ingredients	American
2 medium	onions	2 medium
50 g/2 oz	butter	¼ cup
25 g/1 oz	plain (all-purpose) flour	¼ cup
good pinch	grated or ground nutmeg	good pinch
750 ml/1¼ pints	milk	good 3 cups
350 g/12 oz	canned sweetcorn	¾ lb
to taste	salt and freshly ground black pepper	to taste
To garnish	chopped parsley and/or chives croûtons (see page 305)	

Peel and finely chop the onions. Heat the butter and fry the onions gently for
10 minutes. Do not allow to colour, so stir well during this time. Add the
flour and nutmeg, stir to blend with the onions. Pour in the milk. Stir or
whisk as the liquid comes to the boil and thickens slightly.

Drain the canned sweetcorn, add to the pan and heat thoroughly. Season
to taste, then garnish and serve.

VARIATIONS
- Cook 2 large corn cobs in boiling water, adding a little salt towards the
end of the cooking period. If salt is added to the corn too early, it
toughens the grains. Strip the corn from the cob and add as above. Use
150 ml/¼ pint (⅔ cup) of the liquid in which the corn has cooked
instead of that amount of milk.

- Place 350 g/12 oz (¾ lb) frozen sweetcorn in the soup after adding the milk and cook steadily until tender. You may find you need to add a little extra milk towards the end of the cooking period.

DO NOT FREEZE

Fennel and Tomato Soup

Cooking time: 25 minutes
Serves 4 to 6

The combination of fennel and tomatoes is a very pleasant one. Make sure the white fennel bulbs are firm and that any leaves are bright green. The soup can be served chunky or smooth.

Metric/Imperial	Ingredients	American
2 large	fennel bulbs	2 large
4 medium	tomatoes	4 medium
50 g/2 oz	butter	¼ cup
900 ml/1½ pints	water	3¾ cups
to taste	salt and freshly ground black pepper	to taste
to taste	pinch aniseed, optional	to taste
To garnish	yoghurt fennel leaves	

Remove the fennel leaves, chop them for the garnish and set aside. Wash, dry and finely chop the fennel bulbs. Skin and halve the tomatoes, then remove the seeds. Chop the flesh finely. Heat the butter and cook the fennel and tomatoes for 10 minutes or until softened. Stir well so that the mixture does not brown. Add the water, bring to the boil and cook for 10 minutes. Season to taste. A little aniseed can be added if you want to enhance the fennel flavour.

Serve the soup topped with yoghurt and fennel leaves. If you prefer a smooth soup, sieve or liquidize the ingredients and reheat.

VARIATIONS
- A chopped medium onion and/or 2 crushed garlic cloves can be cooked in the butter with the fennel and tomatoes.

● **FENNEL AND SHRIMP SOUP**

Follow the recipe above and add about 175 g/6 oz (1 cup) peeled shrimps or chopped prawns just before serving. Heat for a few minutes only, as overheating toughens the shellfish.

FREEZING: This soup freezes well.

Lemon and Spinach Soup

Cooking time: 20 to 25 minutes
Serves 4 to 6

If you use frozen chopped spinach, you can make this soup in a very short time.

Metric/Imperial	Ingredients	American
1 medium	onion	1 medium
1 or 2	garlic cloves	1 or 2
25 g/1 oz	butter	2 tablespoons
900 ml/1½ pints	water	3¾ cups
1	vegetable or chicken stock cube	1
350 g/12 oz	frozen chopped spinach	¾ lb
1 teaspoon	finely grated lemon zest	1 teaspoon
2 tablespoons	lemon juice, or to taste	2½ tablespoons
to taste	salt and freshly ground black pepper	to taste
300 ml/½ pint	milk or single (light) cream	1¼ cups
To garnish	blanched, flaked (slivered) almonds or lemon slices	

Peel and finely chop the onion and garlic. Heat the butter and cook the onion and garlic for 5 minutes. Add the water and stock cube. Bring to the boil. If you have a microwave, you can defrost the spinach while preparing the onion and garlic and heating the water. If you do not have a microwave, simply add the spinach to the boiling liquid and stir from time to time to break up the block as the soup cooks steadily.

Add the lemon zest, juice and seasoning. When the ingredients are tender, add the milk or cream and heat without boiling. If preferred, the soup can be sieved or liquidized, then reheated with the milk or cream.

If the soup is too thin for your taste, thicken it by adding a little Beurre Manié (see page 8).

VARIATIONS
- Use about 700 g/1½ lb fresh, young leaf spinach, well washed. Cook in the water and stock cube, or use fish stock (see pages 16 and 17). Sieve or liquidize, then reheat with the milk or cream.

• LEMON AND CABBAGE SOUP
Follow the recipe for Lemon and Spinach Soup on page 37 but use 450 g/ 1 lb finely shredded cabbage instead of spinach. This soup is particularly good if made with beef stock (see page 14). 1 or 2 teaspoons caraway seeds can be added to the other ingredients.

• LEMON AND LETTUCE SOUP
Follow the recipe for Lemon and Spinach Soup on page 37 but use 50 g/2 oz (¼ cup) of butter to enrich the soup and a good 450 g/1 lb shredded lettuce. This variation is best made with real chicken stock (see page 14). Use only 600 ml/1 pint (2½ cups) of stock with 300 ml/½ pint (1¼ cups) milk and 300 ml/½ pint (1¼ cups) double (heavy) cream.

QUICK TIP *Lemon and Spinach Soup is excellent cooked in a microwave. Defrost the spinach first, as suggested in the recipe. The variations can also be cooked in a microwave if the cabbage and lettuce are really young; if older and rather tough, it is better to use a saucepan.*

FREEZING: Freeze without adding the milk or cream; these ingredients can be added when reheating.

10-Minute Tomato Soup

Cooking time: 10 minutes
Serves 4 to 6

Cans of chopped tomatoes are an invaluable ingredient in the store cupboard because tomatoes add flavour to many dishes. As they are already chopped, they cook in a very short time. You can, of course, prepare and freeze chopped tomatoes or tomato purée. If doing this for use in cooked rather than uncooked dishes, it is advisable to choose plum tomatoes, as they have a better flavour than ordinary tomatoes.

Metric/Imperial	Ingredients	American
450 g/16 oz	canned tomatoes	1 lb
900 ml/1½ pints	water	3¾ cups
4 tablespoons	chopped spring onions (scallions)	5 tablespoons
1 small	dessert apple	1 small
to taste	salt and freshly ground black pepper	to taste
½ teaspoon	paprika	½ teaspoon
1 teaspoon	brown sugar	1 teaspoon
To garnish	chopped parsley and/or chives	

Put the tomatoes and their liquid into a saucepan with the water and onions. Bring to the boil. Meanwhile, peel and grate the apple, then add to the pan with a little seasoning, the paprika and sugar. Simmer for 10 minutes and serve, or purée the soup, return to the pan and reheat. Garnish and serve.

Speedy Vegetable Soup

Cooking time: 25 minutes
Serves 4

Grating the suitable vegetables before use either by hand or with the attachment on an electric mixer or food processor shortens the cooking time a great deal.

Softer ingredients, such as onions and tomatoes, are better chopped. Partially cook the onions in a little fat before adding the liquid – this gives them a better flavour.

Metric/Imperial	Ingredients	American
2 medium	onions	2 medium
350 g/12 oz	mixed vegetables, see Note, weight when prepared	¾ lb
25 g/1 oz	butter or margarine	2 tablespoons
900 ml/1½ pints	water	3¾ cups
2 medium	tomatoes, optional	2 medium
2 tablespoons	chopped parsley	2½ tablespoons
1 teaspoon	chopped thyme or tarragon or ½ teaspoon dried thyme or tarragon	1 teaspoon
to taste	salt and freshly ground black pepper	to taste
To garnish	cream or yoghurt	

Note: Choose vegetables that will give a range of colour and textures, e.g.
Spring: broad (fava) beans, carrots, fennel, early potatoes.
Summer: fresh green beans and peas, young carrots and turnip.
Autumn: broccoli, celery, leeks, sweetcorn (fresh, frozen or canned)
Winter: carrots, celeriac, leeks, turnip, parsnip.

Peel and finely chop the onions. Prepare your other vegetables as necessary. Heat the butter or margarine in a saucepan, add the onions and cook gently for 5 minutes. Pour the water into the pan, bring to the boil and add the vegetables. Boil steadily for 10 minutes. If too thick, add a little extra water. Skin and finely chop the tomatoes, then add to the pan with the herbs and seasoning to taste. Continue cooking for a further 5 minutes, then garnish and serve.

VARIATIONS

- Add a vegetable stock cube to the water for extra flavour.
- If fresh tomatoes are not available, add 1 to 2 tablespoons (1¼ to 2½ tablespoons) tomato purée (paste) or use about 300 ml/½ pint (1¼ cups) tomato juice instead of the same amount of water.

- **SPEEDY CREAM OF VEGETABLE SOUP**

Follow the recipe above, but use only 600 ml/1 pint (2½ cups) water.

When the vegetables are tender, blend 1 level tablespoon (1¼ level tablespoons) cornflour (cornstarch) with 150 ml/½ pint (⅔ cup) milk and 150 ml/¼ pint (⅔ cup) single (light) cream. Stir into the vegetable mixture and cook steadily, stirring all the time, until thickened.

Alternatively, purée the vegetables first, then return them to the pan and add the cornflour mixture. In this case, use only 2 level teaspoons cornflour. Cook steadily, stirring all the time, until thickened. Steady, rather than quick cooking is particularly important if tomatoes or tomato juice are in the soup.

FREEZING: The basic soup freezes well. If making the Speedy Cream of Vegetable Soup it is better to freeze the cooked vegetables and add the cornflour mixture when the soup has been defrosted and reheated.

QUICK FISH, MEAT AND POULTRY SOUPS

The soups on the following pages can all be cooked quickly, particularly if you use time-saving devices.

Microwave cooking fish works well, and fish soups are no exception. The flavour is excellent, provided the fish is not overcooked. Over-cooking in the microwave makes fish dry and hard. When the fish is added to the other ingredients, allow just over half the cooking time that it would need in a saucepan. If the fish does not appear to be quite cooked, allow the soup to stand for 2 or 3 minutes after cooking and check again. You will probably find that during the standing time the cooking has been completed and the fish is perfectly tender. If it is not quite ready, replace the bowl in the microwave and cook for a further 1 or 2 minutes.

The recipes based on canned consommé take about two-thirds of the cooking time needed in a saucepan. I would avoid cooking the Consommé and Liver Soup in a microwave because it is all too easy to overcook liver; even a few seconds too long in the microwave makes it dry and tough.

The chicken soups on pages 53 to 57 also take about two-thirds of the ordinary cooking time provided you boil the water before adding it to the other ingredients.

General information about cooking soups in a microwave appear on page 7.

Pressure cooking can be used for fish and chicken soups. They take just under half the ordinary cooking time given in the recipe and require 25 per cent less liquid.

The recipes based on consommé are so quickly cooked in a saucepan that cooking under pressure after the preliminary stages would not save much time.

General information about making soups in a pressure cooker appear on page 6.

Arbroath Smokie Broth

Cooking time: 25 minutes
Serves 4

Arbroath Smokies are small, delicately flavoured smoked haddock. As the smoking process cooks them, subsequent heating can be kept to a minimum. For the best results, use home-made chicken stock (see page 14) rather than a stock cube. A famous Scottish haddock soup, Cullen Skink, is on page 182.

Metric/Imperial	Ingredients	American
1 small	onion	1 small
1 small	leek	1 small
1 medium	potato	1 medium
50 g/2 oz	butter	¼ cup
900 ml/1½ pints	water	3¾ cups
1	chicken stock cube	1
350 to 450 g/12 oz to 1 lb	Arbroath Smokies	¾ to 1 lb
to taste	salt and freshly ground black pepper	to taste
to taste	cayenne pepper, optional	to taste
To garnish	chopped parsley and/or chopped dill	

Peel, then finely and neatly chop the onion, leek and potato. Heat the butter and cook the vegetables for 10 minutes. Add the water and stock cube, bring to the boil and simmer for 10 minutes.

Meanwhile, skin the smokies and divide the fish into neat, bite-sized pieces. Add to the liquid, simmer for 4 to 5 minutes, then season to taste (be sparing with the salt). Garnish and serve.

VARIATIONS

• SMOKED KIPPER BROTH

Cook kippers in a little boiling water, then drain and use the flaked flesh instead of smokies in the soup above. A few tablespoons of the liquid in which the kippers were cooked could be used with the water. In this case, you may have sufficient flavour to omit the stock cube, or to use only half of it.

• SMOKED TROUT BROTH

Use smoked trout instead of smokies. You will need 2 good-sized trout as there is considerable wastage from the heads, skins and bones. These could be simmered to make a fish stock, which could be substituted for the water and chicken stock cube or chicken stock. This trout soup could be garnished with lightly whipped cream flavoured with a little horseradish cream.

DO NOT FREEZE

Crab Soup

Cooking time: 25 minutes
Serves 4 to 6

The combination of leeks, tomato and crab makes this a particularly interesting soup. If possible, use all white crabmeat, but it can be frozen, canned or fresh. There is a famous crab soup, Partan Bree, on page 189.

Metric/Imperial	Ingredients	American
350 g/12 oz	small leeks, weight when prepared	¾ lb
25 g/1 oz	butter	2 tablespoons
25 g/1 oz	plain (all-purpose) flour	¼ cup
600 ml/1 pint	tomato juice	2½ cups
450 ml/¾ pint	water	scant 2 cups
2 teaspoons	lemon juice, or to taste	2 teaspoons
225 to 350 g/8 to 12 oz	crabmeat	½ to ¾ lb
to taste	salt and freshly ground black pepper	to taste
To garnish	little whipped cream or cream cheese lemon wedges	

Wash the leeks, discard the tough green parts of the stalks, but use a little of the tender green. Slice thinly. Heat the butter in the saucepan, add the leeks and cook for 5 minutes. Stir in the flour, then add the tomato juice, water and lemon juice. Stir as the mixture comes to the boil and thickens slightly. Cover the pan and simmer steadily for 10 minutes. Add the crabmeat and stir into the hot liquid. Heat for a few moments only, then season to taste. Spoon into warmed soup bowls, then garnish and serve.

VARIATIONS
- Sieve or liquidize the cooked leeks, then return to the pan, stir in the crabmeat and heat for a few minutes.

- Add half a fish stock cube to emphasize the fish flavour.
- For a more savoury taste, add 1 crushed garlic clove to the leeks.
- If using fresh crabmeat, make stock from the shells and small claws, as described on page 17, and use this instead of water.
- If you have no tomato juice, use about 225 g/8 oz (½ lb) skinned, deseeded and chopped tomatoes, or a small can of chopped tomatoes plus an extra 300 ml/½ pint (1¼ cups) of water or 2 tablespoons (2½ tablespoons) tomato purée (paste) diluted with 600 ml/1 pint (2½ cups) additional water.

- **MUSSEL SOUP**

Use about 225 g/8 oz (½ lb) cooked mussels (weight without shells), prepared as described on page 196, instead of the crabmeat. Take the mussels out of their shells when cooked. (You will need at least 550 g/1¼ lb mussels in their shells to give the required weight.)

- **PRAWN OR SHRIMP SOUP**

Use peeled and chopped prawns or shrimps instead of crabmeat.

QUICK TIP *If using frozen crabmeat, allow it to defrost before using to save time in heating.*

DO NOT FREEZE

Salmon and Ginger Soup

Cooking time: 20 minutes
Serves 4 to 6

This is a delicious creamy soup with the delicate flavour of ginger. Adjust the amount of root ginger used to personal taste. Do not pre-cook the salmon: the small dice of fish cook well in the liquid and retain all their flavour.

Metric/Imperial	Ingredients	American
450 g/1 lb	salmon fillet	1 lb
2 cm/¾ inch	root ginger	¾ inch
900 ml/1½ pints	milk	3¾ cups
100 g/4 oz	frozen peas	¾ cup
to taste	salt and freshly ground black pepper	to taste
1 tablespoon	cornflour (cornstarch)	1¼ tablespoons
300 ml/½ pint	single (light) cream	1¼ cups
1 oz/25 g	butter	2 tablespoons
To garnish	lemon wedges	

Skin the salmon fillet and cut the flesh into 1.25 to 2 cm/½ to ¾ inch dice. Peel and grate the ginger. Bring nearly all the milk to the boil with the ginger, add the salmon and frozen peas (there is no need to defrost them) together with a little seasoning. Simmer for 10 minutes. Blend the cornflour with the rest of the milk, tip into the soup and stir briskly as it thickens. Lastly, add the cream and butter and heat. Taste the soup and adjust the seasoning. Garnish and serve.

DO NOT FREEZE

Seafood Bisque

Cooking time: 20 minutes
Serves 4 to 6

A traditional bisque recipe appears on page 193 and describes how to make a fish stock from the shells of lobsters, crabs or prawns, or the bones of fish. In the speedy recipe below, water, milk and cream are used, plus a few drops of anchovy essence, to give more flavour to the trio of fish used. The bread thickens the soup.

Metric/Imperial	Ingredients	American
3 level tablespoons	soft white breadcrumbs	3¾ level tablespoons
300 ml/½ pint	water	1¼ cups
1	lemon	1
600 ml/1 pint	milk	2½ cups
few drops	anchovy essence	few drops
175 g/6 oz	peeled prawns or shrimps	1 cup
175 g/6 oz	fresh, frozen or canned white crabmeat	1 cup
100 g/4 oz	canned salmon, weight without bones or skin	¾ cup
300 ml/½ pint	single (light) cream	1¼ cups
to taste	salt and freshly ground black pepper	to taste

Put the breadcrumbs into a saucepan with the water. Heat for a few minutes until the water reaches boiling point, then remove from the heat and allow to stand for 5 minutes. Pare the zest from half the lemon and squeeze out the juice. Put the zest into the pan with the breadcrumbs. Cut the other half of the lemon into wafer-thin slices and set aside for garnish.

Pour the milk over the breadcrumbs and liquid in the pan, heat gently. Add the anchovy essence, the fish, cream, lemon juice and seasoning, heat steadily for 5 to 10 minutes. Stir once or twice to break up the salmon. Serve topped with the lemon slices.

VARIATIONS
- Use just one kind of fish; in this case, you need at least 350 g/12 oz (2 cups).

- **SEAFOOD AND FENNEL BISQUE**

Simmer 3 tablespoons (4 tablespoons) finely chopped fennel root for a few minutes in the water before adding the breadcrumbs. Omit the lemon zest and juice in the recipe above but add 2 teaspoons chopped fennel leaves. Garnish with lemon slices and sprigs of fennel leaves.

QUICK TIP *This is an ideal soup to cook in a microwave. Follow the recipe above, but cook the fish only until it is heated; do not overcook.*

DO NOT FREEZE

SOUPS BASED ON CONSOMMÉ

The following soups are all based on consommé, either canned or home-made (see pages 68 to 83). If you have no consommé, dissolve a stock (bòuillon) cube in water; this will make a less rich soup than consommé.

Beef Soup with Parsley Dumplings

Cooking time: 15 minutes

Serves 4 to 6

The liquid must be boiling briskly when the dumplings are added or they will not rise.

Metric/Imperial	Ingredients	American
600 ml/1 pint	canned or home-made consommé (see page 68)	2½ cups
600 ml/1 pint	water parsley dumplings (see pages 308 and 309), made with 50 g/2 oz (½ cup) flour	2½ cups

Bring the consommé and water to the boil. Make the dumplings and form into at least 12 small balls. Drop into the briskly boiling liquid and cook rapidly for 5 minutes, then lower the heat slightly and cook for a further 10 minutes. This cooking time is perfectly adequate for really **small** dumplings.

VARIATIONS

- Use 1.2 litres/2 pints (5 cups) of water with 2 beef stock cubes instead of the consommé and water.
- Add a few diced cooked vegetables to the soup towards the end of the cooking time.
- Use some of the other kinds of dumplings described on pages 309 and 310.

FREEZING: Although this soup freezes well, it does take up a lot of space in the freezer, so you may prefer to make and freeze the cooked or uncooked dumplings separately, then prepare the soup when required.

Beef and Liver Soup

Cooking time: 10 to 15 minutes
Serves 4 to 6

This combination of the two good flavours of liver and beef forms a very tempting soup. It would be ideal for an invalid, but the 'hale and hearty' will enjoy it too. Ideally, calf's liver should be used but lamb's liver is a good alternative.

Metric/Imperial	Ingredients	American
225 g/8 oz	calf's or lamb's liver	½ lb
600 ml/1 pint	canned or home-made consommé (see page 68)	2½ cups
600 ml/1 pint	water	2½ cups
to taste	salt and freshly ground black pepper, but see method	to taste
To garnish	yoghurt paprika	

Mince the liver, or chop it finely in a food processor. Be careful not to over-process, as this makes the liver sticky. You can scrape fine pieces from the pieces of liver by drawing a sharp knife across the meat.

Heat the consommé and water, then add the liver and lower the heat. Cook for about 3 minutes only because overcooked liver becomes tough and unpalatable. Taste the soup and add seasoning if necessary. You may like to add a shake of cayenne pepper or paprika, or a few drops of soy sauce or Worcestershire sauce to give more flavour. Garnish and serve.

VARIATIONS
- Use home-made veal consommé (see page 69) rather than beef.
- Beef Tea, made as described on page 70, makes an excellent soup.

FREEZING: Leftover soup can be frozen to prevent wastage but this is not an ideal soup to freeze. The liver should be slightly undercooked, since reheating after defrosting would make it dry and rather tough.

Beef, Potato and Mushroom Soup

Cooking time: 15 minutes
Serves 4 to 6

When potatoes are grated, they cook very quickly, so care must be taken not to overcook them or they disintegrate and thicken the soup. Choose any type of mushrooms.

Metric/Imperial	Ingredients	American
600 ml/1 pint	canned or home-made consommé (see page 68)	2½ cups
600 ml/1 pint	water	2½ cups
225 g/8 oz	old or new potatoes	½ lb
100 g/4 oz	mushrooms	¼ lb
to taste	salt and freshly ground black pepper	to taste

Bring the consommé and water to the boil. Peel or scrape the potatoes immediately before cooking so they do not discolour. Grate them fairly coarsely and drop into the boiling liquid. Cook for 5 minutes.

Meanwhile, wipe the mushrooms, reserve the stalks for potential use in other soups or stews and cut the caps into very thin strips. Add to the soup and cook for 5 minutes. Taste the soup and add more seasoning if necessary. Lower the heat if the potatoes are not quite tender and continue cooking.

VARIATIONS

- Use 1.2 litres/2 pints (5 cups) water with 2 stock cubes instead of the consommé and water. Add any other seasoning sparingly.
- Use finely shredded leeks, white parts only, or finely chopped fennel instead of mushrooms.
- Substitute grated carrots, mixed root vegetables or celeriac for the potatoes.

- **CHICKEN, POTATO AND MUSHROOM SOUP**
Use chicken or game consommé instead of beef (see pages 71 and 72).

DO NOT FREEZE: the cooked potato seems to lose much of its flavour.

Speedy Mulligatawny Soup

Cooking time: 20 to 25 minutes
Serves 4

This soup has a refreshing and well-spiced flavour. It is equally good made with a chicken- or meat-flavoured stock cube, and excellent with canned consommé.

Metric/Imperial	Ingredients	American
1 tablespoon	sunflower oil	1¼ tablespoons
4 tablespoons	chopped spring onions (scallions)	5 tablespoons
3 teaspoons	curry paste or powder	3 teaspoons
3 tablespoons	grated cooking apple	4 tablespoons
1.2 litres/2 pints	water	5 cups
1	chicken, beef or lamb stock cube, or to personal taste	1
2 tablespoons	seedless raisins	2½ tablespoons
2 tablespoons	long-grain rice	2½ tablespoons
to taste	salt and freshly ground black pepper	to taste

Heat the oil, add the onions and curry paste or powder and cook for 2 minutes. Stir the apple into the curry mixture, then add the water. Bring to the boil, add the stock cube with the remaining ingredients and cook until the rice is tender.

VARIATION
- Use canned consommé instead of the water and stock cube, or use half consommé and half water.

FREEZING: While this soup can be frozen, it is so quickly prepared that it hardly seems worthwhile.

Chicken Broth

Cooking time: 25 minutes
Serves 4 to 6

This is a very satisfying soup which could be served as a light main dish. Make sure the chicken flesh is very finely chopped, minced or processed in order to cook the soup quickly. If speed is not too important, cut the chicken into small, neat dice. As the soup is not sieved or liquidized, chop all the vegetables finely and neatly.

Metric/Imperial	Ingredients	American
225 to 350 g/8 to 12 oz	chicken breast	½ to ¾ lb
2 medium	onions	2 medium
2 medium	tomatoes	2 medium
100 g/4 oz	button mushrooms	¼ lb
2 tablespoons	sunflower oil	2½ tablespoons
1 litre/1¾ pints	water	scant 4½ cups
1	chicken stock cube	1
1 tablespoon	chopped parsley	1¼ tablespoons
to taste	salt and freshly ground black pepper	to taste

Mince or finely chop the chicken. Peel and finely chop the onions and tomatoes (these can be deseeded if desired). Wipe and thinly slice the mushrooms. Heat the oil in a pan, add the chicken and vegetables and cook gently for 10 minutes, stirring all the time.

Boil the water in a kettle, then add to the pan with the stock cube. Bring to simmering point, add the parsley and a little seasoning. Cover the pan and cook for another 10 minutes. Check the chicken is cooked. Taste the soup, add additional seasoning if required and serve.

VARIATION
- Add 1 tablespoon (1¼ tablespoons) long-grain rice. Blend this with the vegetables and chicken after these have been cooked in the oil and before adding the water. If using rice the cooking time must be a little longer than given in the recipe above.

DO NOT FREEZE

Oriental Chicken Soup

Cooking time: 25 minutes
Serves 4 to 6

The combination of chicken with water chestnuts, bamboo shoots and soy sauce makes this soup both interesting and satisfying. In order to cook the chicken within the time given, the breast should be finely chopped or minced. If you have a little more time, choose chicken legs rather than breasts as they have more flavour, but allow an extra 10 minutes' cooking time.

Metric/Imperial	Ingredients	American
225 to 350 g/½ to ¾ lb	chicken breast	½ to ¾ lb
1 small	carrot	1 small
1 small	leek	1 small
1 small bunch	spring onions (scallions)	1 small bunch
1½ tablespoons	sunflower oil	scant 2 tablespoons
2 teaspoons	grated root ginger	2 teaspoons
1 litre/1¾ pints	water	scant 4½ cups
1	chicken stock cube	1
6 to 8	canned water chestnuts	6 to 8
¼ to ½	canned bamboo shoot	¼ to ½
1 tablespoon	soy sauce	1¼ tablespooons

Mince or finely chop the chicken. Peel and grate or finely dice the carrot. Wash and thinly slice the white part of the leek. If the spring onions (scallions) are small, cut them in half; if larger, cut into slices.

Heat the oil in a saucepan, then add the chicken and prepared ingredients together with the root ginger. Stir over a low heat for 10 minutes. Meanwhile, boil the water, add to the pan with the stock cube and simmer for 5 minutes.

Drain the water chestnuts and bamboo shoots and cut into fine strips. Add to the soup with the soy sauce and heat for 5 to 8 minutes. No extra seasoning should be needed in this soup, but taste just before serving and add a little salt and pepper if required.

VARIATIONS

- When time permits, use home-made Chicken or Oriental Stock (see pages 14 and 16) instead of water and a stock cube.
- Add a few tablespoons of finely chopped fresh or canned beansprouts.

• ORIENTAL DUCK SOUP

Use finely diced duck, free from skin and fat, instead of chicken. The cooking time for the soup will then be about 35 minutes. Use a chicken stock cube with the water, or better still, use home-made Chicken or Duck Stock (see pages 14 and 16).

FREEZING: The soup should not be frozen, but you can transfer the remaining water chestnuts and bamboo shoot(s) with their liquid to suitable containers and freeze for future use.

Chicken and Bacon Chowder

Cooking time: 25 minutes
Serves 4 to 6

Although it is ideal to use uncooked chicken in a soup, this particular dish has such a lot of flavour from bacon, vegetables and herbs that cooked chicken can be used. In fact, this soup is a good way of using the small pieces of chicken left on a carcass. You will find the timing for making the soup with uncooked chicken under variation.

Metric/Imperial	Ingredients	American
4 rashers	bacon	4 slices
2 medium	potatoes	2 medium
2 medium	onions	2 medium
100 g/4 oz	button mushrooms	¼ lb
2	celery sticks	2
25 g/1 oz	butter	2 tablespoons
1 litre/1¾ pints	water	scant 4½ cups
1	chicken stock cube	1
2 tablespoons	chopped parsley	2½ tablespoons
1 tablespoon	chopped chives	1¼ tablespoons
1 teaspoon	chopped thyme	1 teaspoon
to taste	salt and freshly ground black pepper	to taste
1 to 2 teaspoons	ready-made English mustard	1 to 2 teaspoons
350 g/12 oz	cooked chicken	¾ lb
To garnish	grated or cream cheese	

Derind the bacon and cut the rashers into small pieces. Peel the potatoes and onions, cut the potatoes into 1.25 cm/½ inch dice and finely chop the onions. Wipe and slice the mushrooms. Finely slice the celery.

Heat the bacon rinds with the butter, add the chopped bacon and vegetables and cook steadily over the heat, stirring from time to time, for 10 minutes.

Bring the water to the boil and pour over the ingredients in the pan. Add the stock cube, herbs, a little seasoning and the mustard. Simmer for 5 minutes.

Dice the chicken neatly, add to the soup and heat for 5 minutes. Remove the bacon rinds and serve the chowder topped with the cheese.

VARIATION
- If using uncooked chicken, cut it into 1.25 cm/½ inch dice. Allow 50 g/ 2 oz (¼ cup) of butter and cook the chicken with the bacon for 5 minutes. Add the vegetables and cook for a further 10 minutes. Add the water and stock cube, or better still, real Chicken Stock (see page 14), plus the remaining ingredients and cook for a further 15 minutes.

DO NOT FREEZE

QUICK FRUIT AND CHEESE SOUPS

There are a number of fruit soups on pages 262 to 276, but the two given in this chapter – one based on avocados and one on groundnuts (peanuts) – are particularly easy and quick to cook. In fact, all the soups that follow are so rapidly cooked in a saucepan that it is not worth using a microwave, and a pressure cooker is unsuitable. By cooking in a saucepan you can check on the various flavours that need to be added.

Avocados are unusual because, unlike other fruits, they provide a certain amount of protein in which groundnuts, like all nuts, are rich.

Warning: Before serving groundnut soup, make absolutely certain that no one who might eat it is allergic to the nuts. The consequences to that person could be very serious, sometimes even fatal.

Avocado Soup

Cooking time: 5 or 10 minutes
Serves 4 to 6

This soup is based upon the well-known spiced dip guacamole, and can be served hot or cold. When serving it cold, I prefer to use ripe, ordinary tomatoes; if serving it hot, I would choose plum tomatoes.

Metric/Imperial	Ingredients	American
900 ml/1½ pints	water	3¾ cups
1	vegetable or chicken stock cube	1
2	garlic cloves	2
6 tablespoons	chopped spring onions (scallions)	7½ tablespoons
350 g/12 oz	tomatoes	¾ lb
3 medium	avocados	3 medium
1 tablespoon	lemon juice	1¼ tablespoons
to taste	salt and freshly ground black pepper	to taste
to taste	Tabasco sauce	to taste
To garnish	lemon slices	

If serving cold: put about 150 ml/¼ pint (⅔ cup) of water into a pan, add the stock cube and heat until dissolved. Remove from the heat, add the cold water and mix together.

Peel and crush the garlic cloves, add to the onions. Skin, deseed and chop the tomatoes. Halve the avocados, remove the stones and skin, chop the flesh and sprinkle with the lemon juice immediately.

Sieve or liquidize all the ingredients with some of the stock. Blend with the remaining stock, then add salt, pepper and Tabasco to taste. Chill well and garnish with the lemon before serving.

If serving hot: heat all the water with the stock cube. Prepare the ingredients as above, then sieve or liquidize with a little of the stock. Return to the pan, add the seasoning and Tabasco sauce, heat for a few minutes only, then garnish and serve.

DO NOT FREEZE

Groundnut Soup

Cooking time: 25 minutes
Serves 4 to 6

The fascinating mixture of ingredients in this West Indian recipe makes a
wonderful special occasion soup, with the advantage that it is quickly prepared
and cooked. Groundnuts are another name for peanuts, and their flavour is
enhanced by adding peanut butter. This butter is *not* good by itself for frying the
onions, so use a little extra butter or margarine.

Metric/Imperial	Ingredients	American
3 medium	onions	3 medium
3 medium	tomatoes	3 medium
50 g/2 oz	peanuts	scant ½ cup
25 g/1 oz	butter or margarine	2 tablespoons
50 g/2 oz	peanut butter	¼ cup
900 ml/1½ pints	water	3¾ cups
1 tablespoon	lime or lemon juice	1¼ tablespoons
1 large	avocado	1 large
to taste	salt and freshly ground black pepper	to taste

Peel and finely chop the onions. Skin and chop the tomatoes. Chop the peanuts
coarsely. Heat the butter or margarine in a saucepan, add the onions and cook
gently for 5 minutes. Put in the tomatoes, peanuts and peanut butter and stir
over a low heat until well blended. Pour the water and lime or lemon juice over
the ingredients and bring to the boil. Cover the pan and simmer for 15 minutes.

Halve and peel the avocado, remove the stone. Dice the flesh and add to
the soup with seasoning to taste. Simmer for a few minutes only, then serve.

VARIATION

● GROUNDNUT AND CHICKEN SOUP
Use the ingredients in the soup above, but substitute chicken stock for water.
Add either 100 g/4 oz (¼ lb) finely diced uncooked chicken to the onions and
cook gently for 10 minutes, stirring constantly, then continue as the recipe, or
add the same amount of cooked chicken to the soup with the diced avocado.

FREEZING: **Do not freeze.**

Golden Cheddar Soup

Cooking time: 15 minutes
Serves 4 to 6

Cheese soups make an excellent light meal; if served as a first course, be fairly sparing with the portions as the soup is very satisfying. Never overcook a cheese soup; when the cheese has melted the soup is ready to serve; long cooking makes the cheese stringy. The addition of firm ingredients, such as sweetcorn and carrots, gives an interesting appearance and texture. Soups are a good way of using up cheese that has become dry; grate or dice it finely so that it melts quickly.

Metric/Imperial	Ingredients	American
1 or 2	garlic cloves	1 or 2
175 g/6 oz	mature Cheddar cheese	1½ cups, when grated
25 g/1 oz	butter	2 tablespoons
25 g/1 oz	plain (all-purpose) flour	¼ cup
900 ml/1½ pints	milk	3¾ cups
2 medium	carrots	2 medium
100 g/4 oz	canned sweetcorn	¼ lb
to taste	salt and freshly ground white pepper	to taste
1 teaspoon	ready-made English or French mustard	1 teaspoon

Peel the garlic cloves but leave them whole. Grate the cheese. Melt the butter in a saucepan, add the garlic and turn in the butter until pale golden. Stir in the flour, then add the milk. Bring to the boil and stir until thickened. Add the carrots and simmer for 2 or 3 minutes (they should remain fairly firm). Add the sweetcorn, then stir in the cheese until melted. Taste the soup and add salt, pepper and mustard to taste. Remove the garlic cloves and serve.

VARIATIONS
- For a more savoury flavour, increase the amount of butter to 50 g/2 oz (¼ cup). Peel and finely chop 1 medium onion and cook with the garlic cloves.

- Use half milk and half chicken stock.
- Diced celery or finely grated celeriac could be used in place of the sweetcorn.
- Choose other good cooking cheeses, such as Double Gloucester, Cheshire or Stilton (see below).

- **GOLDEN STILTON SOUP**

Use diced Stilton cheese in place of the Cheddar.

- **STILTON SOUP**

Omit the carrot and corn in the first recipe and use Stilton instead of Cheddar cheese. Heat 50 g/2 oz (¼ cup) butter and cook 2 finely chopped medium onions and 2 crushed garlic cloves until tender. Add the flour, as in the first recipe, but with 450 ml/¾ pint (scant 2 cups) of chicken stock and only 300 ml/½ pint (1¼ cups) of milk. When thickened, sieve or liquidize. Return to the pan with the cheese and seasoning to taste, and heat until the cheese has melted. Continue as the recipe. Garnish with croûtons before serving.

FREEZING: All these cheese soups freeze well, but take care when defrosted that they are heated for the minimum time.

Pasta and Cheese Soup

Cooking time: 15 to 20 minutes
Serves 4

This is a very satisfying soup, which lends itself to many variations (see below). The actual cooking time depends upon the kind of pasta used. Short-cut, quick-cooking macaroni or small shells are an ideal choice, but long pasta, such as spaghetti, can be broken into small pieces before cooking. Soup noodles could be used if you prefer. Do not overcook the pasta: while it can be served softer in a soup, it retains more flavour if slightly *al dente* (firm to the bite).

Metric/Imperial	Ingredients	American
1 small	onion	1 small
900 ml/1½ pints	canned consommé or water with 1 chicken, meat or vegetable stock cube	3¾ cups
75 g/3 oz	pasta, see above	⅔ cup
300 ml/½ pint	milk	1¼ cups
2 tablespoons	chopped parsley	2½ tablespoons
1 tablespoon	chopped chives	1¼ tablespoons
to taste	salt and freshly ground black pepper	to taste
3 tablespoons	grated Parmesan cheese	3¾ tablespoons

Peel and chop or thinly slice the onion. Bring the consommé or water and stock cube to the boil, add the onion and pasta. Cook in an uncovered pan until nearly tender, then add the milk, herbs and any seasoning required. Heat well then stir in the cheese and serve.

VARIATIONS
- Instead of Parmesan cheese, use about 100 g/4 oz (¼ lb) grated Gruyère, Cheddar or other good cooking cheese.
- For a richer soup use half milk and half single (light) cream.
- Add 1 or 2 finely chopped hard-boiled eggs to the soup with the cheese, or use instead of some of the cheese.

- Add a little finely chopped crisp bacon or cooked ham or chicken to the soup with the milk and herbs.
- Add finely diced cooked vegetables to the soup just before serving.
- Vegetarians could use all water and omit the milk, or use soya milk (see page 29).

- **RICE AND CHEESE SOUP**
Use 75 g/3 oz (scant ½ cup) long-grain rice instead of the pasta. Any of the variations work well with rice.

FREEZING: **Do not freeze.** The first soup is inclined to lose both texture and flavour. The variation with rice freezes better.

EASY GARNISHES

On pages 299 to 331 you will find a selection of classic garnishes for soups. Some of these take a long time to prepare, but the following suggestions are based on ingredients you probably already have in your kitchen.

Cheese: Top vegetable and other soups with a little grated cheese or with a small spoonful of cream or curd cheese.

Cream, etc: A spoonful of cream turns a soup into a more luxurious dish and adds a richer flavour. Yoghurt, soured cream, crème fraîche or fromage frais are other alternatives. Add any creamy topping immediately before serving the soup so that it does not dissolve in the hot liquid.

If you draw a knife through thick cream or yoghurt, you can create an interesting feathered effect. Alternatively, whip the cream and put a blob on top of the soup.

If the recipe requires soured cream and none is available, see page 641.

Directions for freezing soups containing cream or yoghurt appear at the end of the recipe or in the introduction to that particular chapter.

Croûtons: If you have frozen croûtons, take them out of the freezer shortly before they are required (see page 305). Ready-prepared croûtons are on general sale.

Herbs: Chopped herbs make a soup look colourful and add flavour. It saves time if you chop small batches with a sharp knife or kitchen scissors and store them in covered containers in the refrigerator or freezer.

Nuts: Chopped nuts make an interesting garnish on a number of soups and also add to the food value. Blanched and flaked almonds (obtainable in packets) are a particularly good garnish for chicken or vegetable soups.

Soured Cream

This is made commercially from single (light) cream to which a culture has been added, giving it a slightly sharp taste. It gives a subtle flavour to many kinds of dishes, including soup.

To produce the same effect at home, simply add a little lemon juice to fresh cream, tasting as you do so to achieve the desired acidic flavour.

FLAVOURING READY-MADE SOUPS

There may be odd occasions when you do not have the time or the ingredients available to make a home-made soup, so you buy a ready-made variety. The choice of flavours on sale is extensive and I hope you select a soup that pleases you. If you are disappointed with the taste or texture, however, there are simple ways in which it can be improved.

Concentrated Soups

These are ultra-thick, designed to be diluted with a considerable amount of liquid, usually water. Taste the soup and see if it would be better diluted with milk or a mixture of milk and water.

Do not use the full amount of extra liquid at once, blend it in gradually and check the taste and consistency as you do so. I have found that soup with a reasonably good flavour when a little extra liquid is added sometimes becomes flavourless when the recommended full quantity is used. It is better to have slightly less soup with a more definite taste.

Consommés

These are much improved by adding a dash of sherry, port or Madeira wine.

If time permits, add a garnish (see pages 299 to 331).

If the soup is somewhat over-salted for your taste, mix in a little top of the milk or single (light) cream, or a purée of fresh tomatoes.

Fish Soups

The creamy variety may seem a little bland in flavour so add freshly chopped herbs, such as dill, fennel leaves, chives or tarragon. If fresh herbs are not available, use a small quantity of dried herbs. One or two teaspoons of finely grated lemon zest heated with the soup may also improve the taste.

If the creamy taste is not very evident, emphasize this by adding a little top of the milk or cream as you heat the soup, or top each serving with cream, soured cream, yoghurt or cream cheese.

A clear, French-type fish soup can be topped with garlic mayonnaise (see page 205).

Meat and Poultry Soups

Particles of meat or poultry often seem very soft, which gives an overcooked taste to soup. Counteract this by adding finely chopped spring onions (scallions), grated carrot or finely diced celery as you heat the soup.

A little red or white wine or sherry improves the taste, as does a fairly generous amount of chopped parsley or chives, and a very small amount of chopped sage.

Garnish with nuts or chopped crisp bacon to restore texture to the soup.

Vegetable Soups

The variety and flavourings used in these have become very imaginative, but the vegetables often seem over-soft, resulting in lack of taste and texture.

Improve the flavour by adding a little lemon juice and chopped herbs. Take care when making the soup if it contains lemon juice and cream: it must not be allowed to boil.

To restore the texture of the vegetable, add either a peeled grated carrot, or finely diced celery, or chopped spring onions (scallions) or wafer-thin slices of leek. Heat with the soup, but do not allow them to become too soft. A little grated nutmeg, a pinch of dried ginger or a small amount of grated fresh ginger may improve the flavour and make it more interesting. Soups based on root vegetables could be flavoured with a little curry paste or powder.

Tomato soups may be a little sweet for some palates, so counteract this by adding a little dry sherry, dry white wine, soy sauce or lemon juice.

Chapter Three

CLEAR SOUPS

Clear soups are a wise choice for anyone wanting to retain a slim figure, as, apart from the garnish, they are made without high-calorie ingredients.

The finest of all clear soups is undoubtedly a consommé. To achieve a perfect result, the meat, stock and other ingredients must be given long, slow cooking. After that it is important to clarify the stock so that the consommé is beautifully clear. Recipes for making consommés based on various meats, poultry and game are given on pages 68 to 72.

Having prepared a consommé, you can turn it into a wide range of soups by using different garnishes. The French fill pages and pages of their cookery books with these, and I have selected some of the more practical and interesting ones. In these the garnish gives the soup its name.

Vegetarians can add suitable garnishes to the very refreshing and delicious Tomato Consommé on page 80.

This chapter also includes other interesting unthickened soups, including those based on beer and wine.

Clear soups are less satisfying than thicker soups, so you can be more generous with the portions.

Microwave cooking: This method can be used for making a consommé. First make the stock as described on pages 14 to 17, but reduce the amount of liquid by a quarter, e.g. 1.8 litres/3 pints (7½ cups) instead of 2.4 litres/4 pints (10 cups). There is less evaporation in a microwave than in a saucepan, and the total cooking time is shorter.

Having made the stock, prepare the extra ingredients, as described in the recipe, and place them in a very large bowl or casserole suitable for microwave cooking. To save time, bring the stock to the boil in an ordinary pan and pour it over the ingredients in the microwave container. Heat for a few minutes on full power until you see bubbles on the surface of the liquid, then turn to defrost and cook for about 10 minutes. Check the speed of cooking; if the liquid is simmering gently, cover the bowl and continue cooking for 30 minutes. If the liquid is boiling too quickly on defrost, turn to a lower setting.

When cooked, strain the stock. You can then return it to the container for clarifying with egg whites and shells, as described on page 69. Heat for 10 minutes on defrost, then strain.

Pressure cooking: This is a splendid way of making consommé. First make the stock in the pressure cooker, as described on page 12. Put your consommé ingredients in the pressure cooker and add the stock. In the case of Beef Consommé, you will need only 1.2 litres/2 pints (5 cups) of stock, since the total cooking time is short and there is virtually no evaporation of liquid.

Bring the cooker to full pressure (high) and maintain this for 30 minutes only. Allow to drop at room temperature, then strain the stock. Continue as the recipe, using the pressure cooker as an ordinary saucepan if you want to clarify the liquid using egg whites and shells.

Always check on the capacity of your particular pressure cooker if making large amounts of consommé or other soups, and follow the manufacturer's instructions about filling the pan. It should never be more than half full, so if your cooker is small, you may need to prepare the consommé in two batches.

Slow cooking: Electric slow cookers have not been mentioned before in this book, but could be used for making stock and consommé. Always fill the cooker with boiling water or boiling stock before turning down to the recommended position for your particular model. You should allow about 6 to 8 hours to produce a good stock, and the same time for a consommé. At the end of the cooking time, strain the liquid and transfer to an ordinary saucepan if you want to clarify it using egg whites and egg shells, as described on page 69.

Oven cooking: It is also possible to make consommé in a tightly covered casserole in the oven. Follow the instructions about making stocks in the oven on page 6. Use the amount of liquid given in the recipes. In the case of the Beef Consommé on page 68 you need to allow at least 2¼ hours (plus the time to make the stock) in a preheated oven set to 150°C/300°F/gas mark 2. Strain the cooked consommé into a saucepan if you want to clarify it using egg whites and shells (see page 69) and continue as the recipe on page 68.

Beef Consommé

Cooking time: 1¼ hours plus time to make stock
Serves 6 to 8

A really first-class consommé takes a great deal of time and care. The first stage is to prepare a good beef stock (see page 14). In order to darken the colour of the stock, place the beef bones, with any meat adhering to them, in a roasting tin with about 25 g/1 oz (2 tablespoons) butter and cook for 30 minutes in the oven preheated to 200°C/400°F/gas mark 6. Place the bones and all your other ingredients in a large saucepan, add the water and make the stock as described on page 14. Allow the stock to become cold, then remove the fat (see page 12).

Basic additions to the shin of beef and stock are listed below, but the variations list a number of other ingredients that add interest and flavour.

Metric/Imperial	Ingredients	American
675 to 900 g/1½ to 2 lb	shin of beef	1½ to 2 lb
2.4 litres/4 pints	good beef stock (see page 14)	10 cups
to taste	salt and freshly ground black pepper	to taste
1 medium to large	onion	1 medium to large
1 medium	carrot	1 medium
2	fresh bay leaves or 1 dried leaf	2
300 ml/½ pint	dry sherry	1¼ cups
To clarify the consommé	3 egg whites and their shells, optional, see method	

Cut the meat into small pieces, then place in a large saucepan with the well-strained stock and a little seasoning. Peel the onion and carrot, but leave them whole to prevent them breaking up in the liquid. Add the vegetables and bay leaves. Bring the liquid to boiling point and remove any scum floating on top with a spoon. Cover the pan, lower the heat and simmer for 1 hour.

Strain the soup, using an ultra-fine strainer or preferably a sieve lined with several layers of fine muslin (chemists sell this as gauze).

If you feel the consommé is sufficiently clear, simply reheat it with the sherry, then taste and adjust the seasoning. If not, add the egg whites and shells to the boiling consommé and simmer for a further 20 minutes. Any minute particles will adhere to the whites and shells. Strain once more though muslin, as described above, then reheat, add the sherry and serve.

VARIATIONS
● Add several chopped celery stalks and their leaves; a small, whole peeled turnip could be added, plus several peeled garlic cloves, sprigs of parsley, and/or thyme or tarragon. A deseeded and halved red pepper may also be added for an interesting taste.

● JELLIED CONSOMMÉ
If you want the consommé to become lightly jellied to serve cold, cook a small part of knuckle of veal or 2 pig's trotters with the other ingredients.

● LAMB CONSOMMÉ
This is far less popular than its beef counterpart but is none the less delicious. Follow the recipe for Beef Consommé but use the Brown Stock (see page 15) made with lamb bones and about 900 g/2 lb diced lean lamb, plus the ingredients given on page 68.

● VEAL CONSOMMÉ
This is a delicious consommé to have hot or cold. Follow the recipe for Beef Consommé but substitute shin of beef with a knuckle of veal plus 450 g/1 lb diced lean veal and the White Stock (see page 15) made with veal bones. The finished consommé is very pale, so it is advisable to flavour it with Madeira or port instead of sherry.

FREEZING: All these recipes freeze perfectly (see the information about freezing stock on page 13). As alcohol tends to lose some flavour in freezing, add it after defrosting the consommé.

Bouillon

Cooking time: 4 to 5 hours
Serves 4 to 6

The word *bouillon* is often used to denote a clear soup. It may be a true consommé, like the recipes that follow, but it is often a good meat soup based on old-fashioned Beef Tea, offered to invalids to build up their strength.

Metric/Imperial	Ingredients	American
675 g/1½ lb	lean shin or neck of beef	1½ lb
1.2 litres/2 pints	water	5 cups
to taste	salt and freshly ground black pepper	to taste

Cut the meat into small dice and put into a deep casserole with the water and a little seasoning. Do not add vegetables. Cover the casserole tightly and cook for 4 to 5 hours in an oven preheated to 150°C/300°F/gas mark 2. Strain the liquid and serve, this could be garnished as suggested on pages 95 to 99 and 299 to 316.

Chicken Consommé

Cooking time: 1¼ hours plus time to make stock
Serves 6 to 8

While the ingredients are different, the method of making Chicken Consommé
is exactly the same as Beef Consommé.

Metric/Imperial	Ingredients	American
1	900 g/2 lb chicken or several chicken portions	1
2.4 litres/4 pints	chicken stock (see page 14)	10 cups
to taste	salt and freshly ground black pepper	to taste
1 or 2	lemons, as required	1 or 2
¼	celery heart	¼
1 medium to large	onion	1 medium to large
2	fresh bay leaves or 1 dried leaf	2
1 sprig	thyme	1 sprig
300 ml/½ pint	dry sherry or port	1¼ cups

Skin the chicken and cut into portions if necessary. Remove any giblets or dark
parts of the inside, which could spoil the colour of the consommé. Put into a
saucepan with the stock and add a little seasoning. Pare the zest from the
lemons, take care not to use any bitter white pith. Cut the celery into large
chunks. Peel the onion and leave it whole. Put the lemon zest, vegetables and
herbs into the pan and continue as for Beef Consommé (see page 68).

Strain through muslin or clarify with egg whites and shells, as described
on page 69. Add the sherry and a little lemon juice to taste.

VARIATIONS

• DUCK CONSOMMÉ
Follow the recipe for Chicken Consommé, but use duck flesh instead of chicken
and duck stock as described on page 16. Discard any skin and excess fat. Instead of
thyme use a small sprig of sage. You can replace the lemon zest with that of
oranges; bitter Seville oranges give a particularly interesting taste to the soup.

● **GUINEA FOWL CONSOMMÉ**

Follow the recipe for Chicken Consommé, or for Game Consommé (see page 72).

● **TURKEY CONSOMMÉ**

Follow the recipe for Chicken Consommé, but use turkey flesh instead of chicken. If you take a mixture of breast and leg meat, you produce a darker-looking consommé, which has a very good flavour.

The stock used in the recipe can be chicken stock (see page 14), or a similar stock produced from turkey bones or the carcass of the bird.

FREEZING: All these consommés freeze well. Freeze as Beef Consommé (see page 68).

Game Consommé

Cooking time: 1¼ to 2 hours plus time to make stock
Serves 6 to 8

This consommé has a particularly rich and delicious flavour. You can use stewing venison, jointed rabbit or joints of hare, pheasant or other game birds. The cooking time depends on the tenderness of the game used. Elderly game birds make a first-class consommé; to extract the full flavour cook the flesh until tender.

Metric/Imperial	Ingredients	American
900 g/2 lb	game flesh, see above	2 lb
2.4 litres/4 pints	game stock (see page 72)	10 cups
to taste	salt and freshly ground black pepper	to taste
about 6	juniper berries, optional	about 6
1 medium to large	onion	1 medium to large
¼	celery heart or about 100 g/4 oz (¼ lb) celeriac	¼
1 medium	carrot	1 medium
2	fresh bay leaves or 1 dried leaf	2
1 sprig	rosemary	1 sprig
300 ml/½ pint	Madeira or port	1¼ cups

Cut the venison or other game into pieces. Place in a saucepan with the stock, a little seasoning and the juniper berries. Peel the onion but leave it whole. Chop the celery into large pieces but leave the celeriac in one piece. Peel the carrot and leave whole. Put the vegetables and herbs into the pan and follow the directions for Beef Consommé (see page 68).

Strain through muslin or then clear with egg whites and shells, as described on page 69. Add the Madeira or port.

FREEZING: As Beef Consommé (see page 69).

Fish Consommé

Cooking time: 40 minutes
Serves 4 to 6

Fish Consommé is not served as frequently as meat consommés but it is an excellent basis for a clear fish soup to which you can add shellfish or small pieces of prime fish, such as sole, turbot or Fish Balls (see page 304).

There is no need to buy fish to make the consommé if you have sufficient fish heads, bones and trimmings.

This recipe is made in the same way as the Fish Stock on page 16 but with a higher percentage of fish, so giving a stronger flavour to the liquid.

Metric/Imperial	Ingredients	American
1 kg/2¼ lb	fish, see above	2¼ lb
1.8 litres/3 pints	water	7½ cups
to taste	salt and freshly ground white pepper	to taste
1 medium	onion	1 medium
1 medium	carrot	1 medium
1	celery stick	1
2	fresh bay leaves or 1 dried bay leaf	2
1 sprig	chervil or parsley	1 sprig
to taste	little lemon zest	to taste
300 ml/½ pint	dry white wine	1¼ cups

Wash the fish and put into a large saucepan with the water and add a little seasoning. Peel the onion and carrot but leave them whole, add to the water with the chopped celery, herbs and lemon zest. Bring to the boil, remove any scum that may float to the top of the liquid, then cover the pan. Lower the heat and simmer for 35 minutes. Strain through fine muslin (see page 69), then return to the pan with the wine and heat.

VARIATIONS

● Add about 150 ml/¼ pint (⅔ cup) dry sherry to the liquid instead of the white wine.

● SEAFOOD CONSOMMÉ
Make the consommé, strain very carefully, then reheat. Add a mixture of flaked crabmeat (preferably white), peeled prawns and finely diced lobster. Heat for a few minutes only so that the shellfish does not become overcooked and tough. Top each portion of consommé with a little cream.

● SOLE CONSOMMÉ
Skin fillets of sole and cut the flesh into small goujons (ribbons) about 2.5 cm/1 inch in length. Put into the hot consommé and poach for a few minutes. Top the soup with cream and chopped fennel leaves.

Halibut, turbot or other white fish can be used instead of sole.

● FISH AND TOMATO CONSOMMÉ
Follow the main recipe, but add 450 g/1 lb skinned and deseeded tomatoes to the other ingredients. Strain and return to the pan. Taste the liquid and add a little tomato purée (paste) for a stronger tomato taste. For a more piquant flavour add a few drops of Tabasco sauce.

This soup can be topped with cream and small pieces of sun-dried tomatoes.

FREEZING: This consommé freezes well.

CLASSIC CONSOMMÉS

Variety is added to consommés by using different garnishes, and the garnishes themselves give their name to the particular recipe. The classic garnishes on page 75 are based on information from *Larousse Gastronomique* and Henry Smith's Book (Practical Press Ltd, 1949). I have tested and adapted some of these to make them sensible for home cooks.

Add the following garnishes to consommés made with meat, chicken or game. The amounts given are sufficient for 4 good servings based on 1.2 litres/2 pints (5 cups) consommé (see pages 68 to 72).

● **CONSOMMÉ BRUNOISE**

Prepare the vegetables described in Consommé Julienne (below), but fry them in 25 g/1 oz (2 tablespoons) butter until really brown. Add to the consommé and cook for a few minutes, until tender.

● **CONSOMMÉ CAMERONI**

Cook 1 to 2 tablespoons (1¼ to 2½ tablespoons) fine soup noodles in a little salted water, strain and add to the hot consommé. Serve finely grated Gruyère cheese with the soup.

● **CONSOMMÉ CELESTINE**

Make small pancakes (see page 95), then cut one or two into wafer-thin strips. Heat for 1 minute in the hot consommé.

● **CONSOMMÉ COLBERT**

Cut about 225 g/8 oz (½ lb) mixed vegetables, such as carrot, turnip, green beans and cauliflower, into small pieces; mix with a few peas. Cook in a little salted water until tender, then strain. Poach an egg for each person. Pour the hot consommé into hot soup bowls or soup plates, top each portion with the vegetables and egg.

● **CONSOMMÉ JULIENNE**

The term *julienne* describes vegetables that are cut into matchstick-sized pieces. They can be cooked in a little salted water, then drained and added to the consommé, or cooked first in a small amount of butter until pale golden, then simmered in a few tablespoons of consommé before being added to the hot soup. The usual mixture of vegetables are carrot, celeriac, turnip, leek or onion and a very small portion of cabbage. Use about 100 g/4 oz (¼ lb) vegetables (prepared weight) and 25 g/1 oz (2 tablespoons) butter.

● **CONSOMMÉ MADRILÈNE**

Skin, halve and deseed 1 good-sized tomato, then chop the flesh into small pieces. Simmer in the consommé with 2 teaspoons tomato purée (paste). Strain carefully, add a few cooked soup noodles, then reheat. Garnish with finely chopped chervil or parsley.

MODERN CONSOMMÉS

Consommés can also be made more interesting and satisfying by using modern ingredients for garnish. The quantities given are sufficient for 1.2 litres/2 pints (5 cups) of consommé.

● **CONSOMMÉ AMÉRICAINE**

The word *américaine* means that tomatoes are part of the dish. I have found that a mixture of fresh and sun-dried tomatoes make an excellent combination. (Use sun-dried tomatoes in oil if possible.)

Skin, halve and deseed 2 medium fresh tomatoes. Cut the pulp into very small neat dice. Chop 2 well-drained sun-dried tomatoes into very tiny pieces. Put both kinds of tomatoes into the consommé and simmer for 5 minutes.

Tomatoes are particularly good with a Beef or Veal Consommé (see pages 68 and 69).

● **CHINESE MUSHROOM CONSOMMÉ**

This soup is based upon Chicken or Turkey Consommé (see page 71), although a Veal Consommé (see page 69) could be used.

Dried mushrooms are readily available today.

Soak 10 to 12 dried mushrooms in warm water for at least 30 minutes. Drain well, then cut into very small dice. Return to the warm water and simmer for about 30 minutes or until quite tender. Add to the consommé with 2 teaspoons light soy sauce, or a little more if desired, and 1 tablespoon (1¼ tablespoons) lemon juice. Heat the soup then add a little rice wine or dry sherry.

● **LEMON CONSOMMÉ**

The flavour of lemon goes well with Chicken or Veal Consommé (see pages 71 and 69). This can be introduced by adding chopped lemon grass plus a little lemon juice. The lemon grass adds a good appearance to the soup.

Soften 2 thick or 3 thinner stems of lemon grass in cold water for about 15 minutes. Cut into very thin slices. Add to the hot soup with 1 to 2 tablespoons (1¼ to 2½ tablespoons) of lemon juice. Heat for 5 minutes and serve.

FREEZING: The consommés can be frozen as described on page 18, but unless stated otherwise, garnishes are better freshly prepared.

BASED ON BEEF CONSOMMÉ

These garnishes add interest and flavour to the Beef Consommé on page 68. The quantities given below with approximately 1.2 litres/2 pints (5 cups) of consommé make 4 generous portions.

● **CONSOMMÉ BÉARNAISE**

Add diced cooked Beef and Chicken Quenelles (see page 95) to the Beef Consommé. Heat very gently for 2 to 3 minutes.

● CONSOMMÉ CLERMONT

Peel and slice 2 small onions, separate the slices into rings and coat in a little seasoned flour. Fry in hot oil until crisp and golden brown. Drain on absorbent paper. Top the hot consommé with the hot onion rings and serve immediately before the rings become soft.

● CONSOMMÉ DUSTAN

Add a few cooked and diced French (bobby) beans to the hot consommé .

● CONSOMMÉ INDIENNE

Peel and finely dice 2 shallots or small onions. Heat 50 g/2 oz (¼ cup) butter, add the shallots and 1 to 2 teaspoons curry powder or paste. Cook gently, stirring well until cooked. Heat the consommé with 1 tablespoon sultanas (1¼ tablespoons seedless white raisins). Put the hot onion mixture at the bottom of the heated soup bowls and top with the consommé.

● CONSOMMÉ PALESTINE

Peel approximately 150 g/5 oz Jerusalem artichokes (¾ cup when prepared) and cut into small dice or scoop into very small balls with a vegetable scoop. Cook in a very lightly seasoned water until just tender. Add to the hot consommé.

● CONSOMMÉ PORTUGAISE

Skin and halve 2 medium tomatoes, remove all the seeds and cut the pulp into small, neat dice. Add to the hot consommé with 2 tablespoons (2½ tablespoons) cooked long-grain or Basmati rice. Simmer for a few minutes only so the tomatoes retain their texture.

As a change from fresh tomatoes, use diced sun-dried tomatoes instead.

● CONSOMMÉ SAINT-GERMAIN

Add a few tablespoons of cooked garden peas or frozen peas to the consommé.

If you make this consommé with lamb rather than beef, add a very little chopped mint to the consommé with the peas.

BASED ON VEAL CONSOMMÉ

The garnishes for Chicken Consommé on page 71 work equally well with Veal Consommé (see page 69). The following are particularly suitable for this delicately flavoured soup.

Allow 1.2 litres/2 pints (5 cups) of consommé plus the ingredients below to serve 4 people.

- **CONSOMMÉ CARÈME**

Finely chop enough lettuce heart to give 4 tablespoons (5 tablespoons).
Peel and dice young carrots and young turnips to give the same amount of
each. Add the carrots and turnips to the soup and cook for 5 minutes or
until just tender, but not over-soft. Add the lettuce and heat for 1 minute.

If asparagus is in season, allow 1 to 2 tips per person and cook with the
carrots and turnips.

- **CONSOMMÉ CREOLE**

Skin, halve and deseed 2 medium tomatoes and cut the pulp into very small
dice. Peel and slice 2 shallots or small onions. Separate the slices into rings,
halve any that are too large to fit easily on a soup spoon. Cut enough
matchstick-sized pieces of red pepper to give 4 tablespoons (5 tablespoons). Fry the onions in 25 g/1 oz (2 tablespoons) of butter until golden
brown. Add the tomatoes and red pepper to the soup and simmer for 5
minutes. Add the onions and cook for a further 1 minute.

- **CONSOMMÉ VALETTA**

Remove the peel from 2 small tangerines, clementines or satsumas. Cut
enough matchsticks of zest to fill 4 tablespoons (5 tablespoons). Allow to
stand in the cold consommé for about 30 minutes, or longer if time permits.
Bring to simmering point and cook for 5 minutes. Cut out the segments from
the fruit, discarding any skin and pips. Add to the soup and heat for 1 minute.

BASED ON CHICKEN CONSOMMÉ

The following ingredients are excellent with Chicken Consommé (see page
71). To give 4 generous servings make 1.2 litres/2 pints (5 cups) of
consommé and the quantities of additional ingredients given below.

- **CONSOMMÉ DIPLOMATE**

Add a few Chicken Quenelles (see page 95) and sliced peeled prawns or
shrimps to the consommé. In the classic recipe diced truffle is also added. This
soup can be thickened with tapioca, as suggested on page 81, then garnished.

- **CONSOMMÉ FLORENTINE**

Chop a few very young spinach leaves into very small pieces. Add these to the
hot consommé and simmer for a few minutes only. Cut 1 or 2 pancakes (see
page 97) into equally small pieces, add to the hot soup and heat for 1 minute.

- **CONSOMMÉ GRENADE**

Add 2 tablespoons (2½ tablespoons) tomato purée (paste) to the Chicken
Consommé. Garnish with chopped chervil.

To make a change, mix equal amounts of Tomato Consommé (see page 81) with Chicken Consommé and garnish as above.

● CONSOMMÉ À LA SEMOULE

As couscous (coarse semolina) is so popular, this soup will be in keeping with modern tastes. Add 2 tablespoons (2½ tablespoons) couscous to the consommé and simmer for approximately 15 minutes until the soup is thickened. Stir briskly from time to time as the soup cooks. Top with grated cheese and serve with a little extra cheese.

BASED ON GAME CONSOMMÉ

These garnishes below are excellent with a Game Consommé (see page 72). The quantities, added to 1.2 litres/2 pints (5 cups) of consommé, give 4 generous portions.

● CONSOMMÉ CHASSEUR

Neatly dice small portions of cooked breast from game birds, rabbit or hare and add to the consommé. Heat with port or wine to taste.

● CONSOMMÉ DIANE

This soup is similar to Consommé Chasseur (above) but is flavoured with a little dry sherry and a good shake of cayenne pepper.

● CONSOMMÉ NESSELRODE

Wipe, then finely chop enough mushrooms to give 4 tablespoons (5 tablespoons). Make the profiteroles as described on page 98; split them open and insert a very small amount of canned unsweetened chestnut purée. Add the mushrooms to the consommé; simmer for 5 to 10 minutes or until just tender. Top the consommé with the profiteroles immediately before serving.

● CONSOMMÉ OLGA

Finely dice enough peeled celeriac to give 2 tablespoons (2½ tablespoons), and cut the same amount of peeled carrots. Strain, dry and dice enough pickled gherkins to give 1 tablespoon (1¼ tablespoons). Add the celeriac and carrots and simmer for 5 to 10 minutes or until just soft. Stir in the gherkins and heat for 1 minute.

BASED ON FISH CONSOMMÉ

Although a fish consommé is not served as frequently as those based on meat, poultry and game, the following recipes make interesting soups with a good flavour.

Allow 1.2 litres/2 pints (5 cups) of Fish Consommé (see page 73) plus the quantities below to give 4 generous servings.

● **CONSOMMÉ BRABANCONNE**
Cook 12 mussels, as described on page 196, then peel and slice 8 prawns. Add to the hot consommé with a few tablespoons of white wine. Heat for a very short time so that the shellfish does not become tough.

● **CONSOMMÉ COLBERT**
Although this garnish can be added to other consommés, it is excellent with a fish consommé. Peel and dice enough young carrots and turnips to give 3 tablespoons (3¾ tablespoons) of each. Add to the hot consommé with the same amount of shelled peas and tiny cauliflower florets. Poach in the soup for about 5 to 8 minutes. Top each portion of soup with a poached egg and serve. (I use quail's eggs, poached for 2 minutes, as they are very much lighter and better than hen's eggs.)

Tomato Consommé

Cooking time: 30 minutes
Serves 4

This fresh tomato consommé has a most refreshing flavour. It is ideal to serve
hot or cold, and the ideas given for meat, poultry and fish consommés on pages
75 to 79 are equally good with this clear soup. Use really ripe tomatoes so you
can extract the maximum amount of juice and flavour.

Metric/Imperial	Ingredients	American
1 medium	onion	1 medium onion
2	garlic cloves	2
675 g/1½ lb	tomatoes	1½ lb
1.2 litres/2 pints	vegetable stock (see page 15)	5 cups
1 tablespoon	lemon juice	1¼ tablespoons
to taste	salt and freshly ground black pepper	to taste
to taste	cayenne pepper, optional	to taste

Peel and finely chop the onion and garlic. Cut the tomatoes into pieces on a
plate so no juice is wasted. Put the onion, garlic and tomatoes, with any
juice, into a saucepan with the stock, lemon juice and a very little seasoning.
Bring the liquid to simmering point. Lower the heat and cook steadily for 30
minutes. Strain carefully through fine muslin (gauze) placed over a sieve.
(Use a nylon or hair sieve if possible as metal sieves sometimes give a faint
metallic flavour to the liquid.) Reheat and taste the consommé and add any
additional seasoning required.

For details of cold, jellied and iced consommés, see pages 69, 294 and 296.

VARIATIONS

- If you feel the consommé is lacking flavour before straining, add a little
  concentrated tomato purée (paste). Heat for a few minutes, then strain as
  above.
- A red deseeded chilli pepper could be added to the other ingredients but
  in this case omit the cayenne pepper.

● **BEETROOT AND TOMATO CONSOMMÉ**

Use 450 g/1 lb tomatoes and 350 g/12 oz (¾ lb) skinned and grated cooked beetroot with the other ingredients given above, but omit the cayenne. Cook as before, then strain.

● **CUCUMBER AND TOMATO CONSOMMÉ**

Use 1 large peeled and sliced cucumber with 350 g/12 oz (¾ lb) tomatoes, a sprig of mint and the other ingredients given in the recipe above. Omit the cayenne. Cook as before, then strain.

QUICK TIP *Each of these consommés can be cooked in a large bowl in the microwave. Allow about 20 minutes' cooking time.*

FREEZING: All the recipes freeze well.

Consommé en Croûte

Cooking time: 24 to 25 minutes
Serves 4 to 6

The first time I was served this impressive soup was at a special dinner party in South Africa – the end of a busy, but very enjoyable, tour of cookery demonstrations I had given in that beautiful country.

I was pleased to see my fellow diners looked as perplexed as I was – how to insert the spoon into a light, golden crust without creating a spray of soup from underneath. Some people used a knife and gently cut the pastry, others spooned it off layer by layer.

In classic dishes the puff pastry is fitted over ovenproof bowls half filled with cold soup and baked in the oven. If the soup bowls are unsuitable for heating, rounds of pastry are cut to size and baked separately before being added to the hot soup.

I take a 'coward's way' out. I make small fancy shapes of puff pastry, bake them until crisp and brown, then add them to the soup just before serving. Apart from being easier to make, they are also easier to eat.

Metric/Imperial	Ingredients	American
115 g/4 oz	frozen puff pastry	¼ lb

Defrost the pastry until just soft enough to roll out on a lightly floured board to a thickness of about 6 mm/¼ inch. Cut into small rounds, about 3.5 cm/

1½ inches in diameter, or any other shapes that take your fancy. Chill for a short time. Meanwhile, preheat the oven to 220 to 240°C/425 to 450°F/gas mark 7 to 8. Bake the pastry shapes for about 10 minutes or until well risen, golden and firm. Serve freshly baked on the soup.

FREEZING: Open-freeze and then pack.

Consommé à la Danoise

Cooking time: 15 minutes plus time to make stock
Serves 4 to 6

This soup is delicious made with duck or wild duck stock and garnished with bite-sized quenelles of minced duck flesh plus diced mushrooms. Make sure the stock from the duck is free from fat.

Metric/Imperial	Ingredients	American
1.2 litres/2 pints	duck stock (see page 16)	5 cups
to taste	salt and freshly ground black pepper	to taste
150 ml/¼ pint	Madeira	⅔ cup
To garnish	duck quenelles (see page 96)	
100 g/4 oz	mushrooms	¼ lb

Bring the duck stock to the boil, add the seasoning and the wine. Lower the heat slightly so the soup is simmering. Wipe the mushrooms, discard the stalks. Dice the caps neatly. Add to the hot soup with the quenelles and poach for 8 minutes. Serve at once.

VARIATION
- Game stock could be used with quenelles of game (see page 96).

FREEZING: The stock containing the mushrooms can be frozen. Do not freeze the quenelles.

Stracciatella

Cooking time: 10 minutes plus time to make stock
Serves 4 to 6

This is an interesting way to combine a good beef stock or consommé (pages 14 and 68) with cheese and eggs, thus turning it into a light meal. Where possible, grate the Parmesan just before using – it has much more flavour than when ready-grated.

Metric/Imperial	Ingredients	American
1.2 litres/2 pints	beef stock or consommé (see pages 14 and 68)	5 cups
to taste	salt and freshly ground black pepper	to taste
4 to 6	eggs	4 to 6
100 g/4 oz	Parmesan cheese	¼ lb
To garnish	chopped chives	

Bring the stock or consommé to the boil and season to taste. Lower the heat until the liquid is boiling gently. Beat the eggs. Grate the cheese, blend with the eggs and gradually pour the mixture into the soup, stirring with a fork as you do so. Serve as soon as the eggs form ribbons in the liquid. Top with the chives.

FREEZING: While the stock or consommé can be frozen, the soup containing the eggs cannot.

Clear Mulligatawny

Cooking time: as specific recipe, see below
Serves 4 to 6

This will be a very popular soup with those who enjoy the bite of curry. The stock used must have a very pronounced flavour. A little dry sherry could be added to the soup after straining, but do not be too generous or it will overwhelm the curry flavour.

Metric/Imperial	Ingredients	American
	as Chicken Mulligatawny Soup 2 (see page 253) or as Mulligatawny Soup 1 (see page 229)	
To garnish	cooked long-grain rice	
	lemon wedges	

Prepare either of the soups, then strain carefully through muslin (see page 69). Add a little dry sherry if desired, then reheat. Garnish and serve.

VARIATION
- To sharpen the taste of the soup, add a whole small cooking apple to the listed ingredients in either recipe. There is no need to peel or core the apple – the whole fruit gives more flavour and is less likely to cloud the soup than when cut into small pieces.

FREEZING: Both the clear soups freeze well, but the flavour is intensified if the soup is frozen before straining. When serving the soup, reheat and then strain it.

Lemon and Egg Soup (Soupa Avgolemono)

Cooking time: 25 minutes plus time to make stock
Serves 4

This classic Greek soup is wonderfully refreshing. If using chicken stock cubes rather than real chicken stock (see page 14), do not use too many as the delicate flavour of the eggs and lemon should predominate.

Metric/Imperial	Ingredients	American
1.2 litres/2 pints	chicken stock (see page 14)	5 cups
to taste	salt and freshly ground black pepper	to taste
50 g/2 oz	long-grain rice	⅓ cup
2 or 3	eggs, see method	2 or 3
3 tablespoons	lemon juice, or to taste	3¾ tablespoons

Bring the stock to the boil, season lightly if necessary, then add the rice. Cover the pan and simmer for 15 minutes, or until the rice is just tender. Beat the eggs (3 eggs give a richer soup) with the lemon juice in a basin. Gradually whisk in a little of the hot stock from the saucepan until smooth. Tip the egg and lemon mixture into the saucepan and simmer very gently for 3 or 4 minutes only. Do not allow the soup to boil at this stage. Serve at once.

DO NOT FREEZE

QUICK TIP *This soup can be cooked in a large bowl in a microwave. Use full power until the rice is cooked. Blend the eggs and lemon juice as above, add a little stock, return to the bowl; place in the microwave on defrost (or a lower setting if your microwave has a high output, see page 7). Heat for 1 to 2 minutes only, stirring or whisking at ½-minute intervals. Allow to stand for 1 to 2 minutes before serving.*

Clear Avgolemono Soup

Cooking time: 10 minutes plus time to make stock
Serves 4

Although this is not a classic dish, the following ingredients make a delicious soup, which can be served hot or well chilled.

Follow the recipe on page 86, but omit the rice. Bring the chicken stock to the boil. Whisk the eggs and lemon juice together, gradually beat in a little of the hot stock, then return to the pan and cook gently for 3 to 4 minutes. Serve hot topped with a little soured cream or yoghurt and finely grated lemon zest.

If serving cold, top with the soured cream or yoghurt, lemon zest and sprigs of fresh mint.

FREEZING: **Do not freeze.**

Mock Turtle Soup

Cooking time: 3 hours plus time to make stock
Serves 8

The only time you are likely to taste real turtle soup in Britain is if invited to a special event, such as the Lord Mayor's banquet held at the Guildhall in London. It is not possible to make this soup in the home, for fresh turtles are unobtainable. Real turtle soup, sold in cans, has the authentic sticky texture but is improved if a little warmed sherry is added to each serving.

Mock Turtle Soup, based on a calf's head, is an excellent alternative to the real thing.

Metric/Imperial	Ingredients	American
1	calf's head	1
few drops	wine or malt vinegar	few drops
1 large	onion	1 large
2 medium	carrots	2 medium
2 or 3	celery sticks	2 or 3
2.4 litres/4 pints	veal stock (see page 15)	10 cups
to taste	sprigs of basil, chives, marjoram	to taste
2	fresh bay leaves or 1 dried leaf	2
to taste	salt and freshly ground black pepper	to taste
150 ml/¼ pint	dry sherry	⅔ cup
To garnish	lemon wedges	

Ask the butcher to split the calf's head. The brains and tongue can be removed and used separately (see Note on page 89). Wash the head very well in plenty of cold water. Put into a large saucepan with sufficient water to cover plus vinegar. Bring the water to the boil, then remove the calf's head and discard the water. This process is known as 'blanching'.

Peel and chop the onion and carrots, dice the celery. Return the head to the saucepan with the veal stock, vegetables, herbs and a little seasoning. Cover the pan and simmer steadily for 3 hours or until the meat is tender.

Strain the stock. If not sufficiently clear, follow the advice given with Beef Consommé on page 68.

Remove the meat from the head and cut into small, neat dice. Return the stock and meat to the pan and heat thoroughly. Add the sherry and any extra seasoning required. Serve with wedges of lemon.

VARIATION
• Extra sherry can be added to each portion of soup, just as with real turtle soup.

Note: The brain can be served on fingers of toast and served as an accompaniment to the soup above or with meat soups (see page 214).

The tongue can be cooked in well-seasoned water with chopped onion, carrots and celery to flavour. Simmer for approximately 1½ hours, then serve the tongue hot or cold.

Beer and Bread Soup (Ollebrod)

Cooking time: 20 minutes plus time to make stock
Serves 4 to 6

This Danish soup is made with bread and beer flavoured with cinnamon and lemon rind. Although pumpernickel bread gives a rich colour and flavour, any wholemeal bread can be used instead of the mixture of breads. It is imperative to allow adequate soaking time for the bread. It is best to select a light ale unless you know you would appreciate a richer dark beer.

Metric/Imperial	Ingredients	American
225 g/8 oz	pumpernickel bread	½ lb
100 g/4 oz	white or wholemeal (wholewheat) bread	¼ lb
600 ml/1 pint	chicken stock (see page 14) or water	2½ cups
1.2 litres/2 pints	beer or ale	5 cups
2.5 cm/1 inch or	cinnamon stick or	1 inch or
1 teaspoon	ground cinnamon	1 teaspoon
1	lemon	1
4 tablespoons	brown sugar	5 tablespoons
to taste	salt and freshly ground black pepper	to taste

Break the bread, including the crusts, into small pieces. Heat the chicken stock or water, pour over the bread and soak for several hours or even overnight.

Tip the bread and any unabsorbed liquid into a large pan and stir briskly until a smooth mixture. Stir in the beer and cinnamon. Pare the rind from the lemon, avoiding the bitter white pith. If the rind is cut into very narrow strips, it can be retained in the soup; if cut into larger pieces, it is advisable to remove it before serving. Add the rind to the bread mixture. Halve the lemon, squeeze out the juice and add 1 tablespoon (1¼ tablespoons) to the pan but retain the remainder in case it is required.

Heat the soup, stirring well to combine all the ingredients, then stir in the sugar and seasoning. Simmer for about 10 minutes. Remove the cinnamon stick, if using this. Taste and adjust the seasoning and add extra lemon juice if necessary.

FREEZING: This soup freezes well, but the beer or ale loses some of its flavour. It is a better idea to freeze the soaked bread and lemon mixture, adding the remaining ingredients when it has been defrosted and reheated.

QUICK TIP *To shorten the soaking time, make the bread into fine crumbs and soak for about 15 to 30 minutes.*

German Beer Soup (Biersuppe)

Cooking time: 25 minutes

Serves 4 to 6

This soup should be made with one of the light German beers (lagers). The addition of cream gives it a surprisingly mellow taste.

Metric/Imperial	Ingredients	American
50 g/2 oz	butter	¼ cup
50 g/2 oz	plain (all-purpose) flour	½ cup
1 litre/1¾ pints	light beer	scant 4½ cups
1 tablespoon	lemon juice	1¼ tablespoons
300 ml/½ pint	double (heavy) cream	1¼ cups
to taste	salt and freshly ground black pepper	to taste
¼ to ½ teaspoon	ground cinnamon	¼ to ½ teaspoon
2 teaspoons	brown sugar, or to taste	2 teaspoons

Heat the butter in a saucepan, stir in the flour and continue stirring over a low heat for 2 to 3 minutes. Gradually add the beer and lemon juice. Bring to the boil and cook over a medium heat, stirring all the time until the soup thickens slightly. Lower the heat, cover the pan and continue simmering for 10 to 15 minutes.

Remove from the heat so the soup is no longer boiling, add the cream, seasoning and cinnamon. Stir well, then add the sugar. Heat gently, without boiling, for a further 2 or 3 minutes and serve with crisp toast. (Sometimes the toast is placed in hot soup bowls and the soup poured over it.)

VARIATIONS

- Black bread or pumpernickel is an excellent alternative to toast.
- Follow the recipe for Weinsuppe below, but substitute beer for the wine, or use half beer and half chicken stock.
- Use single (light) cream instead of double cream and mix it with 2 level teaspoons of cornflour (cornstarch). Pour into a small saucepan, stir over the heat until thickened, then whisk into the hot, but not boiling, beer soup. (Instead of adding cornflour to the cream, use 1 extra level tablespoon (1¼ tablespoons) of flour at the beginning of the method.)

FREEZING: **Do not freeze.**

Wine Soup (Weinsuppe) 1

Cooking time: 15 minutes
Serves 4 to 6

This German soup has a most refreshing flavour. It is excellent made with a sparkling Moselle wine, but other white wines, still or sparkling, can be used instead. Once the egg yolks are added to the hot, but not boiling, liquid, the soup must be cooked very slowly so there is no fear of it becoming overheated and curdling.

Metric/Imperial	Ingredients	American
1	lemon	1
600 ml/1 pint	white wine, see above	2½ cups
600 ml/1 pint	water	2½ cups
5 cm/2 inches	cinnamon stick	2 inches
2	egg yolks	2
to taste	salt and freshly ground black pepper	to taste
1 teaspoon	caster sugar, or to taste	1 teaspoon

Pare the zest from the lemon in fairly wide strips, avoiding the bitter white pith. Put the wine and nearly all the water into a pan with the lemon zest and cinnamon stick and bring just to boiling point. Simmer for 3 minutes.

Mix the egg yolks with the remaining water in a basin. Add 2 tablespoons (2½ tablespoons) of the very hot liquid, mix thoroughly, then pour into the pan. Lower the heat and whisk briskly until the mixture thickens sufficiently to coat the back of a wooden spoon. Remove the lemon zest and cinnamon stick. Add salt, pepper and sugar to taste, then serve with crisp toast or plain biscuits.

FREEZING: This soup must be freshly made.

QUICK TIP *This soup can be made in a microwave. Use defrost (or a lower setting if your microwave has a high output, see page 7) when the egg yolks are added, and cook for 1 to 2 minutes. Stir or whisk at ½-minute intervals. Allow to stand for 1 to 2 minutes before serving.*

German Wine Soup (Weinsuppe) 2

Cooking time: 25 minutes
Serves 4 to 6

This is a very attractive and light soup, something like a consommé thickened with egg yolks and topped with savoury balls of egg white.

Metric/Imperial	Ingredients	American
600 ml/1 pint	dry white wine	2½ cups
600 ml/1 pint	chicken stock (see page 14)	2½ cups
2.5 cm/1 inch	cinnamon stick or ¼ to ½ teaspoon ground cinnamon	1 inch
4	egg yolks	4
to taste	salt and freshly ground black pepper	to taste
2	egg whites	2
pinch	paprika or cayenne pepper	pinch

Heat the white wine, nearly all the stock and the cinnamon together for about 10 minutes; remove the cinnamon stick.

Whisk the egg yolks until thick and creamy, add the remaining cold stock, then whisk into the hot, but not boiling, soup. Cook over a low heat, whisking or stirring briskly all the time for about 6 or 7 minutes or until the soup thickens. Season to taste.

Whisk the egg whites until they stand in firm peaks, add a pinch of salt and the paprika or cayenne pepper. Drop small spoonfuls on to the simmering soup and poach for 2 minutes on each side. Serve the portions of soup topped with the meringue balls.

VARIATION
• Use all wine or three-quarters wine and one-quarter water. In this case flavour the soup with 1 tablespoon (1¼ tablespoons) lemon juice.

FREEZING: **Do not freeze.**

GARNISHES FOR CLEAR SOUPS

Many recipes in this chapter include explicit instructions about the garnish to be added. Indeed, the garnish often inspires the name of the soup.

Pancakes, quenelles and profiteroles are ideal toppings to add to clear soups, giving texture and visual interest. Recipes for these follow.

Chicken Quenelles

Cooking time: 8 minutes
Makes about 24

A delicate mixture, based upon uncooked poultry, fish or meat, is made into miniature balls or fingers to give an interesting garnish to soups. The flavouring can be varied in many ways (see below). Because the cooking time is short, the meat or fish must be tender and finely minced or chopped.

While the quenelles can be poached in a clear soup, it is easier to cook them separately in a frying pan or wide saucepan containing boiling salted water or appropriately flavoured stock. Add them to the soup immediately before serving.

Metric/Imperial	Ingredients	American
225 g/8 oz	chicken breast, prepared weight	½ lb
½ teaspoon	finely grated lemon zest	½ teaspoon
1 teaspoon	finely chopped thyme or pinch dried thyme	1 teaspoon
1	egg	1
2 tablespoons	chicken stock (see page 14) or white wine or milk	2½ tablespoons
2 tablespoons	very fine breadcrumbs	2½ tablespoons
to taste	salt and freshly ground black pepper	to taste
1	egg white	1

Remove any skin and fat from the chicken, then mince it twice or process it to give a very smooth texture. Add the lemon zest and thyme. Separate the egg, adding the yolk to the chicken mixture together with the stock, wine or milk and the breadcrumbs. Mix well and season to taste.

Whisk the 2 egg whites until they just hold their shape, then beat a good spoonful into the chicken mixture to make it softer. Fold in the remaining whisked whites.

Heat enough salted water or clear soup to give a depth of at least 5 cm/2 inches. Bring to the boil, then lower the heat to keep the liquid simmering steadily. Drop teaspoonfuls of the mixture into the liquid and cook for 4 or 5 minutes or until just firm. The quenelles puff up during cooking. Lift from the liquid with a perforated spoon and serve.

VARIATIONS

- Turkey breast or guinea fowl can be used instead of chicken.

- GAME QUENELLES

Game birds can also be used instead of chicken.

- DUCK QUENELLES

Use the breast of young duckling and 1 tablespoon (1¼ tablespoons) of red wine and 1 tablespoon (1¼ tablespoons) duck stock or milk as the liquid. Flavour the mixture with sage rather than thyme, and use orange zest instead of lemon.

- FISH QUENELLES

Use fine-fleshed white fish, such as sole, plaice, whiting, fresh trout or salmon. Mince or process the fish but be careful not to over-process, as this makes it sticky. Use chopped fennel or dill instead of thyme.

Use 1 tablespoon (1¼ tablespoons) lemon juice and 1 tablespoon (1¼ tablespoons) fish stock or milk as the liquid.

FREEZING: **Do not freeze.**

Pancakes

Cooking time: 2 to 3 minutes per pancake
Makes about 12

It is not worth making just one or two pancakes for garnish, so make a batch and freeze the surplus. The ingredients below make about 12 pancakes, or even more if you have a very small pan. Always add the oil or melted butter to the batter mixture if you intend freezing the pancakes as it improves the texture. It also helps to prevent the pancakes sticking to the pan.

Metric/Imperial	Ingredients	American
110 g/4 oz	plain (all-purpose) flour	1 cup
pinch	salt	pinch
2	eggs	2
275 ml/9 fl oz	milk or milk and water	scant 1¼ cups
1 tablespoon	olive or sunflower oil, or melted butter (optional)	1¼ tablespoons
To cook	oil or butter	

Blend the flour and salt, break the eggs into the bowl, add a little milk, or milk and water, then beat until a stiff, smooth batter. Gradually beat in the remaining liquid. If adding the oil or melted butter as recommended, whisk into the batter just before cooking.

Heat 1 to 2 teaspoons oil or a small knob of butter in a frying pan. Heat well, then pour in enough batter to give a paper-thin coating. Cook for 1 to 1½ minutes, or until the bottom of the pancake is golden. Turn or toss, and cook for the same time on the second side. Turn out of the pan and continue like this until all the batter is used.

You should find that no extra oil or butter is needed in the pan after cooking the first pancake.

VARIATION

● Use just 1 egg and 2 tablespoons (2½ tablespoons) extra milk or milk and water.

FREEZING: Stack the pancakes with a piece of greaseproof paper between each one, then pack and freeze. You can take out the number of pancakes required without defrosting the whole batch.

Profiteroles

Cooking time: 8 minutes to make choux pastry
15 minutes to bake choux buns
Makes about 40

Profiteroles used as a garnish on soups must be very small: they are miniature choux buns. Either spoon the prepared pastry mixture on to the greased baking sheets with a coffee spoon, or pipe it into tiny blobs, using a bag with a small, plain pipe.

The oven must be thoroughly preheated before baking. Always check carefully that the choux pastry is really firm before bringing the profiteroles out of the oven. Never cool choux pastry near a draught: if you do, the well-risen buns could flop.

Metric/Imperial	Ingredients	American
150 ml/¼ pint	water	⅔ cup
50 g/2 oz	butter or margarine	¼ cup
pinch	salt	pinch
65 g/2½ oz	plain (all-purpose) flour	½ cup plus 1½ tablespoons
2	small eggs	2

Pour the water into a saucepan and add the butter or margarine and salt. Heat steadily until the fat has melted. Meanwhile, sift the flour. Remove the saucepan from the heat and add all the flour. Stir well, then return the pan to a low heat and continue stirring all the time until the mixture forms a ball and leaves the sides of the saucepan clean. Allow to stand until cool.

Whisk the eggs in a separate basin, then gradually beat into the flour mixture. Always make sure the egg is thoroughly blended with the other ingredients before adding the next spoonful. Stop adding egg when the dough forms a soft sticky mixture that stands in peaks.

Preheat the oven to 220°C/425°F/gas mark 7, or 200°C/400°F/gas mark 6 if your oven is fan-heated or rather fierce. Grease two baking sheets, then spoon or pipe the mixture into buns the size of a large pea.

Bake for approximately 15 minutes until well risen, pale golden in colour and very firm. Do not remove from the baking sheets until quite cold.

VARIATION

Tomato Profiteroles: use tomato juice instead of water as the liquid in the pastry.

FREEZING: The uncooked choux pastry freezes well for up to 1 month. Remove from the freezer, leave at room temperature, then use as directed.

Cooked profiteroles also freeze well. Freeze on flat trays, so the small buns are kept separate, then pack.

FILLINGS FOR PROFITEROLES

- While small choux buns can be served plain on top of a soup, they are more interesting if filled. When cooked, carefully make a slit in the sides and insert the selected filling. This can be done while the buns are still warm or completely cold, but should not be done too far in advance or the pastry may become soggy.

  Below are some suggested fillings, which should be the consistency of thick whipped cream.

Chestnut purée: The canned variety is excellent, but very firm, so mix it with cream or crème fraîche. Add to beef, chicken or game consommés and to vegetable soups.

Cream or curd cheese: These may be flavoured with finely chopped herbs. Add to chicken, veal or tomato consommés or fish and vegetable soups.

Flaked crabmeat: Mix with mayonnaise or thick cream. Add to fish consommé or fish soups. These profiteroles are also surprisingly good with chicken consommé.

Liver pâté: Mix with cream or soured cream. Use on any of the consommés.

Chapter Four

VEGETABLE SOUPS

The wonderful range of vegetables available today means we have an almost unlimited choice of soups based on them. Many of the recipes in this chapter suggest cooking the vegetables in chicken stock, as this imparts a rich flavour that complements the other ingredients. If you are a vegetarian, simply substitute fresh vegetable stock (see page 15), or use a stock cube dissolved in water. Never overcook vegetable soups, as it is important to retain the flavour and texture of fresh vegetables.

There are several different types of vegetable soup. The first is a *clear liquid soup* in which diced vegetables add interesting flavour and colour. The soup can be exotic, like Beansprout Soup on page 103, or homely, as the Farmhouse Soup on page 125. Always cut the vegetables into a sensible size, as it is difficult to cope with oversized pieces of food on a soup spoon.

Puréed soups, where the vegetables, sometimes mixed with a little flour or other thickening, create a smooth, creamy texture, are easily and quickly prepared thanks to modern liquidizers (blenders) and food processors (see page 10). When using a food processor, remember to remove the blades before pouring out the soup as the blades can easily drop out and create a mess or even damage.

In these weight-conscious times try to use the vegetables themselves as the main thickening agent rather than introducing flour or similar ingredients.

Creamed or *velouté* soups include cream or a similar alternative. As stressed in the recipes, do take care when heating a soup that includes cream, wine or lemon juice: if allowed to boil rapidly, it will curdle (separate).

Low-fat alternatives to cream include yoghurt and fromage frais, both of which give an excellent flavour to soups. However, both need just the same care in heating as cream. Soured cream and crème fraîche have slightly acid flavours, so you may find them more interesting additions than cream.

Do try some of the less usual vegetable soups, such as Bortsch on pages

105 and 106, which is made with beetroot or a combination of cranberries and beetroot, or Okra Gumbo (see page 164), based on the vegetable sometimes known as ladies fingers. These soups are sufficiently satisfying to form a complete light meal.

Microwave cooking: Soups can be cooked very successfully in a microwave, saving time and retaining a lot of flavour. Use this appliance if the vegetables are young and tender. As large amounts of liquid are slow to heat in a microwave, boil it by conventional means and then add to the other ingredients.

It is not possible to give exact microwave timings as soups vary so much, but once they come to simmering point, they will cook in about half the time stated in the recipes. Use 10 per cent less liquid than indicated and cook on the defrost setting. Check and stir the soup from time to time, just as you would do if using a saucepan. General hints about microwaving soups are on page 7.

Pressure cooking: This is an excellent way to soften vegetables and other ingredients in a soup, particularly if they are not particularly young and tender. Check in your manufacturer's book to find the timing for vegetable soups. Onion Soup, for example, takes about 3 minutes under pressure. Use full pressure (high) and never have the cooker more than half filled. Always allow the pressure to drop at room temperature. General hints about pressure cooking soups are on page 6.

Aubergine Soup

Cooking time: 35 minutes
Serves 4 to 6

Aubergines, or eggplants as they are also called, form the basis of many dishes and are excellent in soups. In the past aubergines were salted to remove their slightly bitter taste, but modern varieties do not seem to have this problem. If you fear they may have a bitter flavour, simply peel off the skin, or salt the vegetable before cooking, as described below.

Metric/Imperial	Ingredients	American
450 g/1 lb	aubergines, see method	1 lb
to taste	salt and freshly ground black pepper	to taste
2	garlic cloves	2
1 small bunch	spring onions (scallions)	1 small bunch
225 g/8 oz	tomatoes	½ lb
2 tablespoons	olive oil	2½ tablespoons
1 litre/1¾ pints	chicken or vegetable stock (see pages 14 and 15)	scant 4½ cups
1 tablespoon	lemon juice	1¼ tablespoons
1 teaspoon	chopped oregano or marjoram	1 teaspoon
1 tablespoon	chopped parsley	1¼ tablespoons
150 ml/¼ pint	white wine	⅔ cup
To garnish	yoghurt, fromage frais or cream cheese	

If you are confident that your aubergines are not bitter, wipe them and cut into 1.25 cm/½ inch dice. If not, peel them and weigh to ensure you have 450 g/1 lb. Alternatively, score the skin(s), sprinkle with salt and leave to stand for 30 minutes. Rinse in cold water, then dice. The advantage of retaining the skin is that it gives more flavour and colour to the soup.

Peel and crush the garlic, skin and chop the white part of the spring onions and a very little of their tender green stems. Skin and finely chop the tomatoes. Heat the oil, add the garlic, onions, aubergine(s) and tomatoes and cook gently, stirring, for 5 minutes.

Add the stock, lemon juice, herbs and seasoning. Bring the liquid to the boil, cover the pan and lower the heat. Simmer for 20 minutes.

Pour in the wine, heat for 2 or 3 minutes. Taste the soup and add more seasoning if required. Garnish with yoghurt, fromage frais or small spoonfuls of cream cheese.

VARIATION

● **Purée of Aubergines**: cook the soup as above, then sieve or liquidize. Return to the pan, add the wine and heat for a few minutes. Garnish as above.

FREEZING: This soup freezes well.

Beansprout Soup (Kong Na-mool Kook)

Cooking time: 20 minutes plus time to make stock
Serves 4

This Korean soup is most interesting. The mild flavour of chicken stock forms a pleasing contrast to the stronger flavour of the beef and the delicate beansprouts.

Metric/Imperial	Ingredients	American
1 to 2	garlic cloves	1 to 2
100 g/4 oz	beef fillet steak	¼ lb
900 ml/1½ pints	chicken stock (see page 14)	3¾ cups
2 tablespoons	sliced spring onions (scallions)	2½ tablespoons
2 tablespoons	soy sauce, or to taste	2½ tablespoons
350 g/12 oz	beansprouts	¾ lb
to taste	salt and freshly ground black pepper	to taste

Peel and crush the garlic; cut the meat into 6 mm/¼ inch dice. Pour the stock into a saucepan, add the garlic, beef and spring onions and bring to the boil. Add most of the soy sauce and the beansprouts (chopped, if desired). Simmer for 10 minutes, then add seasoning to taste and the rest of the soy sauce if necessary. Serve hot with crisp biscuits.

VARIATIONS
- If using canned beansprouts, drain carefully and add to the soup after it has been cooking for 5 minutes.
- Use only half the amount of beansprouts and stir in 4 or 5 tablespoons (5 or 6¼ tablespoons) cooked, long-grain rice.
- For a vegetarian soup, use vegetable stock and diced water chestnuts instead of beef.

FREEZING: This soup is better freshly made.

QUICK TIP *A chicken stock cube and water can be used instead of fresh chicken stock.*

This soup is ideal for making in a microwave. Cook for only about 2 minutes on full power once the liquid comes to the boil to make sure the meat is not overcooked.

Bortsch

Cooking time: 1¼ hours plus time to make stock
Serves 4 to 6

There are almost as many variations in the spelling of *bortsch* as there are recipes for making this Russian soup. The name indicates that it originally included blood as one of the ingredients. Nowadays, most recipes are based on beetroot. Although the cooking time is longer with uncooked beetroot, it gives a better flavour than cooked beetroot. Beef stock adds a richer taste, but chicken stock produces a brighter colour to the soup.

Metric/Imperial	Ingredients	American
450 g/1 lb	raw beetroots (beets)	1 lb
1 medium	onion	1 medium
1 medium	carrot	1 medium
2	celery sticks	2
3 medium	tomatoes	3 medium
1.2 litres/2 pints	beef or chicken stock (see pages 14 and 15)	5 cups
1 tablespoon	lemon juice or white wine vinegar	1¼ tablespoons
to taste	salt and freshly ground black pepper	to taste
2 teaspoons	sugar, or to taste	to taste
To garnish	soured cream or yoghurt chopped dill	

Peel the beetroots, onion and carrot, then either cut them into fine shreds or grate coarsely. Cut the celery into small dice. Skin and halve the tomatoes, remove the seeds and chop the pulp.

Put all the vegetables into a saucepan with the stock, lemon juice or vinegar and a little seasoning. Bring to the boil, lower the heat and cover the pan. Simmer for 1¼ hours, or until the beetroot is very tender. Adjust the seasoning and stir in the sugar. Top each serving with a generous amount of soured cream or yoghurt and dill.

VARIATIONS

- This version of Bortsch is excellent served cold. Chill the cooked soup then garnish as on page 105.
- Many other ingredients can be added to the basic soup, including 1 or 2 teaspoons caraway seeds; a little finely shredded cabbage; a thinly sliced leek; about ¼ peeled and shredded small cucumber.
- For a richer flavour, toss the vegetables in 50 g/2 oz (¼ cup) heated butter before adding the stock. This should not be done if serving the soup cold.
- **Using cooked beetroot:** Dice or grate a generous 450 g/1 lb cooked beetroot instead of the raw vegetable, and shorten the cooking time to 30 minutes.

FREEZING: The cooked soup freezes well.

Cranberry Bortsch

Cooking time: 30 minutes plus time to make stock
Serves 4 to 6

Cranberries have so much flavour that this soup can be made with water, rather than stock, if desired. Always keep the lid on the pan when cooking, for cranberries pop so violently that they could force the lid off the pan.

Metric/Imperial	Ingredients	American
1 medium	onion	1 medium
1 large	carrot	1 large
225 g/8 oz	cooked beetroot (beets)	½ lb
2	celery sticks	2
1 litre/1¾ pints	beef or chicken stock (see pages 14 and 15) or water	scant 4½ cups
175 g/6 oz	cranberries	1½ cups
2 teaspoons	lemon juice or white wine vinegar	2 teaspoons
to taste	salt and freshly ground black pepper	to taste
1 tablespoon	sugar, or to taste	1¼ tablespoons
To garnish	soured cream or yoghurt	

Peel and finely dice or coarsely grate the onion, carrot and beetroot. Cut the celery into small dice. Put these ingredients into a saucepan with the stock or water and bring to the boil. Add the cranberries, lemon juice and a little seasoning, then cover the pan, lower the heat and simmer for 20 to 25 minutes, or until all the ingredients are tender. Taste the soup and add the sugar and any extra seasoning required. Serve hot or cold, topped with soured cream or yoghurt.

VARIATION
● Omit the beetroot and use 350 g/12 oz (¾ lb) cranberries. As the fruit is so sharp, you will need to use at least twice the amount of sugar.

FREEZING: This soup freezes well.

Russian Cabbage Soup (Schi)

Cooking time: 45 minutes plus time to make stock
Serves 4 to 6

This sustaining soup depends a great deal on the strong flavour of the stock. While beef stock, or even a stock cube and water, could be used, the classic recipe for the stock is made from beef bones (see page 14), but with the addition of a small amount of lean pork and the carcass of a duck to give a subtle taste.

Metric/Imperial	Ingredients	American
2 medium	onions	2 medium
3 medium	carrots	3 medium
1 very small	turnip	1 very small
2	celery sticks	2
1 medium	leek	1 medium
2 tablespoons	olive or sunflower oil	2½ tablespoons
1.2 litres/2 pints	stock, see above	5 cups
to taste	salt and freshly ground black pepper	to taste
1 medium	crisp young cabbage	1 medium
300 ml/½ pint	soured cream	1¼ cups

Peel and neatly dice the onions, carrot and turnip. Cut the celery and leek into thin slices. Heat the oil in a pan, add all the vegetables and stir over a low heat for 10 minutes. Add the stock and a little seasoning. Cover the pan and simmer for 25 minutes.

Meanwhile, finely shred the cabbage, tip into a small quantity of boiling water and cook for 3 to 5 minutes only, until slightly softened. Drain carefully. Add the cabbage to the hot soup together with half the soured cream. Heat for 5 minutes. Serve the soup topped with the remaining soured cream.

Note: In old recipes for this soup the cabbage is added and the soup cooked for about 30 minutes. Nowadays, we have developed a taste for lightly cooked cabbage and I find the soup much nicer with the shorter cooking time given above.

VARIATIONS

- To make an even more satisfying soup, finely dice about 225 g/8 oz (½ lb) tender beef or lean pork and simmer this with the vegetables. Diced beef steak should be given only about 10 minutes' cooking time.

- **RUSSIAN NETTLE SOUP**

Prepare the mixed vegetables as above but omit the cabbage and use about 225 g/8 oz (½ lb) young nettle tops plus the same amount of sorrel leaves instead. If you have no sorrel, double the amount of nettle leaves. Blanch in the same way as the cabbage, then add to the soup and cook for 10 minutes.

DO NOT FREEZE

Carrot and Coconut Soup

Cooking time: 25 minutes
Serves 4 to 6

Carrots are an important ingredient in a wide range of soups, adding flavour and colour to the other ingredients. They can also be the main ingredient. I find this combination of coconut and young firm carrots delicious.

Metric/Imperial	Ingredients	American
450 g/1 lb	young carrots	1 lb
1 medium	onion	1 medium
1.2 litres/2 pints	chicken or vegetable stock	5 cups
100 g/4 oz	creamed coconut	¼ lb
to taste	salt and freshly ground black pepper	to taste
To garnish	lemon rings little desiccated coconut	

Scrape or peel the carrots, then grate them. Peel and neatly dice the onion. Heat the stock in a saucepan, cut the creamed coconut into pieces and add to the stock, stirring until melted. Add the carrots, onion and seasoning. Bring to the boil and cook fairly briskly for 10 to 15 minutes until the carrots and onion are tender. Serve topped with the lemon rings and a dusting of desiccated coconut.

VARIATIONS
- Make a puréed soup by rubbing the ingredients through a sieve or liquidizing them. Return to the saucepan and heat. Top with a little soured cream, then the lemon slices and coconut.
- Instead of creamed coconut in the soup above, use 300 ml/½ pint (1¼ cups) canned coconut milk. Reduce the amount of stock by this amount.

- CREAMY CARROT AND COCONUT SOUP
Follow the first recipe but use only 600 ml/1 pint (2½ cups) stock with 300 ml/½ pint (1¼ cups) milk. When the soup is cooked, stir in 300 ml/½ pint (1¼ cups) double (heavy) cream.

The puréed version of the soup can be made with a mixture of stock, milk and cream.

● ORANGE, CARROT AND COCONUT SOUP
Follow the first recipe but use only 600 ml/1 pint (2½ cups) stock and 600 ml/1 pint (2½ cups) orange juice. Add several strips of thin orange rind but remove before serving. Top the soup with orange rings and desiccated coconut.

The puréed version of the soup can be made with these ingredients too.

FREEZING: **Do not freeze.**

Cauliflower and Potato Soup (Crème Dubarry)

Cooking time: 40 minutes
Serves 4 to 6

Cauliflower makes a delicious and economical soup because it uses mainly the leaves and stalks; most of the florets can be served as a separate vegetable. This recipe is a classic version of the French soup. If you omit the potatoes, you will need all the cauliflower florets to thicken the soap.

Metric/Imperial	Ingredients	American
1 medium to large	cauliflower	1 medium to large
750 ml/1¼ pints	water	good 3 cups
to taste	salt and freshly ground black pepper	to taste
50 g/2 oz	butter or margarine	¼ cup
1 medium	onion	1 medium
1 medium	leek	1 medium
2 medium	potatoes	2 medium
600 ml/1 pint	milk	2½ cups
150 ml/¼ pint	single (light) cream	⅔ cup
To garnish	cauliflower florets, see method	
	paprika	

Discard any imperfect leaves from the cauliflower, then cut the remaining leaves, stalks and base into small pieces. Bring the water to the boil with a little seasoning, add the chopped leaves and stalks, then cover the pan and cook briskly for 15 minutes. Strain the stock and reserve it. Set aside a few tender cooked stalks and leaves to liquidize with the other ingredients. Divide about 175 g/6 oz (2 American cups) of the cauliflower into small florets. Put these into the hot cauliflower stock and cook for 5 minutes, or until tender. Strain and put a few florets on one side to garnish the soup. Save the stock.

Peel and finely chop the onion, wash and slice the white part and a very little of the tender green stalk of the leek; peel and finely dice the potatoes. Heat the butter or margarine and cook the onion, leek and potatoes for 5 minutes. Add the cauliflower stock, bring to the boil, lower the heat and cover the pan. Simmer for 15 minutes, then sieve or liquidize the soup with the cooked florets, stalks and leaves.

Return to the pan, add the milk and cream and heat. Taste and adjust the seasoning. Garnish with the reserved florets and paprika.

VARIATIONS

- Heat the milk with the puréed ingredients. Blend 1 or 2 egg yolks with the cream in a basin, then spoon a few tablespoons of the hot soup over the egg mixture. Return to the pan, lower the heat and cook gently, whisking briskly, for 5 minutes.

- CAULIFLOWER SOUP

Follow the main recipe but omit the potato and use all the cauliflower florets. When sieving or liquidizing the soup, you can also add a more generous quantity of the cooked stalks and leaves to give body to the soup.

- BROCCOLI SOUP

Use broccoli instead of cauliflower in the main recipe or the variations.

FREEZING: The puréed soup freezes well.

Celeriac Soup

Cooking time: 30 minutes plus time to make stock
Serves 4

Celeriac is a vegetable about the size of a large turnip with a flavour similar to celery. It is often known as celery root. Under the brown skin the flesh is white, it discolours easily when peeled, so should be placed immediately in a bowl of cold water containing at least 1 tablespoon (1¼ tablespoons) lemon juice or white vinegar until needed. A little celeriac is an excellent alternative to celery in any vegetable soup.

Metric/Imperial	Ingredients	American
2 tablespoons	lemon juice	2½ tablespoons
225 g/8 oz	celeriac, prepared weight	½ lb
2 medium	onions	2 medium
1	garlic clove, optional	1
1 teaspoon	finely grated lemon zest	1 teaspoon
40 g/1½ oz	butter	3 tablespoons
900 ml/1½ pints	white stock (see page 15)	3¾ cups
to taste	salt, celery salt and freshly ground white pepper	to taste
To garnish	paprika or finely diced red pepper	
	chopped parsley	

Fill a bowl with cold water, add half the lemon juice. Peel the celeriac, cut into 1.25 cm/½ inch dice, then place in the lemon-flavoured water. Peel and finely chop the onions and garlic. Heat the butter in a saucepan, add the onions and garlic and cook gently for 5 minutes. Drain the celeriac and sprinkle with the remaining lemon juice and the lemon zest. Tip into the pan and cook gently for 5 minutes; take care the vegetables do not brown.

Add the stock with salt, celery salt and pepper to taste. Bring to the boil, cover the pan and simmer steadily for 20 minutes.

Sieve or liquidize the soup, return to the pan and reheat. Garnish and serve.

VARIATIONS
- Omit the lemon juice and zest in the main recipe and flavour the soup with 2 to 3 teaspoons English or French mustard. Add this to the stock.
- Add a few tablespoons cooked rice to the cooked soup or any of the variations that follow.

- **CREAM OF CELERIAC SOUP**
Follow the main recipe, but use only 600 ml/1 pint (2½ cups) stock. Cook the soup, then sieve or liquidize. Return to the pan with 300 ml/½ pint (1¼ cups) single (light) cream and reheat gently without boiling.

    Instead of cream use 300 ml/½ pint (⅔ cup) thin white sauce (see page 28).

- **CELERIAC AND APPLE SOUP**
Follow the main recipe, but cook a small, peeled and diced cooking apple with the celeriac.

- **CELERIAC AND LEEK SOUP**
Omit the garlic in the main recipe or in the Cream of Celeriac Soup and use only 1 medium onion. Cut 2 medium leeks into thin slices, using a little of the tender green part as well as the white. Heat the onions and leeks in the butter then continue as the recipe.

- **CELERIAC AND ORANGE SOUP**
Follow the main recipe, but omit the lemon zest and use only 600 ml/1 pint (2½ cups) of stock. Add 1 tablespoon (1¼ tablespoons) finely grated orange zest with the stock. Sieve or liquidize the cooked soup, then return to the pan with 300 ml/½ pint (1¼ cups) orange juice and reheat. Garnish with orange segments.

    This soup is equally good served cold or lightly frozen (see page 296).

- **CELERIAC AND TOMATO SOUP**
Follow the main recipe, but omit the lemon juice and rind in the soup and use 4 medium tomatoes (these should be peeled, deseeded and chopped, as explained on page 159). Add the tomatoes with the celeriac and continue as the main recipe. This soup is equally good served cold.

- **VIENNESE CELERIAC SOUP**
Known as *Selleriesuppe* in Austria, this soup is often mistakenly translated as celery soup, but it is actually based on celeriac. Prepare the 225 g/8 oz (½ lb) celeriac and cook in boiling water flavoured with 1 tablespoon (1¼ tablespoons) lemon juice and a little seasoning. When tender, strain and sieve the celeriac, then liquidize or mash until smooth.

Make 600 ml/1 pint (2¾ cups) White Sauce (see page 28), add the celeriac and heat. Blend 2 egg yolks with 150 ml/¼ pint (⅔ cup) soured cream and gradually whisk into the hot, but not boiling, soup. Cook slowly for about 6 to 8 minutes. Serve topped with julienne strips of cooked celeriac (see page 75).

FREEZING: All versions of this soup freeze well, but omit the egg yolks and soured cream in Viennese Celeriac Soup; add these to the hot soup and cook quietly for 6 to 8 minutes.

QUICK TIP *Celeriac softens quite easily, so the main recipe on page 112 and all the variations can be cooked in a microwave.*

Corn Chowder

Cooking time: 25 minutes
Serves 4

Sweetcorn is a favourite vegetable in North America, and in chowders it adds flavour and food value as well as colour. The corn must be cooked or canned before use. In this recipe the potatoes are diced, but they can also be mashed to thicken the liquid. Instead of relatively thin slices of bacon you could have one thick slice and cut it into small cubes. The bacon rind is an important garnish.

Metric/Imperial	Ingredients	American
2 medium	onions	2 medium
3 medium	potatoes	3 medium
3 or 4 rashers	streaky bacon	3 or 4 slices
25 g/1 oz	butter, optional	2 tablespoons
450 ml/¾ pint	water	scant 2 cups
to taste	salt and freshly ground black pepper	to taste
600 ml/1 pint	milk	2½ cups
350 g/12 oz	cooked or canned sweetcorn	2¼ cups
6 to 8	plain crackers	6 to 8
To garnish	paprika	

Peel the onions and cut into 6 mm/¼ inch dice. Peel the potatoes and cut into 1.25 cm/½ inch dice. Remove the rind from the bacon and dice the rashers. Heat the rinds for 2 minutes, then add the bacon and cook slowly for a further 2 minutes. If lots of fat runs out, omit the butter. Add the onions and potatoes and cook steadily, stirring from time to time, until they are pale golden. Remove the bacon rinds and set aside. Add the water, bring to the boil and season to taste. Cover the pan and simmer steadily for 10 to 15 minutes. Pour in the milk, then add the hot, well-drained sweetcorn and heat for 5 minutes.

Crumble the crackers into soup bowls, spoon the hot soup on top and garnish with crushed bacon rinds and paprika.

VARIATIONS

- If using frozen sweetcorn, allow it to defrost, then add to the water 5 minutes before the end of cooking time.
- **With creamed potatoes:** instead of diced potatoes use 450 g/1 lb (2 cups) of smooth mashed potatoes mixed with a little butter. Cook the bacon and onions as above, then add the water and simmer until the onions are soft. Add the mashed potatoes. Mix well, then gradually stir in 900 ml/1½ pints (3¾ cups) milk. When hot, add the sweetcorn and continue as above.

- **CHICKEN AND CORN CHOWDER**

Chicken and sweetcorn are perfect partners. Cut 225 g/8 oz (½ lb) cooked chicken breast or leg into neat dice. Follow the main recipe, but use only 225 g/8 oz (1½ cups) sweetcorn. Add the chicken to the hot soup a few minutes before adding the sweetcorn.

- **CRABMEAT AND CORN CHOWDER**

Follow the main recipe or the variation with creamed potatoes. Use only 225 g/8 oz (1½ cups) sweetcorn with 175 g/6 oz (1 cup) flaked white crabmeat. Add the crabmeat after the sweetcorn.

DO NOT FREEZE

Cream of Courgette (Zucchini) Soup

Cooking time: 35 minutes
Serves 4 to 6

Courgettes make an excellent soup. Choose small vegetables with unmarked skins, as they are not peeled.

Metric/Imperial	Ingredients	American
450 g/1 lb	courgettes, prepared weight	1 lb
2 medium	onions	2 medium
2	garlic cloves	2
50 g/2 oz	butter	¼ cup
25 g/1 oz	plain (all-purpose) flour	¼ cup
600 ml/1 pint	vegetable stock (see page 15)	2½ cups
300 ml/½ pint	milk	1¼ cups
to taste	salt and freshly ground black pepper	to taste
1 tablespoon	chopped parsley	1¼ tablespoons
1 teaspoon	chopped oregano or marjoram	1 teaspoon
300 ml/½ pint	single (light) cream	1¼ cups

Wash and dry the courgettes, cut away the tough ends then weigh the vegetables. Cut into 1.25 cm/½ inch slices. Peel and finely chop the onions and garlic. Heat the butter, add the onions and garlic and cook gently for 5 minutes. Add the courgettes and cook for a further 5 minutes. Stir in the flour and mix thoroughly.

Add the stock and bring just to the boil. Cover the pan and simmer for 15 minutes. Sieve or liquidize the soup. Return to the pan, add the milk, seasoning, herbs and cream, then heat and serve.

VARIATION

• CREAM OF ASPARAGUS SOUP 1

Use 450 g/1 lb asparagus instead of the courgettes and omit the herbs. Cut 12 tender tips from the asparagus and set aside. Trim the asparagus stalks, discard the tough ends, then chop into 2.5 cm/1 inch lengths. Follow the method given on page 116. If the asparagus is very young and thin, the simmering time should be only 10 minutes; if thicker, allow 15 to 20 minutes.

Sieve or liquidize the soup then return to the pan with the milk, seasoning and cream. Meanwhile, simmer the tips in a very little lightly salted water, drain and add to the soup just before serving.

FREEZING: Both these soups freeze well, although they have a tendency to separate (see pages 17 and 18). It is better to freeze the courgette or asparagus purée, then add the milk and other ingredients when reheating. The asparagus tips should be cooked, then frozen separately. Pack in a small container when frozen to avoid damaging them.

Cucumber Soup

Cooking time: 35 minutes
Serves 4 to 6

Cucumbers have an excellent flavour when cooked, and this recipe is ideal for really large, mature vegetables. I leave about 5 cm/2 inches of skin on one of the cucumbers to give a delicate colour; any more than that gives a bitter taste to the soup.

The main recipe is very simple, without flavourings to detract from the taste of the cucumber. It makes an excellent basis for the variations that follow.

Metric/Imperial	Ingredients	American
2 large	cucumbers	2 large
50 g/2 oz	butter or margarine	¼ cup
25 g/1 oz	plain (all-purpose) flour	¼ cup
600 ml/1 pint	water	2½ cups
1 tablespoon	chopped parsley	1¼ tablespoons
1 tablespoon	chopped chives	1¼ tablespoons
1	dried bay leaf	1
to taste	salt and freshly ground black pepper	to taste
600 ml/1 pint	milk	2½ cups
150 ml/¼ pint	single (light) cream	⅔ cup
To garnish	croûtons or cheese croûtons (see page 305)	

Peel the cucumbers, retain a small amount of skin in one piece (see above); this makes it easy to remove.

Grate the cucumbers or cut into 1.25 to 2 cm/½ to ¾ inch dice. Heat the butter or margarine and toss the cucumber in this for 5 minutes. Stir in the flour, then add the water with the herbs and a little seasoning. Bring to the boil, stirring or whisking until thickened. Lower the heat and simmer for 20 minutes, then remove the skin and bay leaf and add the milk and cream.

Heat thoroughly, taste and adjust the seasoning then serve topped with the croûtons.

VARIATIONS

- For additional flavour, add 1 or 2 medium onions to the ingredients above. Peel and chop very finely, then cook in the butter or margarine with the cucumber.
- A few strips of lemon zest could be added to the water and herbs.
- Use only 300 ml/½ pint (1¼ cups) milk and the same amount of dry white wine. Heat very gently with the cream, taking care the soup does not boil.

● PURÉED CUCUMBER SOUP

For a fairly thick soup, retain the flour, as in the main recipe; for a thinner soup, omit the flour. When the cucumber has been cooked, remove the bay leaf but retain the skin, if you like, for extra flavour. Sieve or liquidize, then return to the pan with the milk and cream and reheat.

● CUCUMBER AND CHEESE SOUP

Use the main recipe or the recipe for puréed soup. Add 75 g/3 oz (¾ cup) grated Gruyère, Cheddar, Cheshire or any good cooking cheese to the hot soup immediately before serving. Heat for a very short time only.

● CUCUMBER AND CHICKEN SOUP

Use the main recipe or the puréed soup recipe. Substitute good chicken stock (see page 14) for the water. About 100 g/4 oz (¼ lb) finely chopped or minced uncooked chicken breast could be cooked with the cucumber.

● CUCUMBER AND CRABMEAT SOUP

Use the main recipe or the puréed soup recipe. Add about 100 g/4 oz (¼ lb) flaked white crabmeat to the soup with the milk and cream, together with a good shake of paprika and a squeeze of lemon juice. Heat gently, without boiling, then serve.

Other shellfish, such as prawns or shrimps, could be used instead of crabmeat.

● CUCUMBER AND POTATO SOUP

Add onion(s), as suggested in the first variation, and about 225 g/8 oz (½ lb) grated or diced potato to the cucumber. (This is the weight of potato when peeled.) The soup can be served with or without sieving or liquidizing.

FREEZING: The main recipe, using grated or diced cucumber, does not freeze well: it loses texture and flavour. The puréed version of the soup freezes well, although it is advisable to add the milk and cream when reheating.

Austrian Cucumber Soup

Cooking time: 30 minutes plus time to make stock
Serves 4 to 6

Known as *Gurkensuppe* in Austria, this soup consists of a purée thickened with a white sauce. As with other cucumber soups, it is a matter of personal taste as to whether all, or some, of the skin is removed from the cucumbers. The skin adds flavour and colour to the soup, but is slightly bitter for some tastes.

Metric/Imperial	Ingredients	American
1½ to 2 medium	cucumbers, see method	1½ to 2 medium
1 medium	onion	1 medium
1	celery stick	1
750 ml/1¼ pints	veal or chicken stock (see pages 14 and 15)	good 3 cups
to taste	salt and freshly ground white pepper	to taste
25 g/1 oz	butter	2 tablespoons
25 g/1 oz	plain (all-purpose) flour	¼ cup
300 ml/½ pint	milk	1¼ cups
1 tablespoon	lemon juice or white wine vinegar	1¼ tablespoons
To garnish	chopped parsley	

Use only 1½ cucumbers if retaining all the skin, but 2 cucumbers if the skin is to be removed. A good compromise is to discard nearly all the skin except for a few strips; this is enough to give a faint green colour to the soup. Chop the cucumber flesh into small dice.

Peel and chop the onion and dice the celery. Put the vegetables into a saucepan with the stock and a very little seasoning, and simmer for 15 to 20 minutes, or until the vegetables are tender. Sieve or liquidize to make a smooth purée.

Meanwhile, make the white sauce. Heat the butter in the pan, stir in the flour, then add the milk. Stir or whisk briskly as the sauce comes to the boil, add the vegetable purée and heat just to boiling point. Remove the pan from the heat and whisk in the lemon juice or vinegar. Adjust the seasoning and serve topped with the parsley.

VARIATIONS

- Instead of milk in the sauce use single (light) cream.
- An interesting flavour is given to the soup if a sprig of mint is simmered with the vegetables. The soup can be garnished with chopped mint instead of parsley.

- **CUCUMBER AND POTATO SOUP**

Omit the white sauce in the main recipe. Peel and dice 2 medium potatoes and cook with the other vegetables. Sieve or liquidize the vegetables to give a smooth purée. Return to the pan with 300 ml/½ pint (1¼ cups) of milk or single (light) cream and heat. A little finely chopped tarragon makes an interesting garnish to this soup. A small sprig of tarragon can be cooked with the vegetables.

FREEZING: All these soups freeze well. The main version may separate when defrosted, so whisk briefly as it is reheated. (See pages 17 and 18 for hints to prevent soups separating.)

QUICK TIP *This soup cooks very satisfactorily in a microwave if the cucumber is peeled. The skin tends to remain slightly tough when cooked in a microwave.*

Cucumber and Mint Soup

Cooking time: 30 minutes plus time to make stock
Serves 4 to 6

The combination of cucumber and mint is a very happy one. This soup is equally good hot or cold, although I make some slight adaptations when it is served cold (see below). To enhance the colour of the soup leave about 5 cm/2 inches of skin on the cucumber; this softens during cooking and loses any bitter taste.

Metric/Imperial	Ingredients	American
1 very large	cucumber	1 very large
1 medium	onion	1 medium
1 small	sprig mint	1 small
600 ml/1 pint	chicken stock (see page 14)	2½ cups
to taste	salt and freshly ground white pepper	to taste
300 ml/½ pint	single (light) cream	1¼ cups
To garnish	chopped mint and chopped chives croûtons (see page 305)	

Peel the cucumber, as instructed above, then cut into slices. Peel and chop the onion. Put the cucumber, onion and mint into a saucepan with the stock and a little seasoning. Simmer for 15 to 20 minutes, or until the vegetables are tender. Sieve or liquidize and return to the pan with the cream. Heat and adjust the seasoning. Garnish with the herbs and croûtons.

VARIATIONS

- A thicker soup can be made by adding *beurre manié* made with 25 g/1 oz (2 tablespoons) butter and 25 g/1 oz (¼ cup) plain (all-purpose) flour before adding the cream (see page 8).
  Any of the hot soups given below can be thickened in the same way.

- **COURGETTE AND MINT SOUP**
Use 450 g/1 lb small courgettes (zucchini) in place of cucumber. Cut the tough ends from the courgettes, wash well but do not peel. Slice and cook as above.

our-Hot Soup (pages 234 to 235)
he combination of flavours in this unusual meat soup will please all lovers of Oriental foods.

Chicken Consommé (pages 71 to 72)
A consommé is one of the great classic soups. It can be varied by adding different garnishes.

French Onion Soup (page 137)
Perfect for cold winters days; a soup that is warming and full of flavour.

Bortsch (page 288)
A beetroot soup which is a traditional favourite in Russia.

Cream of Courgette Soup (116 to 117)
These popular vegetables make a very appetising soup, which can be prepared at all times of
the year.

Crab and Prawn Gumbo (pages 186 to 187)
An American favourite. Okra and shellfish combine to give a delicious flavour to the soup.

Minestrone (page 131)

The Italian 'big soup'. Ideal for a first course or as a meal in itself.

Pumpkin Soup (pages 150 to 151)
Pumpkins make excellent rich and colourful soups. The flavour can be modified to suit all
tastes.

As courgettes have less flavour than cucumber, you may like to use 2 onions as well.

● **PUMPKIN AND MINT SOUP**
Use 450 g/1 lb peeled pumpkin instead of cucumber.

Various kinds of squash or vegetable marrow can be used instead of pumpkin.

● **CHILLED CUCUMBER AND MINT SOUP**
Use only 450 ml/¾ pint (scant 2 cups) chicken stock in the main recipe. When the soup is cooked, sieve or liquidize it, allow to cool, then stir in 150 ml/¼ pint (⅔ cup) yoghurt, 300 ml/½ pint (1¼ cups) single (light) cream and a little lemon juice. Top the cold soup with chopped chives and chopped walnuts.

Do not thicken this cold soup with *beurre manié*.

FREEZING: It is better to freeze the cucumber, courgette or pumpkin mixture after sieving or liquidizing. Add the cream, yoghurt or lemon juice when the soup is defrosted.

Spiced Cumberland Soup

Cooking time: 35 minutes plus time to make stock
Serves 4 to 6

This interesting soup, with its combination of savoury ingredients and the sweetness of orange juice and redcurrant jelly, has some of the subtle flavour of Cumberland sauce.

Metric/Imperial	Ingredients	American
1 small	onion	1 small
1 small	carrot	1 small
3 medium	mushrooms	3 medium
2 small	tomatoes	2 small
1 rasher	streaky bacon	1 slice
25 g/1 oz	butter	2 tablespoons
600 ml/1 pint	beef stock (see page 14)	2½ cups
3 tablespoons	red wine	3¾ tablespoons
1 teaspoon	allspice	1 teaspoon
to taste	salt and freshly ground black pepper	to taste
150 ml/¼ pint	orange juice	⅔ cup
3 tablespoons	redcurrant jelly	3¾ tablespoons
To garnish	1 to 2 oranges	

Peel and chop the onion and carrot; wipe and slice the mushrooms. Skin and chop the tomatoes; derind the bacon, save the rind and chop the rasher into small pieces. Heat the butter and bacon rind in a saucepan, add the vegetables and diced bacon. Cook gently for 5 minutes. Remove the bacon rind.

Pour the stock into the pan, cover and simmer steadily for 30 minutes. Sieve or liquidize the ingredients, then return to the pan with the red wine, allspice and seasoning to taste. Simmer for 5 minutes, then add the orange juice and redcurrant jelly. Stir over a low heat until the jelly has dissolved.

To garnish the soup cut away the orange rind and pith, then cut out segments of fruit free from skin and pips. Add to the soup just before serving.

VARIATIONS

- Vegetarians should omit the bacon and add an extra onion to give more flavour.

- **COLD SPICED CUMBERLAND SOUP**

Chill the soup and the orange segments and add to the soup immediately before serving.

FREEZING: **Do not freeze.**

Farmhouse Soup

Cooking time: about 45 minutes plus time to make stock
Serves 4 to 6

This is not a classic recipe, but its name describes a homely mixed vegetable soup made with country ingredients. The French make a similar soup called *potage paysanne*. The soup is hearty and satisfying, as it is not sieved or liquidized. To turn it into a complete meal, top with crisp chopped bacon, or diced ham, or cooked sliced sausages, or a thick layer of grated cheese.

Metric/Imperial	Ingredients	American
675 g/1½ lb	mixed vegetables, prepared weight, see method	1½ lb
50 g/2 oz	butter	¼ cup
1.8 litres/3 pints	vegetable, chicken or bacon stock (see pages 14 and 15)	7½ cups
to taste	salt and freshly ground black pepper	to taste
bunch	mixed herbs, see method	bunch
To garnish	cooked bacon, ham or sausages (optional) chopped parsley grated cheese	

The vegetables should consist of 1 or 2 carrots, a few celery sticks, 1 small turnip, 1 small parsnip, 1 small swede (rutabaga), 1 or 2 small leeks, a few cauliflower florets and a red pepper.

Peel and dice or slice the vegetables. Divide the cauliflower into small florets, deseed and dice the pepper. Heat the butter in a saucepan and add all the prepared vegetables, except the cauliflower and pepper. Pour the stock into the pan, bring to the boil and add a little seasoning. Take some sprigs of parsley and chives, plus a very little rosemary and thyme and tie in a bunch or place in a muslin bag. Add to the pan, then cover and simmer the soup for 15 to 20 minutes. Add the cauliflower and pepper and continue cooking for 10 minutes. Add the cabbage and cook for 5 to 7 minutes.

Taste the soup and adjust the seasoning. Add any of the meat garnishes and heat for 1 to 2 minutes. Just before serving, top each portion with parsley. Add the cheese when the soup is served.

VARIATIONS
- Change the vegetables according to the season: in summertime add shelled peas and diced green beans or fresh broad (fava) beans.
- Add small or diced new potatoes with a sprig of mint instead of thyme.
- Substitute shredded lettuce, cabbage kale or spinach for the cauliflower and small skinned tomatoes for the pepper.

DO NOT FREEZE

French Garlic Soup
(Soupe à l'Ail) 1

Cooking time: 35 to 40 minutes plus time to make stock
Serves 4 to 6

Even if you are a lover of garlic, the thought of including a whole head in a soup may sound a little daunting. In fact, by the time the garlic is cooked and puréed with the other ingredients, it has a wonderfully mellow flavour, particularly if you use chicken stock; beef stock makes a rich, strongly flavoured soup.

The second recipe is a favourite in Provence, and the slight variation shows it is just as popular in Spain.

Metric/Imperial	Ingredients	American
2 medium	onions	2 medium
1 medium head	garlic	1 medium head
1 tablespoon	olive oil	1¼ tablespoons
900 ml/1½ pints	chicken or beef stock (see page 14)	3¾ cups
1	fresh bay leaf or ½ dried leaf	1
1 tablespoon	chopped parsley	1¼ tablespoons
1 teaspoon	chopped thyme or ½ teaspoon dried thyme	1 teaspoon
to taste	salt and freshly ground black pepper	to taste
2	egg yolks	2
1 tablespoon	lemon juice	1¼ tablespoons

Peel and chop the onions. Peel the garlic, remove the skin around the cloves, but do not chop them. Heat the oil in a saucepan, add the onions and cook for 5 minutes. If using chicken stock, do not allow them to brown. If using beef stock, cook for 10 minutes, or until the onions are golden brown.

Add most of the stock. Put the herbs and garlic into the pan with a little seasoning. Bring to the boil, lower the heat and simmer for 25 minutes. Remove the bay leaf, then sieve or liquidize the soup, return to the pan and bring almost to boiling point. Blend the egg yolks with the reserved stock and lemon juice. Whisk into the hot soup and cook without boiling for 5 minutes, whisking or stirring constantly. Add extra seasoning if required. Serve with crusty French bread.

VARIATIONS

- For a thicker soup blend 25 g/1 oz (¼ cup) plain (all-purpose) flour with the onions before adding the stock.

- **FRENCH GARLIC SOUP 2**
Use a large head of garlic. Peel the cloves. These can be chopped, if desired, but generally they are served whole. Bring 900 ml/1½ pints (3¾ cups) of water to the boil, add the garlic with a little seasoning, then cover the pan and simmer for 15 to 20 minutes, or until the garlic is tender. Blend 2 egg yolks with a little cold water or milk, whisk into the pan and simmer steadily for 5 minutes, whisking or stirring to keep the soup smooth.

Cut thin slices of French bread, spread with extra virgin oil, then place in heated soup bowls. Ladle the soup over the bread and serve.

This soup is often known as **água bolido**, which means **boiled water soup**. A more interesting version is made if a small sprig of sage, 1 or 2 dried whole cloves or a good pinch of ground cloves and 2 tablespoons (2½ tablespoons) olive oil are added to the water and garlic cloves. Remove the sage and whole cloves before serving the soup. Spread slices of bread with olive oil and grated Gruyère cheese. Place under a preheated grill until the cheese melts. Put into heated soup bowls, then add the soup.

- **SOPA DE AJO**
Spanish Garlic Soup: this is cooked in a similar manner to French Garlic Soup 2, but is enriched by adding 1 tablespoon (1¼ tablespoons) olive oil and 4 whole eggs instead of 2 egg yolks. After thickening with the eggs, the liquid is strained over the bread spread with olive oil. This gives a creamy soup with the flavour of garlic, but without the cloves.

DO NOT FREEZE: The garlic tends to develop an unpleasant flavour in freezing.

Italian Globe Artichoke Soup (Velluttata di Carciofi)

Cooking time: 35 minutes
Serves 4 to 6

Italians love globe artichokes – indeed, I remember seeing piles of freshly prepared artichoke hearts in the market at Padua. The vegetable is so plentiful in Italy that the leaves seem to be discarded quite happily. The fresh hearts (bottoms of the artichokes) are used in this soup but, since they are not sold in this manner in Britain, I have based the recipe on whole artichokes.

Metric/Imperial	Ingredients	American
6 medium	artichokes	6 medium
to taste	salt and freshly ground black pepper	to taste
Velouté base		
50 g/2 oz	butter	¼ cup
50 g/2 oz	plain (all-purpose) flour	½ cup
750 ml/1¼ pints	chicken or white stock (see pages 14 and 15)	good 3 cups
300 ml/½ pint	single (light) cream	1¼ cups
To garnish	diced artichoke heart	

Trim away any tough outer leaves from the artichokes and cut out the centre chokes (hairy middles). Bring a pan of water to the boil, add a little salt and the artichokes. Cover the pan and simmer steadily for 20 to 25 minutes or until tender. To check if ready pull away a leaf and see if the base of this is really soft.

If short of time, cut the hearts out of the artichokes. Dice part of one heart finely to use for garnish. Sieve the remaining hearts or liquidize them with 3 tablespoons (3¾ tablespoons) of stock. If you have time, scrape the soft pulp from the base of the leaves and sieve or liquidize this with the hearts.

While the artichokes are cooking, prepare the *velouté* base. Heat the butter in a saucepan, stir in the flour, then gradually add the stock. Stir constantly as the liquid comes to the boil and thickens, then lower the heat and simmer very gently for 10 minutes. Add the cream and the artichoke purée and heat gently. Adjust the seasoning and garnish with the diced artichoke heart.

VARIATIONS

• Use about 8 small canned artichoke hearts instead of fresh ones. Drain and sieve or liquidize them.

• **ITALIAN ASPARAGUS SOUP (VELLUTTATA DI ASPARAGI)**
This recipe is ideal for the asparagus that has white rather than green stalks. Cut away the very tough ends of the stalks from 450 g/1 lb asparagus. Cut off 8 to 12 tips and cook these separately in a little salted water or stock to use as garnish. Simmer the rest of the asparagus in the same way as the globe artichokes above, then sieve or liquidize.

To make the *velouté* base, add the cream and asparagus purée, reheat gently and add seasoning to taste. Top the soup with the asparagus tips.

FREEZING: Both these soups freeze well, but it is best to do so without the cream; add that when reheating the soup. To save space in the freezer, prepare the artichoke or asparagus purée when the vegetables are in season and freeze until needed. Make the *velouté* base when required. The diced artichoke heart and delicate cooked asparagus tips should be packed and frozen separately.

Minestrone

Cooking time: 2 hours
Serves 4 to 6

Meaning literally 'big soup', traditional minestrone is certainly a satisfying dish. Different regions of Italy have their own versions of this famous soup and some are given below. The method of cooking retains the texture of the various ingredients.

Metric/Imperial	Ingredients	American
225 g/8 oz	dried borlotti or cannellini beans	good 1 cup
1.8 litres/3 pints	water	7½ cups
to taste	salt and freshly ground black pepper	to taste
1 large	onion	1 large
1	garlic clove	1
1 large	carrot	1 large
2 medium	courgettes (zucchini)	2 medium
2	celery sticks	2
225 g/8 oz	tomatoes	½ lb
2 to 4 slices	prosciutto or unsmoked bacon	2 to 4 slices
2 tablespoons	olive oil	2½ tablespoons
100 g/4 oz	pasta, see method	¼ lb
225 g/8 oz	cabbages or other greens	½ lb
3 tablespoons	chopped parsley	3¾ tablespoons
For the topping	grated Parmesan cheese	

Place the beans in a pan, cover with cold water and leave to soak for several hours. Discard the soaking water, then add the amount of water stated above. Bring to the boil and boil briskly for 10 minutes. Add a little seasoning, then cover the pan and lower the heat. Simmer for 1¼ hours or until the beans are nearly tender.

Meanwhile, peel and chop the onion and garlic, peel and dice the carrot. Do not peel the courgettes, but discard the tough ends, wipe the vegetables and cut into small dice. Chop the celery, skin and chop the tomatoes. Cut the prosciutto or bacon into neat pieces, reserving the bacon rinds if possible.

Heat the olive oil with the bacon rinds (if you have them), add the onion and garlic and cook for several minutes, then tip into the pan containing the beans and liquid. Continue cooking for 10 minutes, then remove the bacon rinds and add the carrot, courgettes, celery and tomatoes. Cook for a further 10 minutes. Taste the soup and add more seasoning if required.

If using long pasta, break this into small pieces; small pasta shapes can be left whole. Shred the cabbage or greens finely. Put the prosciutto or bacon, pasta and cabbage into the soup together with half the parsley and cook for a further 10 minutes. Top each serving with chopped parsley and cheese. Serve more bowls of cheese with the soup.

VARIATIONS

- The proportions and variety of vegetables can be changed according to personal preference and what is in season: 1 or 2 peeled diced potatoes can be added to the soup above. Cook them in the oil with the onions.
- Use vegetable or chicken stock instead of water (see pages 15 and 14).

• MINESTRONE ALLA BORGHESE
Follow the main recipe but omit the carrot. Add rather more celery plus 2 or 3 medium peeled and diced potatoes and 2 roasted and diced yellow peppers (see page 152). This soup is generally flavoured with basil, a bay leaf and parsley.

• MINESTRONE ALLA GENOVESE
Follow the main recipe but use both shredded cabbage and the same amount of shredded young spinach leaves. Flavour the soup with chopped basil as well as parsley.

• MINESTRONE ALLA MILANESE
Substitute 100 g/4 oz (good ½ cup) Italian long-grain rice for the pasta. Add a few sliced green beans and peas to the other vegetables and omit the cabbage or other greens.

FREEZING: This soup freezes well but it is better if the ingredients are not completely cooked before freezing.

QUICK TIP *Use canned beans and a selection of frozen vegetables to save time in cooking and preparation.*

MUSHROOM SOUPS

Mushrooms form the basis of a number of excellent soups. Their flavour is delicate, so do ensure that the other ingredients added to the soup do not overwhelm them. I prefer to use shallots instead of onions for this reason.

When cooking the Cream of Mushroom Soup as described below, you make a paler-coloured soup if you use button mushrooms and stir the cooked mushroom purée into the creamy mixture just before serving (see method 1). For a darker soup use large open mushrooms and follow method 2.

The wide selection of mushrooms on the market means that you can vary the flavour of soups by mixing two or three kinds, or choosing one of the lesser known varieties. I am particularly fond of a soup made with chestnut mushrooms.

Cream of Mushroom Soup

Cooking time: 30 minutes
Serves 4 to 6

The skin of cultivated mushrooms adds flavour to soups, so do not peel it off. Simply wipe the mushrooms with damp kitchen paper, or wash in cold water if badly soiled. Always trim and discard the ends of the stalks, but use the remainder with the caps in the recipe.

Metric/Imperial	Ingredients	American
3 medium	shallots or small onions	3 medium
50 g/2 oz	butter or margarine	¼ cup
25 g/1 oz	plain (all-purpose) flour	¼ cup
600 ml/1 pint	chicken stock (see page 14) or water	2½ cups
450 g/1 lb	mushrooms	1 lb
300 ml/½ pint	double (heavy) cream	1¼ cups
to taste	salt and freshly ground white pepper	to taste
To garnish	croûtons (see page 305)	

Method 1: Peel and finely chop the shallots or onions. Heat half the butter or margarine in a saucepan, add the shallots or onions and cook gently for 10 minutes, stirring constantly so that they do not discolour. Mix the flour in carefully, then gradually pour in the stock or water. Whisk or stir as the mixture comes to the boil and thickens. Cover the pan and simmer gently for 15 minutes. Sieve or liquidize the mixture and return to the pan.

Meanwhile, heat the remaining butter or margarine in a separate saucepan and cook the mushrooms gently for 10 minutes. Liquidize or process briefly so you have small pieces of mushroom left. If you do not have the necessary equipment, finely dice the mushrooms before cooking. Add the cooked mushrooms to the stock mixture together with the cream and seasoning. Reheat and serve garnished with croûtons.

Method 2: Cook the shallots or onions in 50 g/2 oz (¼ cup) of butter or margarine; add the roughly chopped mushrooms and cook for a further 5 minutes. Stir in the flour then add the stock or water and simmer for 15 minutes. Liquidize or process the soup, then add the cream and seasoning. Reheat, garnish and serve.

VARIATIONS

- Use 1.2 litres/2 pints (5 cups) milk and omit the cream. Add an extra 2 teaspoons of flour so that the mixture is adequately thickened. This less rich soup can be topped with a little yoghurt or single (light) cream, chopped parsley and a few sliced mushrooms instead of the croûtons.

- **BROWN MUSHROOM SOUP**
Use the main recipe, but substitute good brown stock (see page 15) for the chicken stock or water. A slightly stronger taste can be given to the soup if clarified beef dripping is used instead of butter or margarine. Add the cream as before.

FREEZING: This soup freezes well, but do not add the cream until you reheat the soup.

Nettle and Beef Soup

Cooking time: 15 minutes plus time to make stock
Serves 4 to 6

While nettles may be an enemy to keen gardeners, good cooks regard them with respect as they make a traditional and delicious soup. Choose only young nettle leaves from the tips of plants not exposed to traffic.

The following verse, apparently written on a window, is by Aaron Hill (1685–1750).

> *Tender-handed stroke a nettle,*
> *And it stings you for your pains;*
> *Grasp it like a man of mettle,*
> *And it soft as silk remains.*

Even if you follow this advice, it is wise to wear rubber gloves when picking and preparing nettles: after cooking they do not sting. The quantity of leaves in the recipe below can be varied according to how strong you want the flavour. Never use old, tough leaves.

Metric/Imperial	Ingredients	American
225 to 350 g/8 to 12 oz	young nettle leaves	½ to ¾ lb
1 litre/1¾ pints	beef stock or Beef Consommé (see pages 14 and 68)	scant 4½ cups
to taste	salt and freshly ground black pepper	to taste
To garnish	soured cream or yoghurt	

Wash the nettle leaves in plenty of cold water, do not drain them. Place in a saucepan with the water adhering to the leaves and cover tightly. Cook for 8 to 10 minutes, then sieve or liquidize the leaves. Return the nettle purée to the pan with the stock or consommé, heat and season to taste. Top each portion with soured cream or yoghurt.

VARIATIONS

- Substitute sorrel or spinach purée for the nettle purée in the main recipe.
- Use 225 g/8 oz (½ lb) nettle leaves instead of the sorrel leaves in the first recipe on page 155.
- Use 300 ml/½ pint (1¼ cups) nettle purée instead of spinach purée in the recipe on page 31.

- **CREAMY NETTLE SOUP**

Peel and finely chop 2 medium onions and 2 garlic cloves. Heat 50 g/2 oz (¼ cup) butter and add the onions and garlic. Stir over a low heat for 10 minutes so that they do not colour. Stir in 25 g/1 oz (¼ cup) plain (all-purpose) flour, then add 900 ml/1½ pints (3¾ cups) chicken stock (see page 14). Stir as the soup comes to the boil and thickens slightly. Add 225 g/ 8 oz (½ lb) young nettle leaves and cook for 15 minutes. Sieve or liquidize the soup. Return to the saucepan with 300 ml/½ pint (1¼ cups) single (light) cream and heat gently. Serve with croûtons (see page 305).

FREEZING: All versions of this soup freeze well, but the Creamy Nettle Soup may separate a little (see pages 17 and 18).

French Onion Soup
(Soupe à l'Oignon)

Cooking time: 30 minutes plus time to make stock
Serves 4 to 6

Onion soup is wonderfully warming for a cold day. The first recipe does not include the familiar cheese topping, but this appears in the variations. Onions have a very definite flavour which I feel is enhanced by adding 2 or 3 cloves of garlic. I like strongly flavoured onions but that is a matter of personal choice. Use small onions or cut large ones into manageable pieces so they are easy and elegant to eat with a soup spoon.

Metric/Imperial	Ingredients	American
675 g/1½ lb	onions	1½ lb
2 or 3	garlic cloves	2 or 3
50 g/2 oz	butter	¼ cup
1.2 litres/2 pints	beef stock (see page 14) or water	5 cups
to taste	salt and freshly ground black pepper	to taste
To garnish	chopped chervil or parsley	

Peel the onions, slice thinly and separate into rings. Peel and crush the garlic. Heat the butter, add the onions and garlic and cook over a low heat until the onions are delicately browned. Add the stock or water with seasoning to taste. Bring to the boil, lower the heat and cover the pan. Simmer steadily for about 20 minutes or until the onions are tender. Garnish and serve.

VARIATIONS
- More flavour can be given to the soup by adding a little cayenne pepper or grated nutmeg, a few drops of Worcestershire sauce or a dash of brandy.
- For a richer taste add 1 tablespoon (1¼ tablespoons) olive oil to the butter.

● **SOUPE À L'OIGNON GRATINÉE**

Make the soup as on page 137, then pour into warm bowls. Top with sliced and toasted French bread and cover with grated Gruyère cheese. Place under a preheated grill until the cheese melts. If your bowls are not flame proof (suitable for use under a hot grill), toast the cheese-covered bread separately, then put on the hot soup.

● **CREAMY ONION SOUP**

Use 900 ml/1½ pints (3¾ cups) of chicken stock or water instead of beef stock in the main recipe. Blend 25 g/1 oz (¼ cup) plain (all-purpose) flour with the cooked onions. Continue as the recipe, but add 300 ml/½ pint (1¼ cups) single (light) cream or half milk and half cream to the cooked soup. Heat gently, garnish and serve.

● **ONION AND CHEESE SOUP**

Follow the recipe for Creamy Onion Soup above and serve it topped with thin slices of Gruyère or Cheddar cheese.

● **THICKENED ONION SOUP**

Follow the main recipe but blend 25 g/1 oz (¼ cup) plain (all-purpose) flour with the cooked onions. Add the stock and stir as the soup comes to the boil and thickens slightly.

FREEZING: All these soups freeze well, but those containing flour may separate when frozen; read the hints about counteracting this on pages 17 and 18.

QUICK TIP *All the soups can be cooked in a microwave. Grated or finely chopped onions, although not classically correct for French Onion Soups, cook more quickly than sliced onions.*

Cream of Parsnip Soup

Cooking time: 30 to 40 minutes
Serves 4 to 6

Parsnips are so sweet that other flavourings are needed to prevent them becoming cloying. The lemon in the soup below and the curry paste in the recipe on page 140 turn this vegetable into delicious soups.

Metric/Imperial	Ingredients	American
450 g/1 lb	parsnips, weight when peeled	1 lb
2 medium	onions	2 medium
50 g/2 oz	butter or margarine	¼ cup
25 g/1 oz	flour	¼ cup
750 ml/1¼ pints	vegetable or chicken stock (see pages 14 and 15)	good 3 cups
2	lemons, rind only	2
to taste	salt and freshly ground black pepper	to taste
300 ml/½ pint	milk	1¼ cups
300 ml/½ pint	single (light) cream	1¼ cups
To garnish	lemon segments chopped chives	

Peel and slice the parsnips and onions. Heat the butter or margarine in a saucepan, add the onions and cook gently for 5 minutes, stirring well so they do not brown. Stir in the flour, then add the stock and bring to the boil. Add the parsnips.

Pare the top zest from the lemons, avoid any bitter white pith, add to the pan with a little seasoning. Cover and simmer for 15 to 25 minutes, depending on the age of the parsnips.

Remove most of the lemon zest; you could retain 1 or 2 small strips for extra flavour. Sieve or liquidize the soup, then return to the pan with the milk and reheat; add the cream and any extra seasoning necessary and continue heating.

Cut a few segments from the lemons and add to the soup with the chives immediately before serving.

VARIATIONS
- Use veal stock to give extra flavour.
- Add a pinch of saffron powder or turmeric to the stock to enhance the colour.

- **CREAMED ROOT VEGETABLE SOUP**
Use a mixture of carrots, celeriac, swede (rutabaga) and parsnips.

FREEZING: The puréed soup freezes well, but add the milk and cream when reheating.

Curried Parsnip Soup

Cooking time: 30 to 40 minutes plus time to make stock
Serves 4 to 6

The amount and strength of curry flavouring used in this recipe is a matter of personal taste, but it is better to have a relatively mild flavour for a dish served at the beginning of a meal so that it does not spoil your palate for the food that follows. A recipe for making curry powder appears on page 25.

Metric/Imperial	Ingredients	American
450 g/1 lb	parsnips, prepared weight	1 lb
2 medium	onions	2 medium
2	garlic cloves	2
50 g/2 oz	butter	¼ cup
1 tablespoon	curry paste or powder, to taste	1¼ tablespoons
1.2 litres/2 pints	vegetable or chicken stock (see pages 14 and 15)	5 cups
1 tablespoon	grated or diced creamed coconut	1¼ tablespoons
to taste	salt and freshly ground black pepper	to taste
To garnish	double (heavy) cream	
	chopped red pepper	
	chopped chives	

Peel and slice the parsnips; peel and chop the onions and garlic. Heat the butter in a saucepan, add the onions and garlic and cook gently for 5 minutes, stirring well so they do not discolour. Blend in the curry paste or powder with the onions.

Add the stock, bring to the boil, then add the parsnips and creamed coconut together with a little seasoning. Cover the pan and simmer for 15 to 25 minutes, or until the parsnips are tender.

Sieve or liquidize the mixture, return to the pan and heat thoroughly. Taste and adjust the seasoning. Garnish the soup with the cream, red pepper and chives.

VARIATIONS

- Follow the main recipe, but use 350 g/12 oz (¾ lb) carrots and 100 g/ 4 oz (¼ lb) potatoes.
- Use swedes (rutabagas) instead of parsnips.
- Use turnips in place of parsnips or half turnips and half potatoes.

• CURRIED PARSNIP AND APRICOT SOUP

To emphasize the sweetness of parsnips, add 100 g/4 oz (¼ lb) tenderized apricots to the other ingredients. Increase the amount of stock by 150 ml/¼ pint (⅔ cup). Slice and soak the apricots in the stock for 1 hour before making the soup.

If using non-tenderized apricots, slice and soak overnight in cold water (sufficient to cover them), then simmer in the same water for 1 hour, or until tender. Add the apricots plus 150 ml/¼ pint (⅔ cup) of the cooking liquid to the boiling stock and the other ingredients. Proceed as the recipe above.

FREEZING: All these soups freeze well.

French Pea Soup (Potage St Germain)

Cooking time: 35 minutes
Serves 4 to 6

The availability of frozen peas means that this soup can be made throughout the year, but it is at its best with young fresh peas. Thrifty cooks can use some of the tender green pods to add body, as well as extra flavour, to the soup (see variations).

I like this soup made with stock from boiled bacon, but it has a more delicate taste if chicken stock is used. For a subtle taste use half bacon and half chicken stock.

Metric/Imperial	Ingredients	American
3 medium	shallots or small onions	3 medium
350 g/12 oz	peas	¾ lb
25g/1 oz	butter	2 tablespoons
900 ml/1½ pints	bacon or chicken stock (see page 14)	3¾ cups
small bunch	mint	small bunch
to taste	salt and freshly ground black pepper	to taste
1 teaspoon	caster sugar	1 teaspoon
1 tablespoon	plain (all-purpose) flour, optional	1¼ tablespoons
150 ml/¼ pint	milk	⅔ cup
150 ml/¼ pint	single (light) cream	⅔ cup
To garnish	chopped chervil or parsley	
	croûtons (see page 305)	

Peel and chop the shallots or onions; shell and weigh the peas. If using frozen peas, allow them to defrost slightly so the soup cooks more quickly.

Heat the butter, add the shallots or onions and cook gently for 5 to 8 minutes, stirring well so they do not discolour. Pour the stock into the pan, bring to the boil, then put in the peas, mint, a very little seasoning and the sugar. Cover the pan, lower the heat and cook for 15 minutes.

Remove the mint, sieve or liquidize the soup, then return to the saucepan. If the purée seems rather thin, mix the flour with the milk, add to the soup and stir as it comes to the boil. If sufficiently thick for your taste, omit the flour and simply add the milk. Cook steadily for 5 to 6 minutes. Add the cream and heat for 1 or 2 minutes. Taste and add extra seasoning if required. Serve garnished with the chervil or parsley and the croûtons.

VARIATIONS

- Take a few cooked peas from the soup before sieving or liquidizing it, and add them to the soup just before serving.
- Use about 350 g/12 oz (¾ lb) tender fleshy pea pods, wash then top and tail. The amount of peas could then be reduced to 225 g/8 oz (½ lb) if desired. When using pea pods, the soup *must* be sieved, not liquidized, for a smooth texture. Cook the pods with the peas.
- For extra richness add about 25 g/1 oz (2 tablespoons) butter to the very hot soup just before serving.
- The addition of mint is very much a British taste. The French version of the soup uses chervil or parsley instead.

• GREEN PEA AND MUSHROOM SOUP

Follow the recipe for Potage St Germain on page 142. Slice 100 g/4 oz (¼ lb) small button mushrooms or chestnut mushrooms and cook gently in 25 g/1 oz (2 tablespoons) butter until tender. Stir into the soup with the cream and heat.

• GREEN PEA AND TOMATO SOUP

This is a very happy marriage of flavours. Omit the flour, milk and cream in the main recipe, but add 450 g/1 lb chopped tomatoes. The mint can be retained or omitted. If omitted add 2 or 3 basil leaves instead.

Sieve or liquidize the soup, return to the pan and heat. Top with a little soured cream or yoghurt and croûtons before serving.

FREEZING: All these versions of pea soup freeze well.

French Potato Soup
(Potage Purée de Parmentier)

Cooking time: 35 minutes
Serves 4 to 6

The word *Parmentier* indicates that a recipe should contain potatoes. This very simple soup is delicious and also forms the basis of other puréed soups (see variations).

Metric/Imperial	Ingredients	American
2 medium	leeks	2 medium
50 g/2 oz	butter	¼ cup
350 g/12 oz	floury potatoes, prepared weight	¾ lb
1.2 litres/2 pints	white stock (see page 15)	5 cups
2	fresh bay leaves or 1 dried leaf, optional	2
to taste	salt and freshly ground white pepper	to taste
To garnish	chopped chervil or parsley	
	cayenne pepper or paprika	

Wash and slice just the white part of the leeks. Heat half the butter, add the leeks and cook gently for 5 minutes. Dice the potatoes. Pour the stock over the leeks, bring just to boiling point, then add the potatoes, bay leaves and a little seasoning. Cover the pan, lower the heat and cook gently for 20 minutes, or until the potatoes are just soft.

Remove the bay leaves, sieve or liquidize the soup and return to the pan. Heat thoroughly, add any extra seasoning required and the remaining butter just before serving. Garnish with the herbs and cayenne or paprika.

VARIATIONS

- You could top each serving of the soup with a small knob of butter before adding the garnish.

- **CREAM OF POTATO SOUP**
Reduce the stock by 150 ml/¼ pint (⅔ cup) and add this amount of single (light) cream before serving.

- **JERUSALEM ARTICHOKE SOUP (POTAGE PURÉE DE TOPINAMBOURS)**
This soup is also known as Potage à la Palestine. Follow the main recipe or the variation above, but use Jerusalem artichokes instead of potatoes. You can also use shallots or onions instead of leeks.

- **TURNIP SOUP (POTAGE PURÉE À LA FRENEUSE)**
Substitute very young turnips for the potatoes in the main recipe or Cream of Potato Soup. Turnips develop a stronger flavour as they age, so use only 225 g/8 oz (½ lb) older turnips with 100 g/4 oz (¼ lb) peeled potatoes.
    Leek, shallots or onions can be used to flavour this soup.

FREEZING: All these soups freeze well, but add the cream only when reheating.

Roast Garlic

Garlic is used in a number of recipes in this book. If you find its flavour too pronounced, simply roast it before using.
    Preheat the oven to 190°C/375°F/gas mark 5. If roasting 8 to 10 garlic cloves, heat 1 tablespoon (1¼ tablespoons) olive or sunflower oil in a baking dish. Peel each garlic clove, toss in the hot oil, then cook for 20 minutes or until golden in colour.

Potato Cream Soup

Cooking time: 30 minutes plus time to make the stock
Serves 4 to 6

Do not imagine that a potato soup is dull – that's far from the case. It is full of flavour, particularly if based on ham stock. Alternatives to ham stock appear in the variations.

Metric/Imperial	Ingredients	American
300 g/10 oz	floury old potatoes, prepared weight	1⅔ cups when diced
600 ml/1 pint	ham stock (see page 14)	2½ cups
2 medium	onions	2 medium
1 fresh	bay leaf or ½ dried leaf	1 fresh
to taste	salt and freshly ground black pepper and/or cayenne pepper	to taste
15 g/½ oz	plain (all-purpose) flour	2 tablespoons
300 ml/½ pint	single (light) cream or half cream and half milk	1¼ cups
25 g/1 oz	butter	2 tablespoons
To garnish	chopped chives and/or parsley croûtons (see page 305)	

Peel and dice the potatoes and place in the ham stock so they do not discolour. Peel and finely chop the onions, then add to the stock with the bay leaf. Taste and add whatever seasoning is necessary; you may not need extra salt.

Bring the liquid to the boil, cover the pan and lower the heat. Cook steadily for 15 minutes or until the vegetables are tender. Sieve or liquidize the mixture and return to the pan. Blend the flour with half the cream, add to the soup and stir over the heat until boiling. Whisk in the remaining cream, or milk and cream, add the butter and any extra seasoning required. Heat thoroughly and top with the herbs and croûtons.

VARIATIONS
- Use water with 2 bacon rashers (slices) instead of ham stock. Dice the cooked bacon and use as a garnish on the soup.
- Use chicken stock instead of ham stock.
- Use water with vegetable stock cubes.
- Cook 1 or 2 chopped onions with the diced potatoes.

- **POTATO AND CELERY SOUP**
Use only 225 g/8 oz (1¼ cups) diced potatoes plus ¼ medium-sized heart of celery. Chop the celery and cook with the potatoes. Season the soup with celery salt rather than ordinary salt. Garnish with croûtons and small celery leaves.

- **POTATO AND MUSHROOM SOUP**
Follow the main recipe, but omit butter, cook 1 chopped onion with the potatoes. Dice 100 g/4 oz (1 cup) mushrooms, fry in a little butter and add to the soup just before serving. This method of incorporating the mushrooms does not spoil the colour of the potato mixture.

- **POTATO AND WATERCRESS SOUP**
Follow the basic recipe but add a small bunch of watercress (tied securely) to the other ingredients; the stalks impart a good flavour. Remove the watercress before sieving or liquidizing the ingredients. Reheat as the recipe, adding about 6 tablespoons (7½ tablespoons) coarsely chopped watercress leaves with the butter.

FREEZING: These soups tend to separate in freezing, so whisk or liquidize before reheating.

QUICK TIP *Use dried (dehydrated) potato powder instead of ordinary potatoes. Blend 5 tablespoons (6¼ tablespoons) of the powder with the ham stock. Heat and continue as the main recipe.*

Sweet Potato Soup

Cooking time: 25 to 30 minutes plus time to make stock
Serves 4 to 6

Sweet potatoes and yams (a similar vegetable) have become increasingly popular during the last few years. They can be used in place of ordinary potatoes in many vegetable soups. I like to add a small amount of sharp cooking apple to counterbalance their sweet taste, but tomatoes can also be used.

Metric/Imperial	Ingredients	American
2 medium	onions	2 medium
1 medium	carrot	1 medium
450 g/1 lb	sweet potatoes or yams, unprepared weight	1 lb
2	celery sticks	2
1 litre/1¾ pints	chicken stock (see page 14)	scant 4½ cups
100 g/4 oz	cooking apple, prepared weight	¼ lb
to taste	salt and freshly ground black pepper	to taste
To garnish	croûtons (see page 305)	

Peel the onions, carrot and sweet potatoes or yams and cut into small dice. Keep the potatoes or yams in water until ready to cook to prevent them from discolouring. Chop the celery finely. Bring the stock to the boil and add all the vegetables. Peel, core and dice the apple, then add to the other ingredients with a little seasoning. Cover and simmer for 25 minutes. Check the seasoning, then sieve or liquidize the soup. Return to the pan and reheat. Top with croûtons.

VARIATIONS
- The soup can be topped with a little soured or fresh cream.
- It is excellent made with bacon stock rather than chicken stock.

- **SWEET POTATO AND TOMATO SOUP**
Omit the apple and carrot in the main recipe. Add 3 medium tomatoes, skinned, deseeded and chopped, together with 1 tablespoon (1¼ tablespoons)

tomato purée (paste) and 1 teaspoon finely chopped tarragon. Cook as before, then sieve or liquidize.

● YAM SOUPS

Cook yams in exactly the same recipes as sweet potatoes. Although from a different family of vegetables, they have a similar flavour.

FREEZING: All these soups freeze well.

Cream of Asparagus Soup 2

Cooking time: 25 to 30 minutes
Serves 4 to 6

Metric/Imperial	Ingredients	American
450 g/1 lb	asparagus	1 lb
900 ml/1½ pints	water	3¾ cups
2	roasted garlic cloves (see page 145)	2
to taste	salt and freshly ground black pepper	to taste
300 ml/½ pint	single (light) cream	1¼ cups

Wash the asparagus and cut off a few tips for garnish. Trim off the tough ends of the stalks, place in these the water with the garlic cloves. Simmer for 15 minutes to make stock. Strain the liquid and return most of it to the pan. Cook the tips in the small amount of reserved liquid until just soft. Chop the rest of the asparagus into small pieces; cook in the pan of stock for 10 minutes or until tender. Season to taste.

Sieve or liquidize the soup, add the cream and reheat or chill well. Top with the asparagus tips just before serving.

FREEZING: Freeze the asparagus purée and tips, but add the cream only when defrosted.

Pumpkin Soup

Cooking time: 35 minutes plus time to make stock
Serves 4 to 6

Pumpkins, like all squashes, can be used in both sweet and savoury dishes; they make delicious soups. Since these vegetables do not have a great deal of flavour, they require generous amounts of added spices and herbs. If, however, you prefer a less strongly flavoured soup, you will find this under variations. Although chicken stock can be used for this soup, I prefer it made with vegetable stock.

Metric/Imperial	Ingredients	American
1 medium	onion	1 medium
2	garlic cloves	2
1 medium	carrot	1 medium
550 g/1¼ lb	pumpkin, prepared weight, see method	1¼ lb
50 g/2 oz	butter	¼ cup
¼ teaspoon	ground ginger, or to taste	¼ teaspoon
¼ teaspoon	ground coriander	¼ teaspoon
1.2 litres/2 pints	vegetable or chicken stock (see page 15 and 16)	5 cups
1 teaspoon	chopped sage	1 teaspoon
1 tablespoon	finely chopped parsley	1 tablespoon
to taste	salt and freshly ground black pepper	to taste
To garnish	1 red pepper (optional) cream or yoghurt	

Peel and finely chop the onion, garlic and carrot. Peel the pumpkin, remove all the seeds and stringy bits. In order to have 550 g/1¼ lb pumpkin you will need to buy a good 900 g/2 lb of the vegetable. A few seeds can be retained and cooked as an unusual garnish (see variations).

Heat the butter in a pan, add the onion and garlic and cook gently for 5 minutes. Add the carrot, pumpkin and spices and stir over a low heat for another 5 minutes. Add the stock with the herbs and a little seasoning. Cover the pan and simmer for 20 minutes, then sieve or liquidize the soup. Reheat before serving.

To prepare the garnish, halve and deseed the red pepper and place rounded side uppermost under a preheated grill until the skin turns black. Cool slightly, then remove the skin and dice the flesh very finely. Spoon cream or yoghurt over the soup, then top with the diced pepper.

VARIATIONS

- The seeds of pumpkin and other squashes may be separated and dried on kitchen paper, then cooked slowly in a little oil or butter until golden brown and slightly crisp. They make a pleasing garnish on the soup.
- Instead of ground ginger, peel and grate about 2.5 cm/1 inch fresh root ginger.
- A hotter flavour can be given to the soup if 1 deseeded, chopped red chilli is added to the other ingredients, or a good pinch of chilli powder added to the spices.
- Use peeled and deseeded squash or marrow in place of pumpkin, adding a pinch of turmeric with the other spices to enhance the colour.

• PUMPKIN AND SESAME SOUP

Follow the main recipe but use 2 tablespoons (2½ tablespoons) sesame seed oil instead of the butter. Omit the red pepper and garnish the soup with cream or yoghurt and sesame seeds.

• CREAMY PUMPKIN SOUP

Use the main recipe but add just 600 ml/1 pint (2½ cups) stock to the other ingredients. The spices can be reduced to just a pinch of each. The sage can be replaced with 2 teaspoons chopped thyme. Sieve or liquidize the soup then return to the pan with 300 ml/½ pint (1¼ cups) milk and 300 ml/½ pint (1¼ cups) single (light) cream. Heat and garnish with crisp pumpkin seeds and/or chopped parsley.

Instead of all single cream, use half single cream and half soured cream.

If the soup looks a little pale, mix a good pinch of turmeric with the milk before adding it to the puréed soup.

FREEZING: The main recipe freezes well. The prepared and diced red pepper can also be frozen. When making Creamy Pumpkin Soup, it is better to freeze the puréed pumpkin mixture and add the milk and cream when reheating.

Red Pepper Broth

Cooking time: 35 minutes plus time to make stock
Serves 4 to 6

This very colourful soup is made with finely diced vegetables. Although it is not essential to skin the sweet (bell) peppers, they are more tender if this is done.

Metric/Imperial	Ingredients	American
2 large or 3 medium	red peppers	2 large or 3 medium
2 medium	onions	2 medium
1 or 2	garlic cloves	1 or 2
3 medium	tomatoes	3 medium
2 tablespoons	sunflower or olive oil	2½ tablespoons
900 ml/1½ pints	chicken or vegetable stock (see pages 14 and 15)	3¾ cups
1 teaspoon	chopped basil	1 teaspoon
to taste	salt and freshly ground black pepper	to taste
To garnish	chopped parsley and chopped basil	

Preheat the grill. Cut the peppers in half lengthwise, then remove the seeds and cores. Place the peppers under the heat, rounded sides uppermost, until the skins turn black. Allow to cool slightly, then peel off the skin.

If more convenient the whole peppers can be baked for approximately 30 minutes, or until the skins darken, in an oven preheated to 190°C/375°C/ gas mark 5. Brush the peppers with a little oil before baking. When sufficiently cool to handle, peel off the skin, then halve and remove the cores and seeds.

Cut the flesh of the peppers into very small dice. Skin and finely chop the onions, garlic and tomatoes. Heat the oil in a pan, add the onions and garlic and cook gently for 10 minutes, stirring constantly so they do not brown. Add the peppers, tomatoes, stock, basil and seasoning. Bring to the boil, then cover the pan and simmer for 15 to 20 minutes. Adjust the seasoning, garnish and serve.

VARIATIONS

- Use 1 red, 1 yellow and 1 green pepper instead of 3 red peppers.
- Add a few finely chopped mushrooms to the other ingredients.
- Garnish the broth with small pieces of crisply cooked bacon.

● RED PEPPER SOUP

Use the same ingredients as above, but sieve or liquidize the cooked vegetables. Reheat, then stir in about 150 ml/¼ pint (⅔ cup) single (light) cream or fromage frais. Heat gently, without boiling, then top with more cream or fromage frais and the chopped herbs.

FREEZING: This soup freezes well.

 This is an excellent soup to cook in the microwave.

Spinach and Almond Soup

Cooking time: 35 minutes plus time to make stock
Serves 6

This is a somewhat unusual soup from Yugoslavia, having an interesting taste and texture. As the soup is neither sieved nor liquidized, the onion should be finely chopped and the spinach cut into very thin shreds; use a stainless steel knife to do this so the vegetable does not discolour.

Metric/Imperial	Ingredients	American
1 medium	onion	1 medium
1 tablespoon	olive oil	1¼ tablespoons
450 g/1 lb	young spinach leaves	1 lb
3 tablespoons	ground almonds	3¾ tablespoons
100 g/4 oz	long-grain brown or white rice	½ cup
1 litre/1¾ pints	chicken stock (see page 14)	scant 4½ cups
to taste	salt and freshly ground black pepper	to taste
1 to 2 tablespoons	chopped dill, or to taste	1¼ to 2½ tablespoons
300 ml/½ pint	yoghurt	1¼ cups
To serve	3 large slices toast	
75 g/3 oz	cottage or feta cheese	3 tablespoons

Peel and finely chop the onion. Heat the oil in a really large saucepan, add the onion and gently cook for 5 minutes. Wash, drain and shred the spinach, discarding any stalks. Add the ground almonds to the onion and continue cooking until both ingredients are golden brown. Stir the rice into the onion mixture and add the stock. Bring to the boil, season to taste, then tip in the spinach. Cover the pan and cook steadily for 15 to 20 minutes, or until the rice is cooked.

Stir in half the dill and half the yoghurt and heat gently for 2 or 3 minutes.

Cover the toast with the cheese, cut into fingers or triangles and place on individual plates. Garnish the bowls of soup with the remaining yoghurt and dill.

FREEZING: This soup is better freshly made.

Sorrel Soup 1

Cooking time: 30 minutes plus time to make stock
Serves 4 to 6

Sorrel is one of the early summer herbs that is often sadly neglected. The leaves look very like those of young spinach, and the flavour is not dissimilar. In this recipe the sorrel is used uncooked, but a variation follows which uses rather more cooked sorrel. Always shred sorrel and spinach with a stainless steel knife to avoid discoloration.

Metric/Imperial	Ingredients	American
1 medium	onion	1 medium
25 g/1 oz	butter	2 tablespoons
1 litre/1¾ pints	chicken stock (see page 14)	scant 4½ cups
225 g/8 oz	sorrel leaves	½ lb
to taste	salt and freshly ground black pepper	to taste
225 ml/7½ fl oz	double (heavy) cream	scant 1 cup
To garnish	croûtons (see page 305)	

Peel and finely chop the onion. Heat the butter in a pan and cook the onion gently for 10 minutes, stirring from time to time so it does not discolour. Add the chicken stock, cover the pan and simmer for about 15 minutes.

Meanwhile, wash and dry the sorrel, shred and add to the hot liquid. Sieve or liquidize the soup. Return to the pan, add seasoning to taste and reheat. Whisk the cream into the hot, but not boiling, soup. Reheat gently for a few minutes then serve topped with the croûtons.

VARIATIONS
- Use vegetable stock instead of chicken stock.
- A few tablespoons of cooked rice can be added to the hot soup with the cream. In this case, omit the croûtons.

- **SORREL SOUP 2**

Cook the onion in 50 g/2 oz (¼ cup) butter, then add 450 g/1 lb washed and shredded sorrel. Stir in 1 to 2 teaspoons finely chopped rosemary. Pour 1.2 litres/2 pints (5 cups) boiling water or chicken stock over the ingredients. If using water, add 2 teaspoons lemon juice to give more flavour. Season the soup, cover the pan and simmer for 15 to 20 minutes, or until the sorrel is tender. Sieve or liquidize the mixture and return to the saucepan.

Blend 2 egg yolks and 150 ml/¼ pint (⅔ cup) single (light) cream with a few tablespoons of the hot soup. Stir into the purée and simmer gently for a few minutes. Serve garnished with croûtons.

- **CABBAGE SOUPS**

Follow either of the recipes for Sorrel Soup, but use 2 onions. If using recipe 1, use half the heart of a small, firm green cabbage. If using recipe 2, use a whole small cabbage heart. Cabbage has less flavour than sorrel, so it is advisable to use either chicken or vegetable stock rather than water.

Chopped tarragon, parsley or chives complement cabbage better than rosemary.

- **SPINACH SOUPS**

Follow either of the recipes for Sorrel Soup, but use spinach instead of sorrel.

In recipe 2 tarragon is a better herb to use than rosemary.

FREEZING: All the above soups freeze well.

Tarragon and Tomato Soup

Cooking time: 30 minutes
Serves 4 to 6

Tarragon is not a herb popularly associated with tomatoes, but the two flavours complement each other extremely well. Plum tomatoes give the best flavour in the soup, and French tarragon is much superior to the more robust Russian variety.

Metric/Imperial	Ingredients	American
1 small bunch	tarragon	1 small bunch
900 ml/1½ pints	water	3¾ cups
2 medium	onions	2 medium
2 rashers	streaky bacon	2 slices
675 g/1½ lb	tomatoes	1½ lb
25g/1 oz	butter	¼ cup
to taste	salt and freshly ground black pepper	to taste
1 teaspoon	sugar, or to taste	1 teaspoon
To garnish	soured or fresh cream	
	tarragon leaves	

Put the tarragon leaves into a mortar or strong bowl and crush with a pestle or the back of a spoon; this extracts the maximum flavour. Boil the water and pour a little over the leaves. Allow to stand for about 30 minutes, then strain this liquid into the remaining water.

Peel and chop the onions, derind and dice the bacon, slice the tomatoes. Heat the bacon rinds and butter in a saucepan, add the onions and bacon and cook for 5 minutes, taking care the onions do not discolour. Add the tomatoes and cook gently for a further 5 minutes. Remove the bacon rinds.

Pour the water into the saucepan and bring just to the boil. Add a little seasoning, then cover the pan and simmer for 15 minutes. Sieve or liquidize the mixture (the latter process may leave a few seeds in the soup). Return to the pan, add any further seasoning required plus the sugar. Reheat, then top with the cream and tarragon leaves.

VARIATIONS

- Vegetarians can omit the bacon and add a garlic clove plus a little diced dessert apple to give an interesting flavour.
- This is a very pleasant soup to serve cold or even iced. Follow the main recipe and chill or freeze as suggested on page 296.

FREEZING: This is an excellent soup to freeze.

QUICK TIP *Use approximately 450 g/1 lb canned tomatoes plus a little dried tarragon to shorten the cooking time.*
This soup can be cooked in a large bowl in the microwave.

Tomato and Mushroom Soup

Cooking time: 30 minutes plus time to make stock
Serves 4 to 6

This soup combines two favourite ingredients. It is important not to exceed the weight of mushrooms as this would spoil the tomato flavour. This soup is generally served without sieving or liquidizing the ingredients, so do ensure they are chopped evenly and finely.

Metric/Imperial	Ingredients	American
2 medium	onions	2 medium
675 g/1½ lb	ripe tomatoes	1½ lb
100 g/4 oz	small button mushrooms	¼ lb
50 g/2 oz	butter	¼ cup
600 ml/1 pint	chicken stock (see page 14)	2½ cups
1 to 2 teaspoons	Worcestershire sauce	1 to 2 teaspoons
to taste	salt and freshly ground black pepper	to taste
1 to 2 teaspoons	sugar, preferably brown	1 to 2 teaspoons
To garnish	chopped basil, tarragon or parsley	

Peel and finely chop the onions. Skin and halve the tomatoes, remove the seeds and chop the pulp neatly: this process is known as concassing. Wipe and dice the mushroom caps; the stalks can be trimmed and finely chopped too.

Heat the butter in a saucepan, add the onions and cook gently for 5 minutes. Add the tomatoes and mushrooms and cook for a further 5 minutes, stirring frequently so they do not discolour. Add the stock and remaining ingredients. Bring just to boiling point, then cover the pan and lower the heat. Simmer for 15 minutes, check the seasoning, then garnish and serve.

VARIATION

- The soup can be sieved or liquidized but it then has rather a thin consistency. To overcome this, blend 3 tablespoons (3¾ tablespoons) plain (all-purpose) flour with 4 tablespoons (5 tablespoons) cold stock or sherry, add to the soup and stir over a moderate heat until thickened and smooth. Garnish with soured cream, yoghurt or cream cheese and chopped herbs.

FREEZING: Both versions of this soup freeze well.

 This is an ideal soup to make in the microwave.

Tomato Soup

Cooking time: 30 minutes
Serves 4

In spite of the great variety of soups that can be made at home, or purchased in diverse forms, there is no doubt that tomato soups still head the list of favourites for most people, especially children. There are so many ways of making this soup that I have given a selection of recipes. The first is a very basic one, which is better made with water rather than stock.

In all the recipes the tomatoes, preferably the plum variety, should be fully ripe to give the maximum flavour. Do not overcook the soup, for this will destroy the fresh tomato taste.

The amount of sugar added depends upon personal taste and the season. Freshly picked tomatoes generally have a much sweeter flavour than imported winter produce. Canned plum tomatoes or containers of Italian pomodori make a good soup (see variations).

In the recipes where stock is mentioned, choose one with a mild taste or dilute strong stock with water (unless stated otherwise); or use half the normal amount of stock cubes.

Metric/Imperial	Ingredients	American
675 g/1½ lb	tomatoes	1½ lb
1 medium	onion	1 medium
1	garlic clove	1
2 rashers	lean bacon	2 slices
25 g/1 oz	butter or margarine	2 tablespoons
300 ml/½ pint	water	1¼ cups
1 tablespoon	tomato purée (paste)	1¼ tablespoons
1	bouquet garni*	1
to taste	salt and freshly ground black pepper	to taste
1 teaspoon	sugar, preferably brown, or to taste	1 teaspoon
To garnish	cream, yoghurt or fromage frais chopped parsley or chives	

*Small sprigs of basil, parsley and thyme are ideal for this soup.

Chop the tomatoes into small pieces. If you intend to liquidize rather than sieve the soup and want it to be completely smooth, skin, halve and deseed the tomatoes first.

Peel and chop the onion and garlic, derind the bacon and chop the rashers. Heat the butter or margarine with the bacon rinds in a saucepan, add the onions, garlic and bacon. Cook over a low heat for 5 minutes. Do not allow to brown. Add the remaining ingredients and bring the soup to simmering point. Cover the pan, cook for 20 minutes, then remove the bacon rinds and bouquet garni.

Sieve or liquidize the soup, return to the pan and reheat. You may need to add additional seasoning and sugar. Top with cream, yoghurt or fromage frais and herbs before serving. This soup is also good cold (see page 278).

VARIATIONS

- Vegetarians can omit the bacon and use 40 g/1½ oz (3 tablespoons) margarine plus an extra onion and/or garlic clove to give more flavour.
- Use 550 g/1¼ lb canned chopped tomatoes or pomodori instead of fresh tomatoes.
- **For a thicker soup**, mix 25 g/1 oz (¼ cup) flour with the cooked onion mixture.

- **HERB-FLAVOURED TOMATO SOUPS**

Many herbs combine well with tomatoes, so you may like to omit the bouquet garni, which gives a delicate taste, and emphasize just one herb, such as **basil, fennel leaves, oregano, rosemary, tarragon or thyme**.

Chop enough herbs to give up to 4 teaspoonsfuls. Add gradually to the other ingredients until you achieve the desired flavour. Garnish the soup with the herb used in cooking. Be very sparing if using dried herbs – ½ to 1 teaspoon is generally sufficient.

- **CREAM OF TOMATO SOUP 1**

Follow the main recipe, then sieve or liquidize the mixture and return to the saucepan.

In another saucepan make a White Sauce (see page 28) with 25 g/1 oz (2 tablespoons) butter or margarine, 25 g/1 oz (¼ cup) plain (all-purpose) flour and 300 ml/½ pint (1¼ cups) milk. When thickened, add 150 ml/¼ pint (⅔ cup) of single (light) cream. Whisk the very hot sauce into the very hot, but not boiling, tomato soup and stir over a low heat until well blended. Check the seasoning and serve. This variation serves 6.

- **CREAM OF TOMATO SOUP 2**

Mix 25 g/1 oz (2 tablespoons) butter with 25 g/1 oz (¼ cup) plain (all-purpose) flour to make a *beurre manié*. Gradually drop small amounts of this (see page 8) into the basic hot tomato soup. When absorbed, make sure the soup is no longer boiling, then whisk in 150 to 300 ml/¼ to ½ pint (⅔ to 1¼ cups) single (light) or double (heavy) cream, depending on how rich you want the soup to be. Stir until heated and serve topped with croûtons (see page 305). This variation serves 4 to 6.

- **TOMATO AND BEEF SOUP**

Use fairly strongly flavoured beef stock (see page 14) instead of water in the main recipe, and stir in approximately 6 tablespoons (7½ tablespoons) minced or finely diced cooked beef. Heat for a few minutes before serving.

- **TOMATO AND CHICKEN SOUP**

Use chicken stock (see page 14) instead of water in the main recipe. Stir approximately 8 tablespoons (10 tablespoons) minced or finely diced cooked chicken breast and 4 tablespoons (5½ tablespoons) neatly diced raw mushrooms into the soup just before serving. Heat for a few minutes. In this variation the chicken stock can be quite strongly flavoured.

- **TOMATO AND LEMON SOUP**

Follow the main recipe, but omit the bacon and bouquet garni. Add 1 teaspoon finely grated lemon zest, 2 tablespoons (2½ tablespoons) lemon juice plus 2 stems finely chopped lemon grass to the other ingredients. This soup is equally good hot or cold. Garnish with lemon slices.

● TOMATO AND POTATO SOUP

Follow the main recipe but use chicken stock (see page 14) instead of water and add 2 medium peeled and diced potatoes to the other ingredients. Sieve or liquidize the ingredients to make a thick purée, then add extra stock, milk or cream to produce the right consistency. Heat carefully if using milk or cream and do not allow to boil. This variation serves 5 or 6.

This soup can be served without sieving or liquidizing, but all the ingredients should be neatly and finely diced.

● TOMATO AND VEGETABLE SOUP

Use about 350 g/12 oz (¾ lb) root vegetables (unprepared weight), such as **carrots, celeriac, swede (rutabaga), turnips** or chopped **celery heart** in place of the potatoes above, and adjust the amount of liquid as suggested.

● BULGARIAN TOMATO SOUP WITH CHEESE

Follow the main recipe, omitting the bacon if you wish. Add salt and 1 to 2 teaspoons paprika for flavour. Sieve or liquidize the soup, then return to the pan and reheat. Add about 5 tablespoons (6¼ tablespoons) soft cream cheese or grated cheese and stir until just melted. Do not overcook at this stage or the cheese becomes stringy.

● AUSTRIAN TOMATO SOUP

A typical Austrian tomato soup depends very much on generous amounts of vegetables and herbs. Chop enough parsley, young spinach leaves, celery and carrot to give 2 tablespoons (2½ tablespoons) of each ingredient. Peel and finely chop 1 medium onion. Heat 50 g/2 oz (¼ cup) butter in a saucepan and gently cook the onion, vegetables and parsley for 10 minutes, taking care they do not discolour. Add 675 g/1½ lb chopped tomatoes with 300 ml/½ pint (1¼ cups) water, 150 ml/¼ pint (⅔ cup) red wine and seasoning to taste. Cook for approximately 25 minutes in a covered pan, then sieve or liquidize, return to the saucepan and reheat. This soup can also be served without sieving.

Just before serving 3 tablespoons (3¾ tablespoons) cooked long-grain rice can be added to the soup, and I often add 1 teaspoon caraway seeds at the same time. Top the hot soup with soured cream before serving.

● ITALIAN TOMATO SOUP

Follow the main recipe, but omit the bacon and use 750 ml/1¼ pints (good 3 cups) chicken or other white stock (see pages 14 and 15). Fry the onion and garlic in the butter or margarine, add the tomatoes and liquid with 3 tablespoons (3¾ tablespoons) arborio (Italian risotto) rice. Cook as the recipe. This soup can be sieved or liquidized if you wish. An extra 25 g/1 oz (2 tablespoons) butter should be stirred into the soup just before serving to enrich it.

A few pieces of finely chopped sun-dried tomatoes (preferably those bottled in olive oil) may be added to the soup just before serving, or before sieving or liquidizing if you prefer a smooth puréed soup. These add a particularly interesting flavour.

FREEZING: Most of these tomato soups freeze well, the exceptions being the cream soups, which tend to separate during freezing. (See pages 17 and 18 for hints on returning them to their original smooth texture.) To avoid this problem, freeze the basic tomato purée and combine with the white sauce or cream *after* defrosting. Always reheat creamed soups gently as the acid content of the tomatoes could cause the soup to curdle if allowed to boil vigorously.

Vegetable Gumbo

Cooking time: 30 minutes plus time to make stock
Serves 4 to 6

A gumbo is a soup that contains okra, sometimes called ladies' fingers because of their shape. As these give a slightly odd colour to the soup, I like to add tomatoes for a pleasantly reddish appearance. This recipe uses chicken stock, which I find enhances the flavour of the okra, but vegetable stock could be used instead.

Metric/Imperial	Ingredients	American
350 g/12 oz	okra	¾ lb
2 medium	onions	2 medium
1	garlic clove	1
3 medium	tomatoes	3 medium
2 tablespoons	olive or sunflower oil	2½ tablespoons
1.2 litres/2 pints	chicken stock (see page 14)	5 cups
1 tablespoon	chopped parsley	1¼ tablespoons
to taste	salt and freshly ground black pepper	to taste
To garnish	4 tablespoons (5 tablespoons) cooked rice chopped parsley	

Wipe and slice the okra. Peel and chop the onions, garlic and tomatoes. Heat the oil and cook the onions and garlic gently for 5 minutes, stirring well so they do not brown. Stir in the tomatoes and okra and cook for 5 more minutes.

Pour in the stock, bring to the boil, then stir in the parsley and seasoning. Cover the pan and simmer for 15 to 20 minutes.

Stir in the rice and heat for 1 or 2 minutes. Top the soup with the parsley.

VARIATION

- Before slicing the okra it can be blanched by cooking it for 2 minutes in boiling salted water.

FREEZING: **Do not freeze.**

GARNISHES FOR VEGETABLE SOUPS

In most recipes an appropriate garnish is recommended, but if this is not the case, the soup can be topped with cream, soured cream, crème fraîche, yoghurt or fromage frais. Chopped herbs also complement vegetable soups (see pages 299 to 311). You could also use any of the garnishes on pages 20 and 21. A generous topping of grated cheese, cream cheese or dumplings turns the soup into a more satisfying dish (see page 308).

The recipe for Danish Brown Soup (see page 166) is topped with Parmesan Cheese Balls (see page 301). These turn an appetizing, but fairly light soup into a much more sustaining dish and would be equally good on many other soups in this book, especially the clear soups on pages 66 to 81.

Danish Brown Soup (Brun Suppe)

Cooking time: 15 minutes plus time to make stock
Serves 4

The cheese balls added as a garnish to this recipe are traditional on a thickened brown soup in Denmark. The secret of this soup lies in the quality of the beef stock, which must be strongly flavoured and free from excess fat (see page 12).

Metric/Imperial	Ingredients	American
50 g/2 oz	butter	¼ cup
50 g/2 oz	plain (all-purpose) flour	½ cup
1.2 litres/2 pints	beef stock (see page 14)	5 cups
3 tablespoons	sherry	4 tablespoons
to taste	salt and freshly ground black pepper	to taste
To garnish	Parmesan Cheese Balls (see page 301)	

Heat the butter in a saucepan, stir in the flour, then add the stock. Stir as the liquid comes to the boil and thickens. Simmer for about 10 minutes, then add the sherry and seasoning to taste.

Top each portion with Cheese Balls and serve.

VARIATION

- Although it is not traditional to include vegetables in this soup, you can add finely diced and lightly cooked root vegetables to the basic recipe. Cooked peas may be used as an alternative garnish to Cheese Balls, or in addition to them.

FREEZING: This soup freezes well. Freeze the Cheese Balls separately (see page 301).

QUICK TIP *Use beef stock cubes dissolved in water or canned consommé instead of fresh beef stock.*

Cheddar and Potato Chowder

Cooking time: 30 minutes plus time to make stock
Serves 4 to 6

This is a very satisfying soup. The main recipe and some of the variations are suitable for vegetarians. Other chowders appear on pages 56, 114, 190 and 192.

Metric/Imperial	Ingredients	American
4 medium	potatoes	4 medium
3 medium	onions	3 medium
50 g/2 oz	butter or margarine	¼ cup
900 ml/1½ pints	vegetable stock (see page 15)	3¾ cups
to taste	salt and freshly ground black pepper	to taste
1 teaspoon	ready-made English or French mustard	1 teaspoon
1	bouquet garni*	1
150 ml/¼ pint	single (light) cream or milk	⅔ cup
225 g/8 oz	Cheddar cheese	½ lb
To garnish	chopped parsley and savory	

* Small sprigs of savory, thyme and parsley should be tied together or placed in muslin.

Peel the potatoes and cut into 1.25 cm/½ inch dice. Peel the onions and cut into 6 mm/¼ inch dice. Heat the butter or margarine in a saucepan, add the onions and cook slowly for 5 or 6 minutes. Put in the potatoes and cook, stirring constantly, until both vegetables are a delicate golden colour.

Pour in the stock, bring just to boiling point, then add the seasoning, mustard and bouquet garni. Cover the pan, lower the heat and simmer for approximately 10 minutes or until the vegetables are just tender.

Meanwhile, grate just over half the cheese and cut the rest into 1.25 cm/ ½ inch dice. Remove the bouquet garni, add the cream and grated cheese and stir over the heat until the cheese has just melted – do not overcook. Top with the diced cheese, chopped parsley and savory immediately before serving: the diced cheese should remain firm in the soup.

VARIATIONS

• CHEDDAR AND CELERIAC CHOWDER

Use ½ a small celeriac in place of 2 of the potatoes. Peel the celeriac and cut into 1.25 cm/½ inch dice; keep in cold water with a little lemon juice until ready to cook. Toss in the butter with the onions and potatoes.

• CHEDDAR AND MIXED VEGETABLE CHOWDER

Use 350 g/12 oz (¾ lb) mixed diced root vegetables instead of 1 of the onions and 2 of the potatoes. A few shelled or frozen peas and/or sliced green beans can be added to the stock during the cooking period.

• CHEDDAR AND BACON CHOWDER

Derind 2 or 3 rashers (slices) of bacon and heat the rinds with the butter or margarine. Dice the bacon and sauté with the potatoes. Chicken stock (see page 14) can be used instead of vegetable stock. The amount of cheese can be reduced slightly in this particular recipe.

Remove the bacon rinds with the bouquet garni.

• CHEDDAR AND TOMATO CHOWDER

Omit the cream in the main recipe or any of the variations above. Skin, halve and deseed 450 g/1 lb ripe tomatoes. Cut the flesh into neat dice. Add to the soup just before the vegetables are quite cooked. Heat for a few minutes, then add the grated cheese and continue as above.

DO NOT FREEZE: The vegetable pieces are inclined to become too soft.

SOUPS WITH PULSES

All the pulses – beans, peas and lentils – make excellent soups. Their food value is high, being excellent sources of protein and fibre.

Check the consistency of soups made with *dried pulses* because they require long, slow cooking and may become too thick, especially if the lid of the pan is not a good fit and too much liquid has evaporated. It is, however, quite easy to add a little extra stock or water at the end of the cooking time so that the soup has the consistency of thick cream.

Microwave cooking: Although this method can be used to cook these soups, dried beans never become quite as soft as when cooked by other means.

The amount of liquid given in the recipe can be reduced by 10 per cent. As large quantities of liquid take a long time to heat in the microwave, save time by bringing the pulses, their soaking water and any other ingredients to the boil in a saucepan. Allow the soup to boil for several minutes (10 minutes in the case of dried beans to make sure harmful enzymes are destroyed). Transfer the very hot mixture to a heated microwave bowl, cover and continue cooking on defrost setting for approximately half the time it would take in a saucepan. The time will vary slightly according to the output of the microwave being used.

Pressure cooking: Dried pulses cook quickly and easily in a pressure cooker. Soak them as directed in the recipes, then place in the pressure cooker with the liquid and other ingredients. Fix the lid and bring up to full pressure (high). Maintain at this pressure throughout the cooking time. It is essential that the pressure cooker is never more than half filled with the ingredients. Always allow the pressure to drop at room temperature.

Dried bean soup takes about 20 minutes at pressure, or a little longer if the beans are large. Dried pea soup takes 15 minutes at pressure, and lentils 10 to 15 minutes, depending upon the type.

You can reduce the amount of liquid given in the recipe by 25 per cent.

If milk or cream is added to the soup, this must be done after the pressure has dropped. Use the cooker like an ordinary saucepan at this stage.

Slow cooking: The soaked pulses with the stock and other ingredients must be brought to the boil in an ordinary saucepan first. When using dried beans, boil for 10 minutes to kill harmful enzymes. Transfer the soup to the heated container in the slow cooker and allow to cook for 5 to 6 hours, or even more if convenient. The pulses will then be very tender.

Use the same amount of liquid as given in the recipes.

Arabic White Soup

Cooking time: 1¼ hours
Serves 4

It may seem strange that this soup with its generous amount of beans should be served cold, but it is traditional. It is also sustaining and refreshing.

Metric/Imperial	Ingredients	American
175 g/6 oz	haricot (navy) beans	⅔ cup
to taste	salt and freshly ground white pepper	to taste
100 g/4 oz	almonds	scant 1 cup
1	garlic clove	1
1 to 2 tablespoons	virgin olive oil	1¼ to 2½ teaspoons
as required	ice-cold water	as required
3 tablespoons	soft breadcrumbs	3¾ tablespoons
1 tablespoon	chopped parsley	1¼ tablespoons
2 teaspoons	chopped mint	2 teaspoons

Soak the beans in cold water for several hours. Drain, then cover in fresh cold water. Bring to the boil and boil briskly for 10 minutes. Lower the heat and add a little seasoning. Cover the pan and simmer until the beans are tender. Strain and allow to become cold.

Blanch and chop the almonds. Peel and crush the garlic. Mix the almonds, garlic and olive oil into the beans and gradually add enough water to make the consistency of a thick soup. Stir in the breadcrumbs, parsley and mint and season well. Chill before serving.

DO NOT FREEZE

 Use canned beans, drained and rinsed in cold water.

Butter Bean Soup

Cooking time: 2 hours
Serves 4 to 6

This dried bean soup is ideal for a light main meal and lends itself to many variations. The other ingredients included add a great deal of flavour and colour to the beans.

Metric/Imperial	Ingredients	American
225 g/8 oz	dried butter (lima) beans	½ lb
1.8 litres/3 pints	bacon or chicken stock (see page 14)	7½ cups
2 medium	onions	2 medium
2	garlic cloves	2
2 medium	carrots	2 medium
2	celery sticks	2
350 g/12 oz	tomatoes	¾ lb
to taste	salt and freshly ground black pepper	to taste
1 teaspoon	chopped savory leaves or pinch dried savory	1 teaspoon
1 tablespoon	chopped parsley	1¼ tablespoons
1 teaspoon	finely grated lemon rind	1 teaspoon
To garnish	soured cream	

Wash the beans, place in the stock and soak overnight, or bring just to the boil and simmer steadily for 10 minutes. Cover the pan and allow to stand for 2 or 3 hours.

Peel and finely chop the onions and garlic; peel and slice the carrots; chop the celery and tomatoes. Add to the pan of beans and stock with some seasoning, be sparing with the salt if using bacon stock. Add the herbs and lemon rind. Cover the pan, bring to the boil and boil briskly for 10 minutes. Lower the heat and simmer gently for 1½ to 1¾ hours or until the beans are tender.

Sieve or liquidize the soup, add a little additional stock if it is rather thick, then return to the pan and reheat. Check the seasoning and serve topped with soured cream.

VARIATIONS

- Substitute basil for savory in the main recipe.
- Use white or red haricot (navy) beans instead of butter (lima) beans.

- **BUTTER (LIMA) BEAN BROTH**

Do not sieve or liquidize the soup above. Top with plenty of freshly chopped parsley and the soured cream.

- **ADZUKI BEAN SOUP**

These dried reddish beans make a delicious soup. They are more expensive than other beans and have a distinctly sweet taste, so you might like to add a little lemon juice to the main recipe.

Follow the main recipe on page 171 but use only 2 medium tomatoes and 1 garlic clove.

Prepare the adzuki beans in the same way as the butter beans, but simmer with the other ingredients for only 45 minutes to 1 hour. Check the seasoning and serve.

- **BLACK BEAN SOUP**

If possible, always use bacon stock (see page 14) for a soup based on these excellent black beans. Add several chopped bacon rashers (slices) to the other ingredients listed in the main recipe, and use 1 teaspoon ground cumin instead of the savory.

If you like a hot flavour, add ½ to 1 teaspoon chilli powder with the other seasoning, or include 1 deseeded and chopped red chilli pepper with the rest of the ingredients. Garnish this soup with sliced lemon instead of soured cream.

- **CANNELLINI BEAN SOUP**

Follow the main recipe, but use only 1 medium tomato and 1 garlic clove as cannellini beans have a very delicate flavour. Prepare the cannellini in the same way as butter beans, but simmer with the other ingredients for only 45 minutes.

This soup is delicious topped with cream cheese.

- **VEGETARIAN DRIED BEAN SOUPS**

Use vegetable stock (see page 15) instead of bacon or chicken stock in any of the recipes on pages 170 to 174.

FREEZING: All the puréed bean soups freeze well. The beans in Butter (Lima) Bean Broth are inclined to become over-soft with freezing, so undercook the soup slightly if you intend to freeze it.

Haricot Bean Soup

Cooking time: 25 minutes
Serves 4

This is a good soup to make from store-cupboard ingredients when time is short. The various ingredients give such a good flavour that there is no need to make stock.

Metric/Imperial	Ingredients	American
2 medium	potatoes	2 medium
2 medium	onions	2 medium
2 or 3	bacon rashers	2 or 3 (slices)
1 × 450 g/1 lb can	chopped tomatoes	1 × 1 lb can
600 ml/1 pint	water	2½ cups
1 × 225 g/8 oz can	baked (navy) beans in tomato sauce	1 × ½ lb can
to taste	salt and freshly ground black pepper	to taste
1 teaspoon	chopped fresh oregano or marjoram or ½ teaspoon dried herbs	1 teaspoon
To garnish	chopped chives	

Peel and grate or finely dice the potatoes and onions. Cut the rinds from the bacon and chop the rashers into bite-sized pieces. Put the vegetables, bacon rinds and rashers and the canned tomatoes into a saucepan with the water. Bring to the boil, lower the heat and cover the pan. Simmer for 15 minutes or until the onions and potatoes are just soft.

Add the baked beans, seasoning and herbs. Simmer for 5 minutes, then remove the bacon rinds. Serve topped with chives.

VARIATIONS
- Vegetarians can omit the bacon and add a little finely chopped celery instead.
- Use cooked haricot (navy) beans or other varieties of beans plus 1 tablespoon (1¼ tablespoons) tomato purée (paste) to give extra flavour.

DO NOT FREEZE

Lentil Soup

Cooking time: 1 hour plus time to make stock
Serves 4 to 6

This is the soup I make when I have some stock left from boiling a piece of bacon. In my opinion the two flavours – bacon and lentils – are a perfect partnership. I generally use the small orange lentils although for a more delicate flavour I sometimes substitute the delicious French lentilles de Puy. These green lentils do take about 50 per cent longer to cook, so increase the amount of stock to 900 ml/1½ pints (3¾ cups).

Metric/Imperial	Ingredients	American
2 medium	onions	2 medium
1	garlic clove	1
1 medium	carrot	1 medium
1 small	dessert apple	1 small
600 ml/1 pint	bacon stock	2½ cups
1 bunch	bouquet garni*	1 bunch
225 g/8 oz	lentils	1 cup
to taste	salt and freshly ground black pepper	to taste
1 tablespoon	cornflour (cornstarch)	1¼ tablespoons
300 ml/½ pint	milk	1¼ cups
50 g/2 oz	butter	¼ cup
To garnish	chopped parsley croûtons (see page 305)	

---

* In this recipe tie together a small bunch of parsley, 1 sprig of thyme and 1 sprig of sage, or use ¼ teaspoon of each of these dried herbs.

Peel and finely chop the onions and garlic; peel and thinly slice the carrot and the apple (discard the core). Bring the stock to the boil, add the vegetables, plus the apple, bouquet garni and lentils. Lower the heat and season to taste, being sparing with the salt at this stage. Cover the pan and simmer for 45 minutes. Remove the bunch of fresh herbs.

Blend the cornflour with the milk, add to the hot soup and stir as it thickens. Sieve or liquidize the mixture, then return to the pan and heat thoroughly. If the soup is a little thick, add more stock or milk to give the perfect consistency. Stir in the butter just before serving and adjust the seasoning. Top with parsley and croûtons.

VARIATIONS

• AMERICAN LENTIL SOUP

Large American green and brown lentils give a wonderful flavour to soups. It is important to soak them in the stock (or other liquid) overnight. Use 1.2 litres/2 pints (5 cups) bacon stock (or half stock and half water for a milder flavour) to 225 g/8 oz (1 cup) lentils. You can use water or chicken stock, in which case add 2 to 3 diced uncooked rashers (slices) of bacon to the other ingredients when cooking the soup for a richer taste.

Put the lentils and their soaking liquid into a saucepan, add 2 medium sliced carrots, 2 chopped celery sticks, 2 medium chopped onions and 2 medium diced potatoes. Cook for 1½ to 2 hours, or until the lentils are tender. Season well and add 2 tablespoons (2½ tablespoons) dry sherry. Sieve or liquidize the mixture, then return to the pan and reheat. Stir 5 tablespoons (6¼ tablespoons) soured or fresh double (heavy) cream into the soup just before serving. Do not allow to boil.

This soup can be turned into a complete meal if about 350 g/12 oz (¾ lb) sliced cooked sausages or frankfurters are heated in the soup.

• AUSTRIAN LENTIL SOUP (LINSENSUPPE)

This is made in a similar way to the main recipe, but the lentils are cooked in 900 ml/1½ pints (3¾ cups) water rather than bacon stock. Omit the apple. The soup is given a sharp flavour by adding 1 tablespoon (1¼ tablespoons) red wine vinegar towards the end of the cooking time. Sieve or liquidize the soup. Heat 50 g/2 oz (¼ cup) butter in a saucepan, stir in 50 g/2 oz (½ cup) plain (all-purpose) flour and the lentil purée. Stir over the heat until thickened. Garnish with profiteroles (see page 98).

• LENTIL AND TOMATO SOUP

Follow any of the three recipes on pages 174 and 175, using half stock or water and half tomato purée made with fresh or canned plum tomatoes. Where milk or cream are included, it is important that the soup is stirred well and heated thoroughly but not allowed to boil: this ensures it will not curdle.

FREEZING: All versions of this soup freeze well.

Indian Lentil Soup

Cooking time: 45 to 55 minutes
Serves 4 to 6

In this recipe the tiny red or orange lentils, known as *dhal* in India, are ideal. It is not essential to soak them before cooking, but if you do so, it shortens the cooking time by about 10 minutes. To bring out the maximum flavour of the spices, heat them in a dry frying pan. If you do not have the varieties mentioned, use curry powder (see variations).

Metric/Imperial	Ingredients	American
2 medium	onions	2 medium
2	garlic cloves	2
1 tablespoon	ground cumin, or to taste	1¼ tablespoons
2 teaspoons	ground coriander, or to taste	2 teaspoons
2 teaspoons	ground ginger, or to taste	2 teaspoons
½ teaspoon	ground coriander, or to taste	½ teaspoon
50 g/2 oz	ghee* or butter	¼ cup
1.2 litres/2 pints	water	5 cups
225 g/8 oz	lentils, preferably red or orange	1 cup
150 ml/¼ pint	coconut milk**	⅔ cup
to taste	salt and freshly ground black pepper	to taste

* **To make ghee**, cover a quantity of butter with water and heat gently until the butter melts. Allow to become quite cold, then lift the clarified butter from the top of the water. It is possible to buy ghee from Indian shops and good supermarkets.

** **To make coconut milk**, cover 2 tablespoons (2½ tablespoons) desiccated coconut with 225 ml/7½ fl oz (scant 1 cup) boiling water. Allow to cool then strain and use the liquid. Another method is to heat 25 g/1 oz (good tablespoon) coconut cream with 150 ml/¼ pint (⅔ cup) water until dissolved.

It is possible to buy ready-made coconut milk.

Peel and finely chop the onions and garlic. Put the four spices into a dry frying pan and heat gently, stirring well, for 4 minutes. Add the ghee or butter, heat until melted, then tip in the onions and garlic. Cook over a low heat for 5 minutes, stirring well. Pour in the water, bring to the boil, then add the lentils, coconut milk and seasoning to taste. Bring just to boiling point, stir briskly, then cover the pan and lower the heat. Simmer gently for 30 to 40 minutes, or until the lentils are soft.

Serve the soup with the whole softened lentils or sieve or liquidize. Reheat before serving.

VARIATIONS

- Omit the four spices and use 1 to 2 tablespoons (1¼ to 2½ tablespoons) curry powder. The amount and strength of this depends upon personal taste.
- Many Far Eastern lentil recipes include tamarind purée. This comes from a very acid-flavoured fruit shaped like a broad bean and is sometimes available canned: add 1 tablespoon (1¼ tablespoons) with the seasoning. If you find it in powder form, add ½ to 1 teaspoon. If you can't find it at all, add a little lemon or lime juice to give a sharper flavour.

• LENTIL AND VEGETABLE SOUP

Follow the main recipe but add 3 small, thinly sliced carrots, 1 diced aubergine and small pieces of peeled, diced marrow or 2 unpeeled, sliced courgettes (zucchini) to the liquid with only 175 g/6 oz (¾ cup) of lentils.

FREEZING: This soup freezes well in any form.

Dutch Dried Pea Soup (Erwtensoep)

Cooking time: 1¾ hours
Serves 4 to 6

This soup has a very meaty flavour because it includes brown stock, pork, frankfurters and bacon.

The British version (see variations) has a different, but equally good, taste. It was given the name of 'London Particular' by the author Charles Dickens, who felt it resembled a real 'pea souper' – the term used to describe London fogs in his day.

Metric/Imperial	Ingredients	American
300 g/10 oz	dried split peas	1¼ cups
2 litres/3½ pints	brown stock (see page 15)	8¾ cups
2	fresh bay leaves or 1 dried leaf	2
225 g/8 oz	lean pork, weight without bone	½ lb
2 medium	onions	2 medium
2 medium	leeks	2 medium
2	celery sticks	2
to taste	salt and freshly ground black pepper	to taste
2 or 3	frankfurter sausages	2 or 3
To garnish	2 or 3 bacon rashers (slices)	

Wash the peas in cold water, drain and place in the pan with the stock. Leave to soak overnight, or bring to the boil, simmer for 10 minutes, then allow to stand in the covered pan for 2 or 3 hours before cooking.

Add the bay leaves or leaf to the soup. Chop the pork very finely. Peel and chop the onions; wash and slice the white part of the leeks and a small part of the tender green stems; chop the celery. Add the meat and vegetables to the pan with a little seasoning.

Bring the stock to the boil, lower the heat, cover and simmer for approximately 1½ hours, or until the peas are tender. Sieve or liquidize the soup and return to the pan. If the soup is too thick, add a little more stock. Slice the frankfurters and simmer in the soup for 5 minutes.

Meanwhile, grill or microwave the bacon until crisp, then chop into small pieces. Check the seasoning in the soup and serve topped with the bacon.

VARIATIONS
- Salted pork is often used instead of fresh pork.
- Substitute the pork with 225 g/8 oz (½ lb) chopped bacon rashers.

• DRIED PEA SOUP
Place 225 g/8 oz (1 cup) split dried peas in 1.8 litres/3 pints (7½ cups) bacon or chicken stock (see pages 15 and 14) and soak overnight, or bring to the boil, cook for 10 minutes and allow to stand for 2 to 3 hours in the covered pan.

Add 2 chopped bacon rashers, 2 chopped medium-sized onions, 2 chopped large carrots, 1 or 2 sprigs of mint leaves or ½ to 1 teaspoon dried mint. Season with freshly ground black pepper, but be sparing with the salt if using bacon stock. Cover the pan and simmer for 1½ hours or until the peas are tender. Sieve or liquidize the mixture, then return to the pan. Add a little milk to thin slightly, check the seasoning and reheat. Garnish with croûtons (see page 305) and serve.

• VEGETARIAN DRIED PEA SOUP
Omit the pork and bacon in the main recipe and the bacon in the second recipe, and use vegetable stock (see page 15).

To compensate for the lack of meat fat and for a stronger flavour add 2 or 3 chopped garlic cloves to the chopped onions in the main recipe and cook in 2 tablespoons (2½ tablespoons) olive or sunflower oil for 10 minutes. Add to the peas and stock.

Cooked vegetarian sausages could be added to the main recipe instead of frankfurters.

• CHICKPEA SOUP
Follow any of the pea soup recipes, substituting chickpeas for dried peas.

When following either of the variations add 2 chopped garlic cloves to give a more pronounced flavour to the chickpeas.

FREEZING: All the dried pea soups freeze well. Use within 4 to 6 weeks if including bacon in the ingredients.

The bacon garnish in the main recipe should be cooked just before serving the soup.

Chapter Five

FISH SOUPS

Some of the most luxurious and delicious soups are based on fish, and a selection appears in the following pages.

When preparing fish soups, as with all fish dishes, it is absolutely essential to use really fresh fish. Look for bright eyes, firm body and scales and absolutely no smell of ammonia.

Shellfish keeps less well than white fish, so check the freshness particularly carefully. You can tell if a lobster is fresh by pulling the tail: if it springs back, you have no worry; if it is limp, the lobster is not fresh. Crabs should smell pleasant and feel heavy for their size; if surprisingly light, they are watery. Mussels have to be inspected carefully when preparing and cooking (see page 196). Small shellfish, such as prawns (shrimp) and scallops, should be firm, bright in colour and smell pleasant.

COOKING SHELLFISH

Most people like to buy shellfish ready-cooked, but it is quite easy to cook them yourself.

Lobsters and crabs may be cooked in two ways. The method considered most merciful is to put the shellfish into warm water and gradually bring this to the boil. The alternative is to plunge the shellfish into boiling water. With either method, lobsters and crabs change colour when they are cooked.

Prawns are sold fresh or frozen. They can be defrosted at room temperature or in a microwave oven.

The golden rule with seafood is not to overcook it: this results in loss of flavour and texture in white fish and toughness in shellfish.

Microwave cooking: A microwave is splendid for cooking fish dishes, but I have some reservations about using it for fish soups. It is so difficult to assess the cooking time to the exact minute. Fish overcooked in a microwave does not become dry, as it can in a conventional oven – it becomes very hard and tough, really inedible. You must therefore be

prepared to check the cooking process continually or not use this method.
Pressure cooking: Again, I would stress that cooking has to be done with
the utmost care, otherwise the fish in the soup will break badly. That may
not matter if the soup is sieved or liquidized, but in a chowder the
appearance is very important.

As cooking times for most fish soups are fairly short, I would be inclined to
rely on a good old-fashioned method, using a saucepan.

Aberdeen Soup

Cooking time: 25 minutes
Serves 4 to 6

I first made this soup many years ago when I had a portion of uncooked smoked
haddock left. It is not only quick and easy to make, but is also very sustaining,
especially if milk alone is used as the liquid. The slight curry flavour gives a
piquancy to the soup.

Metric/Imperial	Ingredients	American
2	eggs	2
1 medium	onion	1 medium
1 to 2 teaspoons	curry paste	1 to 2 teaspoons
1.2 litres/2 pints	milk or milk and water	5 cups
50 g/2 oz	long-grain rice	⅓ cup
to taste	salt and freshly ground black pepper	to taste
225 g/8 oz	smoked haddock, weight without bone	½ lb
25 g/1 oz	butter	2 tablespoons
To garnish	croûtons (see page 305)	

Hard-boil the eggs. Shell them and chop the yolks and whites separately.
Peel and finely chop the onion. Blend the curry paste with a little of the milk
or milk and water until smooth, then add to a large pan with the onion and
remaining liquid. Bring just to boiling point, then add the rice plus a very
little salt and pepper.

Bring the liquid to the boil, put in the smoked haddock. Cover the pan and simmer for 8 to 10 minutes, or until the fish is just cooked. Transfer the fish to a plate and continue simmering the rice for a further 5 minutes. Meanwhile, flake the fish, return to the pan with the egg whites. Taste the soup, adjust the seasoning and continue cooking for a further 3 to 4 minutes. Serve topped with the egg yolks. Add the crisp croûtons at the last minute.

FREEZING: This soup freezes reasonably well. If possible, undercook the rice so that it does not become too soft on reheating. Omit cooked eggs until soup is defrosted. These become leathery in freezing.

Cullen Skink

Cooking time: 1 hour
Serves 4 to 6

This rather extraordinary name is given to a soup made from smoked haddock – finnan haddie as it is called in Scotland. There are many versions, depending on where in Scotland you are offered the soup. The version below is homely and very satisfying because a generous amount of mashed potatoes is mixed with the other ingredients.

Metric/Imperial	Ingredients	American
350 g/12 oz	potatoes, unpeeled weight	¾ lb
to taste	salt and freshly ground black pepper	to taste
1 large	finnan haddock or 350 g/12 oz (¾ lb) smoked haddock fillet	1 large
1 or 2 medium	onions, amount depends on personal choice	1 or 2 medium
750 ml/1¼ pints	milk	good 3 cups
25 g/1 oz	butter	2 tablespoons
4 tablespoons	double (heavy) or single (light) cream	5 tablespoons
To garnish	chopped parsley	

Peel the potatoes and cook in a little salted water until just soft. Strain and mash until very smooth. Remove the skin and set aside with the fins and tail. Cut the haddock into pieces. Peel the onion(s) but leave them whole. Place the haddock in a large pan, cover with water and cook until just tender. Remove from the liquid, flake the fish and take out all bones. Put these with the skin, fins and tail back into the liquid and cover the pan. Simmer steadily for 20 minutes, then strain 300 ml/½ pint (1¼ cups) of the fish liquid and put into a clean pan.

Add the milk, the flaked fish and the mashed potatoes; stir briskly to mix well, then bring to boiling point. Lower the heat and add the butter and cream. Simmer for a few minutes. Adjust the seasoning and serve topped with parsley.

VARIATIONS
- Omit the butter and cream and use a little more milk.
- Chop the onion(s) finely. Use only 2 small potatoes, diced and cooked until just tender. Add the chopped onions to the water when cooking the fish and keep them in the fish liquid when making the stock. Remove the skin etc. from this liquid, but retain the onions. Put the stock, with the onions, diced potatoes, flaked fish and milk into the saucepan. Add the butter and cream and heat as instructed in the main recipe.

- ### LUXURY CULLEN SKINK
Omit the potatoes and use a very large finnan haddock or 450 g/1 lb haddock fillet. Skin, cook and flake the haddock. Pound or liquidize with 2 hard-boiled eggs and a little milk until smooth. Stir in 900 ml/1½ pints (3¾ cups) of milk and 300 ml/½ pint (1¼ cups) single (light) cream. Season to taste and heat gently. Top with chopped parsley.

FREEZING: The first version of this soup freezes well. Do not freeze the version containing hard-boiled eggs.

Cockle Soup

Cooking time: 30 minutes
Serves 4 to 6

My mother had a great fondness for cockles and from time to time used to make the following soup. I now realize that it has a great similarity to an American chowder, but as children we knew it simply as Mother's soup.

Metric/Imperial	Ingredients	American
1.8 litres/3 pints	cockles	7½ cups
2 medium	onions	2 medium
2 small	leeks	2 small
2 medium	potatoes	2 medium
2 or 3	bacon rashers	2 or 3 slices
25 g/1 oz	butter	2 tablespoons
900 ml/1½ pints	water	3¾ cups
½ to 1 teaspoon	anchovy essence	½ to 1 teaspoon
2 tablespoons	chopped parsley	2½ tablespoons
1 tablespoon	chopped chives	1¼ tablespoons
to taste	salt and freshly ground black pepper	to taste
300 ml/½ pint	single (light) cream	1¼ cups
To garnish	chopped parsley	

Wash the cockles in plenty of cold water as they are inclined to be sandy; drain well. Peel and neatly dice the onions; slice the leeks, including a little of the tender green part. Peel the potatoes and cut into 1.25 cm/½ inch dice. Remove the rind from the bacon and cut the rashers into neat fingers.

Heat the butter and bacon rind, add the onions and bacon and cook until the onions become golden brown and the bacon crisp. Pour the water into the pan, bring it to the boil, then add the anchovy essence and remaining vegetables, herbs and a little seasoning.

Cover the pan and simmer for 20 minutes, or until the vegetables are soft, but still a good shape. Remove the bacon rinds. Add the cockles and heat for 4 to 5 minutes – no longer – then serve topped with a generous amount of parsley.

DO NOT FREEZE

Crab and Avocado Soup

Cooking time: 30 minutes plus time to make fish stock
Serves 4 to 6

The combination of crabmeat and avocados in this Caribbean soup is a very pleasant one. The soup is beautifully creamy and satisfying. If you do not want the trouble of making stock from the crab shell, see variations.

Metric/Imperial	Ingredients	American
1 medium	cooked crab	1 medium
900 ml/1½ pints	fish stock (see page 16)	3¾ cups
1 small	onion	1 small
2	garlic cloves	2
50 g/2 oz	butter	¼ cup
1 tablespoon	plain (all-purpose) flour	1¼ tablespoons
2	ripe avocados	2
2 teaspoons	lemon juice	2 teaspoons
150 ml/¼ pint	single (light) cream	⅔ cup
to taste	salt and freshly ground black pepper	to taste

Remove all the flesh from the crab; put a little of the white crabmeat on the side for garnishing the soup.

Put the body, shell and claws of the crab into the fish stock and bring to simmering point. Cover the pan and simmer for 15 minutes, then strain the liquid. By this time it should be reduced to 750 ml/1¼ pints (good 3 cups).

Peel and finely chop the onion; peel and crush the garlic. Heat the butter in a saucepan, add the onion and garlic and cook gently for 5 minutes. Stir in the flour then add the crab stock. Stir as the liquid comes to the boil, then add most of the crabmeat and heat for 3 minutes. Do not overcook as this toughens the crab. Halve the avocados, remove the skin and stones and cut the flesh into 6 mm/¼ inch dice. Add to the soup with the lemon juice, cream and seasoning. Heat gently and serve topped with the reserved white crabmeat.

VARIATIONS
- Use water instead of fish stock; this provides a less colourful liquid with slightly less flavour.

- If you do not want to use the crab shell, add a few drops of anchovy sauce or essence to give a stronger fish flavour and slightly pink colour to the liquid.
- Canned or defrosted frozen crabmeat can be used in this recipe.

- **LOBSTER AND AVOCADO SOUP**
Use a small lobster in place of the crab. The shell can be simmered in the liquid before making the soup.

- **PRAWN AND AVOCADO SOUP**
Use about 100 g/4 oz (¼ lb) prawns (shrimp) instead of crabmeat. The weight refers to the prawns when peeled. Simmer the prawn shells in the stock or water to give extra flavour.

FREEZING: Do not add the avocado if you plan to freeze this soup; it is best added when the soup is defrosted.

QUICK TIP *This soup can be cooked in a microwave. Be very careful about heating the liquid when once the shellfish has been added because overcooking toughens all fish.*

Crab and Prawn Gumbo

Cooking time: 35 minutes plus time to make stock
Serves 4 to 6

This is another Creole soup in which okra is used to give a special taste and texture. Fresh or frozen crabmeat can be used.

Metric/Imperial	Ingredients	American
1 medium	onion	1 medium
1	red pepper	1
3 medium	tomatoes	3 medium
450 g/1 lb	okra	1 lb
50 g/2 oz	butter	¼ cup
1.2 litres/2 pints	fish stock (see page 16) or water	5 cups
to taste	salt and freshly ground black pepper	to taste

Metric/Imperial	Ingredients	American
450 g/1 lb	crabmeat and peeled prawn (shrimp)	1 lb
To garnish	4 tablespoons (5 tablespoons) cooked rice, optional	
	chopped parsley	
	lemon segments	

Peel and finely chop the onion; deseed the pepper and cut the flesh into 1.25 cm/½ inch dice; skin and chop the tomatoes. Wipe and slice the okra.

Heat the butter in a pan, add the onion and cook gently for 5 minutes, stirring well so this does not brown. Stir in the pepper and tomatoes, then add the fish stock or water. Bring to the boil and cover the pan. Simmer for 15 minutes. Add the okra and seasoning to taste and continue cooking for a further 10 minutes.

Lastly, add the crabmeat and prawns and stir well. Spoon some of the rice in with the fish. Cook for 5 to 8 minutes, or until the soup is very hot, but take care not to overcook the crab. Garnish and serve.

DO NOT FREEZE

Crab and Tomato Soup

Cooking time: 20 minutes plus time to make stock
Serves 4

The fresh flavour of tomato combines well with crabmeat. You could use all white flesh or a mixture of white and dark. The soup is best made with fresh crab and a stock from the shells, but defrosted frozen, or even canned, crabmeat could be used.

Metric/Imperial	Ingredients	American
225 g/8 oz	tomatoes	½ lb
225 g/8 oz	crabmeat, when removed from shell	½ lb
300 ml/½ pint	fish or shellfish stock (see pages 16 and 17)	1¼ cups
150 ml/¼ pint	milk	⅔ cup
300 ml/½ pint	single (light) cream	1¼ cups
to taste	salt and freshly ground white pepper	to taste
To garnish	chopped dill or fennel leaves	

Chop the tomatoes if you plan to sieve the soup. If liquidizing, then skin, halve and deseed the tomatoes. Flake the crabmeat. Place the tomatoes and stock in a saucepan, cover and simmer for 10 minutes. Sieve or liquidize the mixture and return to the pan.

Add the milk, cream, crabmeat and a little seasoning and heat without boiling. Garnish and serve.

VARIATIONS
- The soup can be heated in the top of a double saucepan or basin over a pan of hot, but not boiling, water to prevent any possibility of it curdling.
- Use 2 tablespoons (2½ tablespoons) tomato purée (paste) instead of fresh tomatoes. Add to the stock and other ingredients and heat carefully.
- A squeeze of lemon juice can be added to the soup.

● **CHILLED CRAB AND TOMATO SOUP**

Sieve or liquidize fresh uncooked tomatoes. Add to the cold stock with the milk, cream and flaked crabmeat. Season to taste and chill well before serving. Garnish with the herb and lemon wedges.

FREEZING: **Do not freeze.**

Partan Bree

Cooking time: 30 to 35 minutes plus time to make stock
Serves 4 to 6

Meaning literally 'crab broth', Partan Bree is a Scottish recipe and one of the most famous crab soups in the world.

Metric/Imperial	Ingredients	American
1 large	cooked crab	1 large
75 g/3 oz	long-grain rice	½ cup
600 ml/1 pint	fish stock (see page 16)	2½ cups
600 ml/1 pint	milk	2½ cups
½ teaspoon	anchovy essence	½ teaspoon
to taste	salt and freshly ground white pepper	to taste
150 ml/¼ pint	single (light) cream	⅔ cup
To garnish	chopped parsley croûtons (see page 305)	

Remove all the flesh from the body and claws of the crab. Save a little white and dark meat to garnish the soup.

Put the rice and stock into a large saucepan, bring to the boil, then simmer for 20 minutes or until the rice is nearly tender. Add the milk towards the end of the cooking time and heat gently. Stir in the anchovy essence and crabmeat and add seasoning to taste. Avoid using too much salt. Simmer for a few minutes only until the crab is really hot, do not overcook. Stir the cream into the soup before serving and heat gently. Garnish with the reserved crabmeat, parsley and croûtons.

FREEZING: **Do not freeze.**

CHOWDERS

These soups are extremely popular in Canada and the USA. The word chowder comes from the French word *chaudière*, meaning a fish kettle. The most popular chowders are based on fish, sometimes mixed with pork, but those made with vegetables and meat are excellent.

Chowders should be full of ingredients – almost like a stew. It is important to cut the ingredients into even-sized pieces so that the soup looks attractive. Never overcook them because they should retain texture as well as flavour.

Although it is possible to cook chowders in a large bowl in a microwave, it is important to check the cooking process regularly so that the ingredients do not become too soft.

Freezing is not very successful with these soups because the vegetables tend to lose their firmness.

New England Clam Chowder

Cooking time: 30 minutes
Serves 4

Although Clam Chowder is a favourite in many parts of America, the New England version is the best known. If fresh clams are not available, use the canned variety or substitute cockles. Most cooks chop or mince the clams, but if they are very small this is not essential. If using fresh clams, save the liquid from the shells. A thick slice of salt pork is traditionally added to the soup but smoked bacon rashers (slices) can be used instead. Never overcook this soup because clams, like all shellfish, become tough.

Metric/Imperial	Ingredients	American
2 medium	onions	2 medium
3 medium	potatoes	3 medium
225 g/8 oz	salt pork or bacon rashers (slices)	½ lb
900 ml/1½ pints	water	3¾ cups
900 ml/1½ pints	minced fresh clams and their liquid or equivalent in canned clams	good 4 cups
600 ml/1 pint	milk or half milk and half single (light) cream	2½ cups
to taste	salt and freshly ground white pepper	to taste
	6 to 8 plain crackers	
To garnish	paprika	
	chopped parsley	

Peel and finely chop the onions. Peel the potatoes and cut into 1.25 cm/½ inch cubes. Derind the pork or bacon and dice the meat. Heat the rinds for 2 minutes, add the pork or bacon and cook for 2 to 3 minutes. Mix the onions and potatoes with the meat and stir over a moderate heat until pale golden in colour.

Remove the pork or bacon rinds, add the water and bring to the boil. Cover the pan, lower the heat and cook steadily for 10 to 15 minutes or until the ingredients are tender. Meanwhile, simmer the clams with their liquid for 2 to 3 minutes; if using canned clams, this is not necessary, just tip the clams and liquid into the soup, then pour in the milk or milk and cream. Taste the soup and add seasoning; you may not need salt. Heat thoroughly but do not boil.

Crumble the crackers into the soup bowls, add the hot soup and garnish with paprika and parsley.

VARIATIONS
- For a stronger flavour add 2 or 3 crushed garlic cloves to the onions.
- Use chicken or fish stock instead of water (see pages 16 and 17).
- To give more colour and flavour to the soup, add 2 or 3 finely diced celery sticks and ½ finely diced green pepper to the potatoes.
- Omit the milk and/or cream and use tomato juice instead.

• WHITE FISH CHOWDER
Follow the main recipe or incorporate some of the variations above. If possible use fish stock (see page 16) instead of water. Lightly cook and dice 450 to 550 g/1 to 1¼ lb cod or other white fish, making sure it is free from skin and bone. Add to the soup instead of the clams.

• SHELLFISH CHOWDER
Follow the main recipe or incorporate some of the variations above. If possible, use fish stock made from white fish and shellfish (see pages 16 and 17). Add the diced flesh of a good-sized cooked lobster or crab, or 350 g/ 12 oz (2 cups) peeled shrimps, prawns (shrimp) or cooked mussels instead of the clams.

A female lobster containing the roe (coral) gives an especially good colour to the soup.

DO NOT FREEZE

Lobster Bisque

Cooking time: 25 minutes plus time to make stock
Serves 4

A *bisque* is a rich fish soup that includes cream. The secret of the good flavour is to use the shell of the fish to produce the stock. If you can buy a hen lobster, the red coral (roe) gives the soup a wonderful colour. (The tail of a hen lobster is broader than that of the male.)

Metric/Imperial	Ingredients	American
1 medium	cooked lobster	1 medium
900 ml/1½ pints	water	3¾ cups
1 medium	onion	1 medium
sprig	parsley	sprig
sprig	thyme	sprig
few	fennel leaves	few
to taste	salt and freshly ground white pepper	to taste
40 g/1½ oz	butter	3 tablespoons
25 g/1 oz	plain (all-purpose) flour	¼ cup
225 ml/7½ fl oz	double (heavy) cream	scant 1 cup
To garnish	little double (heavy) cream, optional chopped fennel or basil leaves	

Remove all the flesh and coral from the lobster.

To make the stock, crush the shell and place in a saucepan with the water, the peeled whole onion, herbs and a little seasoning. Cover and simmer for 30 minutes, then strain. You should have 600 ml/1 pint (2½ cups) of stock.

Heat the butter in a saucepan, add the flour and stir over a low heat for 2 or 3 minutes. Add the stock, bring to the boil and stir until thickened.

Flake the lobster flesh very finely; it can be pounded, if you wish, or processed for a very short time. Stir the flesh, coral and cream into the thickened mixture. Heat gently and serve with the garnish.

VARIATIONS

- Add 2 tablespoons (2½ tablespoons) brandy or dry sherry to the hot lobster soup: do not allow to boil.
- Another way of thickening a *bisque* is to omit the flour and stir 50 g/2 oz (1 cup) fine breadcrumbs into the soup before adding the lobster.

- **CRAB BISQUE**

Use the flesh from a medium crab instead of the lobster. The colour of this *bisque* is improved by adding 2 to 3 teaspoons tomato purée (paste).

- **SALMON BISQUE**

Use 350 g/12 oz (¾ lb) cooked or canned salmon instead of lobster and fish stock (see page 16). The stock can be flavoured with a little chopped fennel and parsley.

QUICK TIP *Instead of making fresh stock, use ready-prepared fish stock.*

FREEZING: These soups freeze well provided the lobster and crab are *not* cooked in the hot liquid. Simply blend them into the thickened liquid, then cool and freeze. Add the cream and any alcohol when reheating the soup.

Mussel Cream Soup (Moules à la Crème)

Cooking time: 30 minutes
Serves 4 to 6

This is a really delicious soup, combining mussels with the sharpness of white wine and a creamy sauce.

Metric/Imperial	Ingredients	American
1.8 litres/3 pints	fresh mussels	7½ cups
1 medium	onion	1 medium
300 ml/½ pint	dry white wine	1¼ cups
1 tablespoon	chopped parsley	1¼ tablespoons
50 g/2 oz	butter	¼ cup
50 g/2 oz	plain (all-purpose) flour	½ cup
600 ml/1 pint	milk	2½ cups
to taste	salt and freshly ground black pepper	to taste
150 ml/¼ pint	single (light) cream	⅔ cup
To garnish	chopped parsley lemon slices	

Clean the mussels, as described on page 196. Peel and chop the onion; place in a pan with the mussels, wine and parsley. Heat until the mussels open, then strain the liquid and take the mussels off the shells.

Heat the butter in a saucepan, stir in the flour and cook gently for 1 or 2 minutes. Add the milk, stirring as the mixture comes to the boil and thickens. Add a little seasoning, then stir in the cream and mussel liquid. Heat gently, taking care not to boil the soup. Finally, add the mussels and continue cooking gently for 2 or 3 minutes. Top with the parsley and lemon slices.

VARIATION

● **CREAM OF SCALLOP SOUP**
Slice 8 medium scallops or halve about 24 queenies (tiny scallops). Poach them in 300 ml/½ pint (1¼ cups) dry white wine for a few minutes only until they turn opaque.

Make the sauce with butter, flour and milk, as in the main recipe. Add the cream. Heat thoroughly, then stir in the scallops and their poaching liquid. Heat for a few minutes without boiling, then serve topped with chopped parsley or fennel leaves and lemon slices.

FREEZING: **Do not freeze.**

Mussel and Tomato Soup

Cooking time: 40 minutes
Serves 4 to 6

The combination of mussels and tomatoes is a very pleasant one, and basil the perfect herb. I have been fairly generous with the amount of basil, so if it is not your favourite herb, use fewer leaves.

Metric/Imperial	Ingredients	American
1.8 litres/3 pints	fresh mussels	7½ cups
3 medium	onions	3 medium
300 ml/1½ pint	dry white wine	1¼ cups
1 tablespoon	chopped parsley	1¼ tablespoons
550 g/1¼ lb	tomatoes	1¼ lb
2 tablespoons	olive or sunflower oil	2½ tablespoons
1.2 litres/2 pints	water	5 cups
to taste	salt and freshly ground black pepper	to taste
12 to 18	basil leaves, or to taste	12 to 18

To cook mussels: scrub shells in cold water, discard any that are open and do not close when tapped sharply. Remove any beards (seaweed-like growth on the shells). Put the mussels into a large pan. Peel and finely chop one of the onions; add to the pan with the white wine and chopped parsley. Place over a medium heat for 5 to 8 minutes, or until the mussels open. Discard any that remain closed. Watch this stage carefully for overcooking will make the fish tough. Cool sufficiently to handle. Remove the mussels and strain the liquid. Discard the shells, then return the mussels and the liquid to the pan.

While the mussels are cooking prepare the rest of the soup. Peel and finely chop the remaining onions; skin and chop the tomatoes. Heat the oil in another saucepan, add the onions and cook for 5 minutes over a low heat, stirring well so the onions do not brown. Add the tomatoes and continue cooking for another 10 minutes over the low heat. Add the water, seasoning and basil. Bring to the boil, lower the heat and cover the pan. Cook for 15 minutes, then add the mussels and the liquid from the second pan. Heat for a few minutes and serve with plenty of fresh crusty bread.

VARIATIONS

- To give a slightly crisp texture to the tomato mixture, chop a small celery heart very finely and add to the tomatoes halfway through the cooking period.

- **MUSSEL, TOMATO AND RICE SOUP**
Follow the main recipe but use 1.5 litres/2½ pints (6¼ cups) water. Add 50 g/2 oz (4 tablespoons) long-grain rice to the onions and tomatoes, then add the liquid and proceed as the main recipe.

FREEZING: **Do not freeze.**

Oyster Cream Soup
(Velouté aux Huîtres)

Cooking time: 25 minutes plus time to make stock
Serves 4 to 6

Nowadays oyster soup is considered something of a luxury, but in the nine-teenth century oysters were regarded as poor man's food. In fact, Sam Weller in Charles Dickens' *Pickwick Papers* stated 'that poverty and oysters always seem to go together'.

Metric/Imperial	Ingredients	American
18 to 24 small	oysters	18 to 24 small
50 g/2 oz	butter	¼ cup
50 g/2 oz	plain (all-purpose) flour	½ cup
600 ml/1 pint	fish stock (see page 16)	2½ cups
300 ml/½ pint	milk	1¼ cups
300 ml/½ pint	single (light) cream	1¼ cups
to taste	salt and freshly ground white pepper	to taste
To garnish	cayenne pepper	
To serve	halved lemons	

When you, or the fishmonger, open the oysters, try to retain as much liquid in the shells as possible. Pour this into a container, then remove the oysters from the shells and cut into neat dice.

Heat the butter in a saucepan, stir in the flour and cook gently for 1 or 2 minutes. Add the fish stock and bring to the boil. Lower the heat, cover the pan and cook gently for 10 to 15 minutes. Add the milk and cream, heat a little and season to taste; remember oysters are very salty.

Add the diced oysters and oyster liquid, heat gently and serve dusted with cayenne pepper. Offer the lemons separately.

VARIATIONS

- For a lighter soup omit the milk and use that amount of extra fish stock.

- **WELSH OYSTER SOUP (CAWL WYSTRYS)**

This is a very unusual soup in that the oysters are combined with meat. You need about 24 small oysters to serve 4 to 6 people.

Peel 2 onions but leave them whole; put into a saucepan with about 225 g/8 oz (½ lb) scrag end of mutton or lamb, a few meat bones, 1.8 litres/3 pints (7½ cups) of water and a blade of mace or pinch of ground mace. Bring to the boil and remove any scum. Cover the pan and simmer gently for 1½ hours. Strain the liquid. If not clear, clarify as described on page 69. You should have no more than 900 ml/1½ pints (3¾ cups) or a little less. If necessary, boil vigorously in an open pan to reduce to this amount.

Heat 50 g/2 oz (¼ cup) butter in a saucepan, stir in 50 g/2 oz (½ cup) plain flour, then add the meat stock. Bring to the boil and cook, stirring well, until it thickens. Tip in the oyster liquid and season to taste. Either add the oysters and cook gently for 2 minutes or put the oysters into soup plates and top with the very hot soup. Garnish with raw sliced leek and lemon wedges.

FREEZING: **Do not freeze.**

Salmon and Fennel Soup

Cooking time: 40 minutes plus time to make stock
Serves 4 to 6

Wild salmon from Scotland and other parts of Britain, together with farmed salmon, means this delicious fish is not only readily available but reasonable in price. The recipe below has the delicate taste of aniseed from fennel, but there are several variations without this.

Metric/Imperial	Ingredients	American
1 medium	onion	1 medium
1 medium	carrot	1 medium
1 medium	head of fennel	1 medium
450 g/1 lb	salmon, weight without bones and skin	1 lb
50 g/2 oz	butter	¼ cup
600 ml/1 pint	fish stock (see page 16)	2½ cups
to taste	salt and freshly ground black pepper	to taste
300 ml/½ pint	milk	1¼ cups
300 ml/½ pint	single (light) cream	1¼ cups
To garnish	fennel leaves croûtons (see page 305)	

Peel and chop the onion and carrot; remove any tough parts of the fennel and save the leaves for garnish.

Cut the fish into small pieces. Heat the butter, add the vegetables and fish and cook for 5 minutes; do not allow the ingredients to brown. Add the stock with a little seasoning, cover the pan and simmer for 25 minutes. Sieve or liquidize the mixture, then return to the pan with the milk and cream and heat. Taste and adjust the seasoning. Garnish with the fennel leaves and croûtons.

VARIATIONS

- If a head of fennel is not available, crush 2 to 3 teaspoons fennel seeds and tie in muslin. Cook with the soup and remove before sieving or liquidizing.
- Salmon trout or fresh trout can be used instead of salmon.

- **SALMON BROTH**

Omit the fennel. Use 2 medium onions, 2 carrots and 2 tablespoons (2½ tablespoons) long-grain rice. Peel and dice the vegetables neatly, cook in 50 g/2 oz (¼ cup) butter for 5 minutes, then add the rice and fish stock. Simmer for 15 minutes, add the neatly diced salmon and cook for 5 minutes. Add the milk and cream and complete the cooking. Season and serve with lemon slices.

- **SALMON AND CUCUMBER SOUP**

Follow the main recipe, but use ½ medium peeled and diced cucumber instead of the fennel. Add 2 or 3 teaspoons lemon juice to the fish stock. When heating the soup with the milk and cream, do not allow it to boil.

- **SALMON AND LEEK CREAM**

Peel and dice 1 medium onion and 2 medium potatoes. Slice 2 medium leeks. Toss the vegetables in 50 g/2 oz (¼ cup) hot butter for 5 minutes. Add 600 ml/1 pint (2½ cups) fish stock and 300 ml/½ pint (1¼ cups) milk. Cover the pan and simmer gently for 20 minutes. Sieve or liquidize, then return to the pan, add 225 to 350 g/8 to 12 oz (½ to ¾ lb) cooked flaked salmon and 300 ml/½ pint (1¼ cups) double (heavy) cream. Heat and serve.

FREEZING: The puréed soups freeze well. Those containing whole pieces of fish etc. become rather over-soft in freezing.

Trout Soup

Cooking time: 35 minutes plus time to make stock
Serves 4 to 6

Metric/Imperial	Ingredients	American
2 medium	trout	2 medium
2 medium	leeks	2 medium
2 small	onions	2 small
50 g/2 oz	butter	¼ cup
1 litre/1¾ pints	fish stock (see page 16)	scant 4½ cups
1 tablespoon	lemon juice	1¼ tablespoons
small bunch	parsley	small bunch
to taste	salt and freshly ground black pepper	to taste
To garnish	chopped chervil	

Clean the trout, but do not remove the heads as these give extra flavour to the stock. Wash and thinly slice the leeks, using a little of the tender green part to add colour to the soup. Peel and finely chop the onions.

Heat the butter in a saucepan, add the leeks and onions and cook gently for 10 minutes or until pale golden in colour.

Add the fish stock, lemon juice, parsley and a little seasoning. Cover the pan and simmer for 10 minutes. Put in the fish, this can be chopped into fairly large pieces to fit in the pan. Cook gently for 10 to 15 minutes. Transfer the trout to a plate and flake the flesh. Remove the bunch of parsley from the stock.

Return the flaked fish to the pan and heat. Serve garnished with chopped chervil.

VARIATIONS

● Whiting can be used instead of trout.

● PURÉED TROUT SOUP

Make the soup as described above, but sieve or liquidize the finished mixture. Return to the pan and reheat. Do not overcook.

For a richer soup add 3 to 4 tablespoons (3¾ to 5 tablespoons) double (heavy) cream and 1 or 2 teaspoons horseradish cream to the purée.

FREEZING: The puréed soup freezes well, but the soup containing the flaked fish does not, because the fish becomes too soft.

Provençal Fish Soup

Cooking time: 1 hour 15 minutes
Serves 4 to 6

This is a very popular soup in the South of France, and restaurants in Provence vie with each other to produce the most noteworthy version. Basically it is a clear soup which has small pieces of perfectly cooked fish floating in it. While it can be based on only one type of fish, a mixture of fish greatly improves the flavour. Use whatever is available on the day.

This soup is often served with croûtons, French bread and a small bowl of Rouille or Aïoli (see pages 208 and 205).

Metric/Imperial	Ingredients	American
1 to 1.35 kg/2¼ to 3 lb	assorted fish, such as bream, sole, red mullet, skate, monkfish, cod and whiting	2¼ to 3 lb
1.8 litres/3 pints	water	7½ cups
2	shallots or small onions	2
3 to 4	garlic cloves	3 to 4
to taste	salt and freshly ground black pepper	to taste
few	fennel leaves	few
½ teaspoon	ground saffron or strands	½ teaspoon
1 tablespoon	chopped chervil	1¼ tablespoons
1 tablespoon	chopped fennel leaves	1¼ tablespoons
150 ml/¼ pint	white wine	⅔ cup
To serve	croûtons (see page 305)	
	Rouille or Aïoli (see pages 208 and 205)	

Cut the heads, tails and fins off the fish and place in a pan of water. Peel and chop the shallots or onions and garlic; add to the water with a little seasoning and the whole fennel leaves. Cover the pan and cook steadily for 1 hour.

Strain the stock; you should have about 1 litre/1¾ pints (scant 4½ cups). Cut the fish into neat pieces, add to the stock with the saffron, chervil and chopped fennel leaves. Simmer for 10 to 15 minutes, then remove the fish and flake or dice as much as desired; discard all the skin and bones.

Return the fish to the pan with the wine and heat well, but do not overcook. Adjust the seasoning and serve with croûtons and Rouille or Aïoli.

VARIATIONS

- To add more colour and interest to the soup, cook thin slices of carrot with the diced fish. If you have a fancy cutter, use this to give a more attractive shape to the carrots. Diced celeriac or fennel may also be added.
- If you prefer an absolutely clear soup, follow the instructions for Fish Consommé on page 73 instead of the method above.

- FISH, PEPPER AND TOMATO SOUP

Make the fish stock as described above or on page 16, then add small pieces of diced uncooked fish (free from skin and bones), 2 to 3 tablespoons (2½ to 3¾ tablespoons) finely diced red pepper and 4 to 5 tablespoons (5 to 6 tablespoons) diced tomato pulp. Cook for 10 to 15 minutes. Serve garnished with crème fraîche.

FREEZING: The clear stock freezes well, but do not freeze the soup with the cooked fish because this becomes over-soft.

Aïoli (Garlic Mayonnaise)

No cooking
Serves 6 to 8

This mayonnaise, strongly flavoured with garlic, is a pleasing accompaniment to the fish soup on page 203. Although Rouille (see page 208) is often served with it, in Provence, Aïoli makes a pleasant change.

Metric/Imperial	Ingredients	American
4	large garlic cloves	4
2	egg yolks	2
to taste	salt and freshly ground black pepper	to taste
up to 250 ml/8 fl oz	extra virgin olive oil	up to 1 cup
1 tablespoon	lemon juice or white wine vinegar, or to taste	1¼ tablespoons
1 tablespoon	boiling water, see method	1¼ tablespoons

Peel and crush the garlic cloves with 1 of the egg yolks; ideally, this should be done in a pestle and mortar to get a very smooth mixture, but it can be done in a liquidizer. Add the second egg yolk with the seasoning and blend thoroughly.

Gradually add as much oil as necessary to obtain a really thick consistency. Blend in the lemon juice or wine vinegar.

The boiling water is not essential, but it does give a slightly lighter mayonnaise. It should be beaten into the other ingredients very slowly.

VARIATION
• Use half olive oil and half sunflower oil.

DO NOT FREEZE

Bouillabaisse

Cooking time: see method – about 45 minutes
Serves 6 to 8

This is the most popular soup around the French Mediterranean coast. Its name comes from *boul abaisso* (boil up and serve). In praising this soup, I cannot do better than quote the words of Henry Smith, the chef and writer, in his book on Soups (Practical Press, 1949):

> *This Bouillabaisse a noble dish is,*
> *A sort of soup, or broth or stew,*
> *Or hotchpotch of all sorts of fishes,*
> *That Greenwich never could outdo;*
> *Green herbs, red peppers, mussels, saffron,*
> *Soles, onions, garlic, roach and dace,*
> *All these you eat at Errl's tavern,*
> *In that one dish of Bouillabaisse.*

Although one cannot hope to get a totally authentic flavour when cooking this soup outside the Mediterranean, it can still be a triumph. Remember – the wider the assortment of fish used, the better the dish will be. As it takes quite a time to gather all the ingredients together, I think this is a soup for a large number of people who will delight in its sight, aroma and flavour.

Metric/Imperial	Ingredients	American
1.35 kg/3 lb	assorted fish, see method	3 lb
few	baby crabs or small lobsters	few
about 18	mussels	about 18
about 18	large prawns	about 18
to taste	salt and freshly ground black pepper	to taste
3 large	onions	3 large
3	garlic cloves	3
350 g/12 oz	tomatoes	¾ lb
2	red peppers	2
6 tablespoons	olive oil	7½ tablespoons

Metric/Imperial	Ingredients	American
3.3 litres/5½ pints	water or fish stock, see method	scant 14 cups
1 tablespoon	chopped fennel leaves	1¼ tablespoons
1 tablespoon	chopped parsley	1¼ tablespoons
2	fresh bay leaves or 1 dried leaf	2
300 ml/½ pint	white wine, optional	1¼ cups
¼ teaspoon	ground saffron or strands	¼ teaspoon

Trim the fish, reserving the heads, tails and fins. Mediterranean sole are often very small, so you may like to halve larger soles, or fillet them; keep the bones, tails and heads. Other fish that could be included are bream, red mullet, small pieces of skate wing, monkfish, cod and whiting. The choice depends on what is available and really fresh. The shellfish can be cooked, if not done already (see page 180).

Place the fish trimmings in a pan with just over 3.3 litres/5½ pints (about 14 cups) lightly seasoned water to cover. Simmer for about 25 minutes to extract the flavour, then strain and use the liquid as fish stock.

Peel and finely chop the onions and garlic. Skin, halve, deseed and chop the tomatoes. Deseed the peppers, cut the flesh into neat strips. Heat the oil in a very large pan, add the onions and garlic, cook for 5 minutes. Add the tomatoes and peppers and cook for 10 minutes. Pour in the water or fish stock, add the herbs and boil briskly for about 15 minutes until the amount of liquid is reduced slightly and the stock and onions are well mixed.

Add the selection of fish and cook for about 10 minutes. Put the shellfish in at the end of the cooking time with the white wine, saffron and a little extra seasoning. Heat for another minute. Do not overcook.

Transfer the soup to a large tureen and let everyone help themselves.

Rouille (garlic mayonnaise, see page 208) is an excellent accompaniment and you will need plenty of hot rolls or French bread to mop up the delicious liquid.

As the shellfish are served in their shells, provide finger-bowls.

VARIATION
• If using saffron strands, you may like to infuse them in a little water or fish stock. Strain the liquid and add to the soup, discarding the strands.

FREEZING: **Do not freeze.**

Rouille

No cooking

Serves 4 to 6

In Provence this garlic-flavoured mayonnaise is given extra colour and flavour by adding red pepper. If you like a hot sauce, use a deseeded red chilli pepper; for a sweeter taste use an ordinary pepper. It is possible to make this mayonnaise in a liquidizer or food processor and to use the whole egg rather than just the egg yolk. Adding fine breadcrumbs makes the sauce firmer and ideal to put on soup. Extra virgin oil, which comes from the first pressing of the olives, has the finest flavour.

Metric/Imperial	Ingredients	American
1	red chilli pepper or sweet red pepper	1
3	garlic cloves	3
1	egg yolk	1
up to 300 ml/½ pint	extra virgin olive oil	up to 1¼ cups
3 level tablespoons	fine, soft breadcrumbs	3¾ level tablespoons
to taste	salt and freshly ground black pepper	to taste

Split the chilli pepper or sweet pepper, remove the seeds, then finely chop the flesh; wash your hands carefully after handling chillies because the juice can sting. Peel and finely chop the garlic.

Whisk the egg yolk in a bowl, then gradually whisk in the oil until the desired thickness is achieved. Add the breadcrumbs, garlic and pepper. Season to taste.

VARIATIONS
- Instead of breadcrumbs, soak a crustless slice of bread in a little water for 10 minutes, squeeze dry and mash until smooth.
- Add a little lemon juice or wine vinegar for a sharper flavour.
- Add 1 or 2 teaspoons chopped fennel leaves to the mayonnaise.

● LIQUIDIZER OR FOOD PROCESSOR MAYONNAISE

It can be tricky to whisk a single egg or egg yolk in certain machines as they only work efficiently with larger amounts. In most cases it is better to double the quantities and store any excess sauce in the refrigerator for up to one week.

Place the egg yolk(s) or whole egg(s) in a liquidizer or food processor and switch on for a second or two. With the motor running, pour the oil slowly through the funnel or hole in the lid until the desired thickness is achieved. Transfer to a bowl and add the remaining ingredients.

QUICK TIP *Add the pepper and a few breadcrumbs to ready-made garlic mayonnaise. If the garlic flavour is not sufficiently strong, add 1 or 2 chopped garlic cloves or a little garlic purée.*

FREEZING: **Do not freeze.**

Norwegian Fish Soup (Fiskesuppe)

Cooking time: 15 minutes plus time to make stock
Serves 4

Fish is of excellent quality in Norway and the country has a number of recipes for fish soup. Some of the most delicious appear on page 210.

Metric/Imperial	Ingredients	American
50 g/2 oz	butter	¼ cup
25 g/1 oz	plain (all-purpose) flour	¼ cup
1.2 litres/2 pints	fish stock (see page 16)	5 cups
to taste	salt and freshly ground white pepper	to taste
2 tablespoons	thinly sliced spring onions (scallions)	2½ tablespoons
3 tablespoons	soured cream (see page 64)	4 tablespoons
To garnish	Fish Balls (see page 304)	

Heat the butter in a large saucepan, stir in the flour and add the fish stock. Stir or whisk as the soup comes to the boil, then simmer for a good 5 minutes. Add seasoning to taste, stir in the onions and cream and heat for 1 minute (the onions should remain firm). Add the Fish Balls and heat for a further 2 to 3 minutes.

VARIATIONS

● To give more colour to the soup, garnish with finely chopped chives.

● **BROWN FISH SOUP 1**
Boil 3 medium-sized carrots and 1 chopped celery stick until soft, then sieve or liquidize with the fish stock. Follow the main recipe and add 3 tablespoons (4 tablespoons) dark brown sherry to the thickened stock. Omit the spring onions, soured cream and fish ball garnish in this and the following variation.

● **BROWN FISH SOUP 2**
Boil a selection of vegetables, such as onion, leek, carrots and celery, in the fish stock; strain and use as in the main recipe. Flavour the soup with 3 tablespoons (4 tablespoons) dark brown sherry and 2 tablespoons (2½ tablespoons) tomato purée.

FREEZING: All versions of the soup freeze well, but it is advisable to omit the spring onions and soured cream in the main recipe and add them when reheating the soup. Fish balls freeze well but they retain more flavour and texture if frozen separately from the soup (see page 304).

 Use fish stock cubes and water instead of fresh fish stock.

Spanish Fishermen's Soup (Sopa de Pescadores)

Cooking time: 55 minutes plus time to make stock
Serves 4 to 6

This is a sustaining soup which has plenty of flavour. Shellfish should be included if possible, but can be omitted if more white fish is used. Choose a firm white fish such as cod, hake or fresh haddock. Spanish fishermen would use fish readily available on the day and would mix several varieties.

Metric/Imperial	Ingredients	American
1 medium	onion	1 medium
2	garlic cloves	2
450 g/1 lb	tomatoes	1 lb
2 tablespoons	olive oil	2½ tablespoons
1.2 litres/2 pints	fish stock (see page 16)	5 cups
1 teaspoon	grated lemon rind	1 teaspoon
1 to 2 tablespoons	lemon juice, or to taste	1¼ to 2½ tablespoons
2 teaspoons	chopped mixed herbs, or 1 teaspoon dried mixed herbs	2 teaspoons
50 g/2 oz	short-grain rice, see **variation**	4 tablespoons
pinch	saffron powder or a few saffron strands	pinch
to taste	salt and freshly ground black pepper	to taste
675 g/1½ lb	white fish	1½ lb
225 g/8 oz	cooked shellfish, crab, prawns, etc.	½ lb
To garnish	diced cucumber	

Peel and dice the onion; peel and crush the garlic. Skin the tomatoes and chop neatly. Heat the oil in a large saucepan, add the onions, garlic and tomatoes and cook for 5 minutes. Pour in the stock, add the rind and lemon juice and bring to the boil. Stir the herbs, saffron and a little seasoning into the liquid. Cover the pan and cook steadily for 30 minutes, stirring once or twice during this time; this helps the starch in the rice to thicken the soup.

Skin and bone the fish, cut into 2.5 cm/1 inch dice. Add to the soup and simmer for 10 to 15 minutes or until the fish is just tender: do not allow it to break. Add the shellfish and a little of the diced cucumber and heat for a few minutes. Serve garnished with more cucumber.

VARIATION
● Use long-grain instead of short-grain rice and shorten the cooking time by 15 minutes.

DO NOT FREEZE

White Fish Soup

Cooking time: 30 minutes plus time to make stock
Serves 4 to 6

This is an excellent way of serving white fish in a soup. The variety of fish can depend on what is in season and personal preference.

Metric/Imperial	Ingredients	American
450 g/1 lb	white fish, weight without bones	1 lb
2 medium	potatoes	2 medium
100 g/4 oz	fennel root	¼ lb
750 ml/1¼ pints	fish stock (see page 16)	good 3 cups
to taste	salt and freshly ground white pepper	to taste
300 ml/½ pint	milk	1¼ cups
150 ml/¼ pint	single (light) cream	⅔ cup
To garnish	chopped red pepper chopped fennel leaves	

Skin the fish and cut into 2.5 cm/1 inch dice. Peel the potatoes and cut into similar-sized dice. Chop the fennel finely. Bring the fish stock to the boil, then add the fish, potatoes, fennel and a very little seasoning. Cover the pan and cook for 15 minutes, then sieve or liquidize the mixture.

Return to the pan with the milk and cream and reheat. Taste the soup and add extra seasoning if required. Serve topped with the chopped pepper and fennel leaves.

VARIATIONS
- This soup is very pale, so a pinch of saffron powder, a few saffron strands or a pinch of turmeric could be added to the fish stock.
- A very little anchovy essence or anchovy sauce may also be added. This colours and flavours the soup but does increase the salt taste.
- Add skinned tomatoes to the other ingredients and serve without sieving or liquidizing.
- Use diced celeriac or celery instead of fennel and garnish with chopped parsley, chives or basil.
- Use peeled cucumber instead of fennel and garnish with matchstick pieces of cucumber and chopped parsley.

FREEZING: This soup freezes well.

Chapter Six

MEAT SOUPS

Meat soups have been part of family fare for centuries. Their great advantage is that they combine a limited amount of meat with plenty of homely vegetables, thus making a filling meal for hungry folk with the minimum of expenditure. Some of the world's most interesting meat soups come from Britain. For example, it's hard to beat home-made Oxtail Soup, with its succulent flavour and special texture (see page 231).

Serve a meat soup when the main course is based on fish or vegetables, or make it the main dish itself. Follow it with salad and fruit and you have a really satisfying meal.

COOKING MEAT SOUPS

Meat soups can be cooked in various ways. The timings in the recipes assume you are using a saucepan but, if more convenient, any of the methods below can be used.

Oven cooking: Allow about 50 per cent longer cooking time than that given in the recipes. Preheat the oven to 160°C/325°F/gas mark 3 or 150°C/300°F/gas mark 2. Use a casserole with a tight-fitting lid so that the liquid in the soup does not evaporate too much. If the lid is loose, put a piece of foil under it to guarantee a good seal.

Microwave cooking: If the meat is tender, you can cook the soup in a large covered bowl. It needs 10 per cent less liquid and will be ready in about half to two-thirds of the time it would take to cook in a saucepan. Microwaves are less efficient for tougher cuts of meat, such as stewing beef. Use the defrost setting but check that the soup is simmering gently. If cooking too quickly, lower the setting. For more about microwaving soups, see page 7.

Pressure cooking: Pressure cookers are excellent for cooking meat because they tenderize even the toughest cuts and the short cooking time helps retain both flavour and texture. The Scotch Broth on page 233, for example, would take only 10 to 12 minutes, depending on the quality of the meat, compared to 2 to 2½ hours in a saucepan.

Never have the pressure cooker more than half-filled with the liquid and ingredients. For further information about pressure cooking soups, see page 6.

Slow cooking: Always bring the ingredients to the boil in a saucepan before putting them in a slow cooker, or add boiling water or boiling stock. Allow 5 to 6 hours cooking time for most meat soups.

GARNISHING MEAT SOUPS

The mixture of vegetables used in a soup often provide sufficient colour; where this is not the case, the recipes suggest a specific garnish.

If you know that the vegetables need lengthy cooking in order to flavour the meat, and will therefore have lost some colour, it is a good idea to hold back a few diced raw vegetables and cook them briefly in stock or seasoned water to garnish the soup. They not only have bright colours but a firm texture and fresh flavour.

Argentine Beef Soup (Locro de Trigo)

Cooking time: 1 hour plus time to make stock
Serves 4 to 6

This meat soup, with its colourful mixture of ingredients, tastes as good as it looks. Canned butter (lima) beans are used to save cooking time, but cooked dried beans could be substituted. Soak and cook these as instructed on page 169.

Metric/Imperial	Ingredients	American
2 medium	onions	2 medium
3 medium	tomatoes	3 medium
1 large	red pepper	1 large
3	bacon rashers	3 slices
2 tablespoons	olive oil	2½ tablespoons
350 g/12 oz	minced (ground) beef	¾ lb
1 teaspoon	paprika, or to taste	1 teaspoon
1.2 litres/2 pints	brown stock (see page 15)	5 cups
to taste	salt and freshly ground black pepper	to taste
225 g/8 oz	garlic sausage	½ lb
225 g/8 oz	canned butter (lima) beans	½ lb
225 g/8 oz	canned sweetcorn	½ lb

Peel and chop the onions and tomatoes. Deseed the pepper and cut the flesh into neat dice. Remove the rind from the bacon and chop the rashers.

Heat the bacon rinds and oil in a large saucepan, remove the rinds and add the minced beef, bacon and onions. Stir over a low heat for 10 minutes or until the beef is slightly brown. Stir the paprika into the ingredients, add just a little stock to moisten and stir well to ensure the minced beef does not form into lumps. Pour in the remainder of the stock, then add a little seasoning, the pepper and tomatoes. Bring to the boil, stirring briskly. Cover the pan and simmer for 40 minutes, stirring from time to time.

Cut the garlic sausages into neat dice, add to the soup with the well-drained beans and sweetcorn and heat for a further 10 minutes. Taste and adjust the seasoning before serving.

FREEZING: The basic soup freezes well, but it is advisable to add the sausage, beans and sweetcorn when reheating.

Goulash (Gulyas)

Cooking time: 1¼ hours
Serves 4 to 6

Although Hungarian goulash is more often served as a stew, a similar blend of ingredients makes a satisfying soup that is full of flavour. Sweet rather than spicy paprika is used to colour and flavour the dish. Do make sure it is fresh: when stale, it develops an unpleasant, musty taste.

Metric/Imperial	Ingredients	American
3 medium	onions	3 medium
2 large	tomatoes	2 large
100 g/4 oz	lean pork	¼ lb
100 g/4 oz	veal or tender beef	¼ lb
40 g/1½ oz	butter or lard (shortening)	3 tablespoons
1 tablespoon	paprika, or to taste	1¼ tablespoons
1.2 litres/2 pints	brown stock (see page 15) or water	5 cups
to taste	salt and freshly ground black pepper	to taste
2 medium	potatoes	2 medium
To garnish	yoghurt or soured cream	

Peel and finely chop the onions. Skin and chop the tomatoes. Cut the meat into 1.25 cm/½ inch dice. Heat the butter or lard in a saucepan, add the onions and cook gently for 5 minutes. Add the two meats and the paprika and continue cooking slowly, stirring well, for another 5 minutes. Add the tomatoes and stock, season lightly and bring to the boil. Lower the heat, cover the pan and simmer for 45 minutes.

Peel the potatoes and cut into 1.25 cm/½ inch dice. Add to the soup and cook for a further 15 minutes. Serve garnished with the yoghurt or soured cream.

VARIATION

● Use only one kind of meat instead of several.

FREEZING: This soup freezes well.

Harira

Cooking time: 50 minutes

Serves 4 to 6

I have visited Morocco on a number of occasions and have a great regard for their imaginative cuisine. A friend of mine, who lived there for many years, gave me this recipe and its variations. Harira is traditionally served after sunset during the holy month of Ramadan when devout Muslims fast between sunrise and sunset.

Metric/Imperial	Ingredients	American
2 medium	onions	2 medium
450 g/1 lb	tomatoes	1 lb
2 or 3	celery sticks	2 or 3
225 g/8 oz	lamb, boned weight	½ lb
225 g/8 oz	chicken, see method	½ lb
50 g/2 oz	butter	¼ cup
2 teaspoons	garam masala, or to taste	2 teaspoons
¼ teaspoon	ground saffron	¼ teaspoon
1 litre/1¾ pints	water	scant 4½ cups
2 tablespoons	couscous	2½ tablespoons
2 tablespoons	lemon juice	2½ tablespoons
to taste	salt and freshly ground black pepper	to taste
To garnish	chopped parsley lemon wedges	

Cream of Vegetable Soup (page 41)
This soup provides a wonderful blend of vegetables with a creamy taste. It can be adapted throughout the year to use vegetables in season.

Farmhouse Soup (pages 125 to 126)
A true country-style soup which is both wholesome and interestingly flavoured.

ouillabaisse (page 206)
traditional soup from the South of France. The use of different fish gives this dish a unique avour.

White Fish Soup (page 213)
The most economical of fish can be used to make this nourishing soup.

old Tomato Soup (page 288)

omato soups are popular with all ages. Chilled soups are excellent dishes for hot weather.

Lobster Bisque (page 193)
One of the all time favourite fish soups, ideal for special occasions.

ream of Asparagus Soup (page 117)

his elegant soup is cooked within minutes. It has a smooth texture and a creamy taste.

Creamy Game Soup (page 260)
A traditional British soup, ideal for all types of game.

Peel and finely chop the onions. Skin, halve and deseed the tomatoes. Chop the celery finely, and if the leaves are fresh, chop these too. Cut the lamb and chicken into 1.25 cm/½ inch dice; it is quite usual to add chicken wings rather than chicken flesh, in which case be rather more generous with the weight.

Heat the butter, add the onions, lamb, chicken and garam masala and cook slowly for 10 minutes. Take care the ingredients do not become too brown. Add the tomatoes, celery and saffron and cook for a further 5 minutes. Pour in most of the water, bring the liquid to the boil and stir well. Cover the pan, lower the heat and simmer for 20 minutes.

Blend the couscous with the remaining water and lemon juice, add to the soup and stir over the heat for 5 minutes until smooth. Season to taste and simmer for a further 10 minutes, stirring from time to time.

Serve topped with the parsley and lemon wedges.

VARIATIONS

- Omit the couscous and add about 75 g/3 oz (⅜ cup) washed split lentils halfway through the cooking period.
- Omit the couscous. Cover 75 g/3 oz (scant ½ cup) chickpeas in water and soak overnight. Drain and rub the skin off the peas. Place the peas in a pan, cover with fresh water, add a little salt and simmer for 1 hour. Add the peas to the other ingredients in the main recipe after cooking the vegetables and meats in the butter. The liquid in which the peas were cooked can be added as part of the total liquid in the soup.
- If garam masala is not available, flavour the soup with ½ teaspoon ground ginger, ½ to 1 teaspoon ground cinnamon and ½ teaspoon ground coriander instead.
- If saffron is not available, use ½ teaspoon turmeric instead.
- This soup is often flavoured with a generous amount of freshly chopped parsley and a few chopped fresh coriander leaves.

DO NOT FREEZE

Ham Chowder

Cooking time: 30 minutes plus time to make stock
Serves 4 to 6

This is an excellent way of serving cooked ham, and the apples really complement the flavour of the meat. This satisfying soup is a complete meal in a bowl.

Metric/Imperial	Ingredients	American
450 g/1 lb	potatoes, peeled weight	1 lb
450 g/1 lb	onions	1 lb
50 g/2 oz	bacon fat or butter	¼ cup
350 g/12 oz	ham	¾ lb
600 ml/1 pint	chicken stock (see page 14)	2½ cups
600 ml/1 pint	milk	2½ cups
to taste	salt and freshly ground black pepper	to taste
2 or 3	sweet eating apples	2 or 3
150 ml/¼ pint	single (light) cream	⅔ cup
To garnish	skinned and diced tomatoes	

Peel the potatoes and grate coarsely or cut into 1.25 cm/½ inch dice. Peel and grate the onions or chop finely.

Heat the bacon fat or butter, add the potatoes and fry gently over a very low heat until golden. Cut the ham into small dice.

Pour the stock and milk over the vegetables, add a little seasoning and bring to the boil. Cover the pan and simmer for 15 minutes. Meanwhile, peel and dice the apples. Add to the soup with the ham and heat for a further 10 minutes. Stir in the cream, heat gently for a few minutes, then taste and adjust the seasoning. Serve topped with the diced tomatoes.

VARIATIONS
- For a less filling soup, reduce the amount of potatoes and onions to 350 g/12 oz (¾ lb) and the ham to 225 g/8 oz (½ lb).

- Use all or part bacon stock (see page 14), and boiled bacon instead of chicken stock and ham. Check the flavour of the stock to ensure it is not too salty.
- Omit the apples and cook approximately 225 g/8 oz (½ lb) diced celeriac or celery with the potatoes and onions.
- Use half grated potatoes and half grated carrots.

- **HAM AND CHICKEN CHOWDER**
Omit the apples from the main recipe and use celeriac or celery as suggested above. Add 225 g/8 oz (½ lb) cooked diced chicken with 100 g/4 oz (¼ lb) diced ham.

FREEZING: **Do not freeze.**

Cardinal Ham and Noodle Soup

Cooking time: 20 minutes plus time to make stock
Serves 4 to 6

This is a satisfying soup made from everyday ingredients. Take care the noodles are cooked only *al dente* so they retain a good texture. Rinsing the pasta in cold water gets rid of any stickiness.

Metric/Imperial	Ingredients	American
600 ml/1 pint	water	2½ cups
to taste	salt and freshly ground black pepper	to taste
50 g/2 oz	small noodles	scant ½ cup
1 medium	onion	1 medium
50 g/2 oz	butter	¼ cup
50 g/2 oz	plain (all-purpose) flour	½ cup
900 ml/1½ pints	chicken stock (see page 14)	3¾ cups
2 tablespoons	tomato purée (paste)	2½ tablespoons
100 g/4 oz	cooked ham	¼ lb
1	egg yolk	1
150 ml/¼ pint	single (light) cream	⅔ cup

Bring the water to the boil, add salt and a shake of pepper. Drop in the noodles and cook quickly, as packet instructions, until barely al dente. Strain and rinse the noodles in cold water.

Peel and finely chop the onion. Heat the butter and cook the onion slowly, until tender but not coloured. Stir in the flour, then add the stock and tomato purée. Stir or whisk as the liquid comes to the boil and the soup thickens.

Cut the ham into small neat dice, add to the soup with the noodles and bring just to boiling point. Blend the egg yolk with the cream, whisk into the hot, but not boiling, soup. Cook gently for 2 to 3 minutes, then serve.

VARIATION

● Use diced, cooked chicken or turkey, or flaked cooked fish or shellfish instead of the cooked ham. Chicken stock is surprisingly good with fish, but fish stock (see page 16) could be used instead.

DO NOT FREEZE

Lamb Broth

Cooking time: 1 hour
Serves 4 to 6

Now that minced (ground) lamb is readily available, I make this old-fashioned and sustaining soup with it. Alternatively, dice a slice of lean uncooked lamb from the leg or shoulder and use that instead. The cooking time will be a little longer.

Metric/Imperial	Ingredients	American
1 tablespoon	pearl barley	1¼ tablespoons
2 medium	onions	2 medium
2	garlic cloves	2
4 medium	carrots	4 medium
1 small	turnip	1 small
¼ small	celery heart	¼ small
1 tablespoon	sunflower oil	1¼ tablespoons
450 g/1 lb	minced (ground) lamb	1 lb
1.2 litres/2 pints	water	5 cups
to taste	salt and freshly ground black pepper	to taste
1 tablespoon	chopped parsley, or to taste	1¼ tablespoons
2 teaspoons	chopped mint, or to taste	2 teaspoons
3 medium	tomatoes	3 medium
To garnish	chopped mint and/ or chopped parsley	

Place the barley in a saucepan and cover with cold water. Bring to the boil, then strain the barley. This process is known as **blanching** and it makes the barley whiter.

Peel and chop the onions and garlic. Peel the carrots and turnip and cut into small dice. Chop the celery.

Heat the oil in a pan, add the onions, garlic and lamb and stir over a very low heat for 10 minutes or until the meat is slightly coloured. Add a little of the water and stir briskly to ensure the meat does not form into lumps. Pour in the rest of the water, add the prepared vegetables, barley, a little seasoning and the herbs. Bring to the boil, cover the pan and lower the heat. Simmer for 30 minutes.

Skin, halve and deseed the tomatoes. Cut the pulp into neat pieces. Add to the broth and continue cooking for 10 minutes. Adjust the seasoning and serve the soup topped with parsley and/or mint.

FREEZING: This soup freezes well.

Kidney Soup 1

Cooking time: 1¼ to 1½ hours plus time to make stock
Serves 4 to 6

The recipe below is based on ox kidney, which has a stronger taste than lamb's kidneys, and thus makes a richer-flavoured soup. It does take a fairly long time to cook in a saucepan, so use either a pressure cooker or slow cooker (if available) or cook on a very low heat (see page 225).

The second version, made with lamb's kidneys, is ready in 30 minutes, so is ideal for busy people. Kidney soup provides a satisfying light meal, especially if a poached egg is added to each bowl of piping hot soup.

Metric/Imperial	Ingredients	American
2 medium	onions	2 medium
350 g/12 oz	ox kidney	¾ lb
2 rashers	streaky bacon	2 slices
50 g/2 oz	butter	¼ cup
1.5 litres/2½ pints	beef stock (see page 14)	6¼ cups
2 tablespoons	chopped parsley	2½ tablespoons
2 or 3	fresh sage leaves or pinch of dried sage	2 or 3
to taste	salt and freshly ground black pepper	to taste
25 g/1 oz	plain (all-purpose) flour	¼ cup
To garnish	croûtons (see page 305)	

Peel and chop the onions. Skin the kidney and remove any gristle and fat. Cut the meat into 1.25 cm/½ inch dice. Derind the bacon and chop the rashers into small pieces. Heat the butter with the bacon rinds, add the onions, bacon and kidney and cook gently for 5 minutes. Remove the bacon rinds.

Pour in nearly all the stock, then add the herbs and seasoning. Cover the pan and simmer for 1 hour, or until the kidney is tender.

Blend the flour with the remaining stock, whisk into the soup and stir over the heat until thickened. Simmer for a further 5 to 10 minutes. Take out the sage leaves and add any extra seasoning required. Garnish with croûtons just before serving.

VARIATIONS

● Use a little less stock and add Madeira or port wine to soups 1 or 2.

● **PURÉED KIDNEY SOUP**
Remove a little cooked kidney and chop this finely for garnish. Prepare the soup as above, and when thickened, sieve or liquidize. The sage leaves do not need removing in this case. Garnish with the chopped kidney and croûtons. Chopped hard-boiled egg makes an interesting garnish.

● **KIDNEY SOUP 2**
Peel and chop 1 medium onion and 2 bacon rashers, save the rinds. Dice 225 g/8 oz (½ lb) skinned lamb's kidneys. Coat in 1 tablespoon (1¼ tablespoons) seasoned flour. Heat 25 g/1 oz (2 tablespoons) butter and the bacon rinds, add the onion and bacon and cook gently for 5 minutes. Remove the bacon rinds. Put the kidneys into the pan with the onions and bacon and cook for a further 5 minutes.

Add 900 ml/1½ pints (3¾ cups) brown stock, preferably made from lamb bones (see page 15) and bring to the boil. Cover the pan and simmer for 15 minutes, then serve the soup. If preferred, sieve or liquidize the soup, then reheat. Garnish as above.

FREEZING: All these soups freeze well.

Meatball Soup
(Jou Wantze T'ang)

Cooking time: 5 minutes plus time to make stock
Serves 4

This Chinese clear soup depends a great deal on having a well-flavoured chicken or meat stock (see page 14). Use very good quality lean pork for the meatballs and do not overcook them.

Metric/Imperial	Ingredients	American
750 ml/1¼ pints	beef or chicken stock (see page 14)	good 3 cups
For the meatballs		
115 g/4 oz	lean pork fillet	¼ lb
1 teaspoon	chopped spring onions (scallions)	1 teaspoon
½ to 1 teaspoon	finely chopped root ginger	½ to 1 teaspoon
1 tablespoon	soy sauce	1¼ tablespoons
1 tablespoon	rice wine or dry sherry	1¼ tablespoons
to taste	salt and freshly ground black pepper	to taste

Strain the stock into a saucepan, make quite sure it has no fat (see page 12 for details of skimming stock).

Mince or finely chop the pork, blend with the remaining ingredients and form into balls 2 to 2.5 cm/¾ to 1 inch in diameter. If the mixture seems a little soft, chill it well for a time before shaping. Bring the stock to the boil, add the meatballs, simmer for 3 to 5 minutes, then serve.

VARIATIONS
- Mix 1 tablespoon (1¼ tablespoons) finely chopped water chestnuts and/or the same amount of beansprouts with the pork and other ingredients.
- Add ½ teaspoon monosodium glutamate to the meatball ingredients. This is obtainable from Chinese food shops.

FREEZING: The soup and meatballs freeze well.

Mexican Soup
(Sopa Mexicana)

Cooking time: 40 minutes plus time to make stock
Serves 4 to 6

This is a satisfying meat soup which has much the same ingredients as Chilli con Carne. The amount of chilli powder used is generous, so add it gradually to achieve a flavour you like. Makes of chilli powder vary a great deal in their strength – another reason for adding it gradually.

Metric/Imperial	Ingredients	American
2 medium	onions	2 medium
2	garlic cloves	2
2	celery sticks	2
1	green pepper	1
2 medium	tomatoes	2 medium
2 tablespoons	olive oil	2½ tablespoons
1 to 1½ teaspoons	chilli powder	1 to 1½ teaspoons
750 ml/1¼ pints	beef stock (see page 14)	good 3 cups
2 tablespoons	tomato purée (paste)	2½ tablespoons
175 to 225 g/6 to 8 oz	raw minced (ground) beef	¾ to 1 cup firmly pressed down
to taste	salt and freshly ground black pepper	to taste
175 g/6 oz	canned red kidney beans, weight when drained	1 cup
To garnish	chopped parsley	

Peel and chop the onions and garlic. Cut the celery into thin strips. Deseed the pepper and cut the pulp into small dice. Skin and finely chop the tomatoes: there is no need to remove the seeds. Heat the oil, add the onion and garlic and cook gently for 5 minutes. Put in the celery, pepper, tomatoes and chilli powder. If you have not made this soup before, use only ½ teaspoon of the powder at this stage, then taste the soup when it is nearly cooked and whisk in any extra chilli powder you require.

Stir well and add the stock, tomato purée and minced beef. Bring to the boil, stir briskly and add a little seasoning. Cover the pan and simmer gently for 20 minutes. Put in the beans and simmer for a further 10 minutes. Add any extra seasoning required. Serve topped with parsley.

VARIATION
- Vegetarians can make this soup using vegetable stock (see page 15) and canned or cooked sweetcorn or chickpeas instead of the beef. (Add these with the beans.) The total cooking time of this variation would be about 25 minutes.

FREEZING: This soup freezes well.

Mulligatawny Soup

Cooking time: 1 hour plus time to make stock
Serves 6

Here is my favourite recipe for this popular curried soup. It has a good mixture of savoury and sweet ingredients. Old recipes for making the stock suggest it is based on boiling a sheep's head in water, but lamb bones produce an excellent result. Mutton bones give a stronger taste to the stock, but this meat is somewhat scarce nowadays. Chicken versions of this soup appear on pages 251 to 254.

If you would rather use a mixture of spices instead of curry powder, see the recipe on page 25.

Metric/Imperial	Ingredients	American
1 medium	dessert apple	1 medium
1 large	carrot	1 large
2 medium	onions	2 medium
50 g/2 oz	lamb or mutton dripping or butter	¼ cup
25 g/1 oz	plain (all-purpose) flour	¼ cup
1 tablespoon	curry powder, or to taste	1¼ tablespoons
1.2 litres/2 pints	lamb or mutton stock (see page 15)	5 cups
1 tablespoon	sweet chutney	1¼ tablespoons
25 g/1 oz	sultanas (seedless white raisins)	3 tablespoons
1 teaspoon	sugar, or to taste	1 teaspoon
to taste	salt and freshly ground black pepper	to taste
1 to 2 teaspoons	lemon juice or vinegar	1 to 2 teaspoons

Peel and neatly dice the apple, carrot and onions. Heat the dripping or butter and fry these ingredients gently for 5 minutes. Stir in the flour and curry powder and cook for 2 minutes, stirring well. Pour in the stock, stirring as it comes to the boil and thickens slightly.

Add the chutney, sultanas, sugar and seasoning to taste. Simmer gently for 45 minutes. Serve the soup as it is, or sieved or liquidized to make a smooth purée. Add the lemon juice or vinegar just before serving.

VARIATIONS

- Mince (grind) 225 g/8 oz (½ lb) uncooked lean lamb or mutton and cook with the apple, carrot and onion in the dripping or butter.
- Add a little finely cooked lamb or mutton just before serving or puréeing the soup.
- Beef stock (see page 14) makes a pleasing alternative to lamb stock. Minced (ground) uncooked or cooked beef can be added in place of the lamb or mutton suggested above.
- Add 1 tablespoon (1¼ tablespoons) long-grain rice when the stock comes to the boil and the mixture thickens slightly.

FREEZING: This soup freezes well.

Oxtail Soup

Cooking time: 2½ to 3 hours plus time to make stock
Serves 4 to 6

It is not only the British who esteem oxtail – it is a great favourite in other countries too. The ingredients stipulate 900 g/2 lb oxtail, which is about 5 large pieces, 7 to 8 medium ones, or 10 to 12 small pieces. The cooking time depends on the tenderness of the meat. Whatever version of the soup you cook, allow it to cool overnight so the fat can be easily removed the next day.

Metric/Imperial	Ingredients	American
900 g/2 lb	oxtail	2 lb
1 large	onion	1 large
350 g/12 oz	root vegetables, see method	¾ lb
50 g/2 oz	beef dripping or butter	¼ cup
1.8 litres/3 pints	beef stock (see page 14)	7½ cups
1	bouquet garni*	1
to taste	salt and freshly ground black pepper	to taste
50 g/2 oz	plain (all-purpose) flour	½ cup
To garnish	chopped parsley	

* In this recipe use parsley, rosemary, sage and thyme.

Cut the oxtail into joints if this has not already been done by the butcher. Soak in cold water for 30 minutes, then drain well. Peel and chop the onion. Prepare the vegetables and cut into bite-sized pieces. (Use mostly carrots, a small amount of turnip, swede or parsnip plus a little celeriac or celery.) If you intend sieving or liquidizing the soup, use a generous amount of vegetables and then you can omit the flour for thickening.

Heat the dripping or butter, add the onion and other vegetables and cook gently for about 10 minutes or until they are golden in colour. Add most of the stock together with the herbs, oxtail and seasoning. Cover the pan and simmer gently for 2½ to 3 hours or until the meat is tender. Remove the bouquet garni and the oxtail. Cut the meat from the bones and discard any surplus fat.

Blend the flour with the remaining stock, whisk or stir into the hot soup. Continue stirring until thickened. Return the oxtail to the pan and heat, then garnish and serve.

If possible leave the soup overnight. When cold store in the refrigerator. Next day remove all the fat from the top of the soup and thoroughly reheat.

VARIATIONS
- Add several tablespoons port or red wine to the soup.
- Omit 300 ml/½ pint (1¼ cups) stock and use that amount of strong beer.
- Add 2 to 3 tablespoons (2½ to 3¾ tablespoons) tomato purée (paste) or 3 skinned and deseeded tomatoes to the other ingredients.

- **PURÉED OXTAIL SOUP**

Remove the meat from the bones, then sieve or liquidize with the other ingredients and reheat. If you prefer, you can sieve or liquidize the soup without the oxtail. Chop the meat finely and return to the soup. Take great care when using a liquidizer or food processor that no splinters of bone are left in the liquid, as these could damage the appliance.

- **AMERICAN-STYLE OXTAIL SOUP**

Coat the oxtail in seasoned flour and fry in the dripping or butter. Add 1.5 litres/2½ pints (6¼ cups) stock, a little seasoning, a generous pinch of cayenne pepper, 2 teaspoons Worcestershire sauce and 6 juniper berries. Cover the pan and simmer for the time stated in the main recipe. Remove the oxtail, cut the meat from the bones and discard any surplus fat.

Strain the stock and return to the pan. Add 3 medium, neatly diced carrots, 2 small, thinly sliced leeks, 3 diced celery sticks and the oxtail. Cook for about 15 minutes or until the vegetables are tender.

- **ITALIAN-STYLE OXTAIL SOUP**

This is based on a delicious Italian recipe – *coda di bue alla vaccarinara*.

Fry the onion plus a crushed garlic clove, as in the main recipe. Add 1.2 litres/2 pints (5 cups) brown stock, plus 300 ml/½ pint (1¼ cups) white wine, the oxtail, 1 sliced leek and 1 sliced carrot, the bouquet garni and seasoning. Cook as before. When tender, remove the oxtail from the stock. Chop the meat finely and discard any fat. Strain the stock and return to the pan with 3 sieved tomatoes or 3 tablespoons (3¾ tablespoons) tomato purée (paste) and ½ a small, finely chopped celery heart. Heat for 10 minutes, then add 100 g/4 oz (¼ lb) chopped prosciutto, 2 tablespoons (2½ tablespoons) pinenuts and the chopped oxtail. Heat for 5 minutes and serve.

● OXTAIL CONSOMMÉ

It is essential to use a well-flavoured beef stock for cooking the oxtail. Follow the main recipe, but omit the flour. When the oxtail is cooked, strain the stock through fine muslin or a fine sieve. Cut the oxtail from the bones and discard any fat. Return the meat to the stock with a little Madeira and reheat. Garnish with thinly sliced fried mushrooms and cooked green peas.

FREEZING: The puréed version of this soup freezes best. The tiny pieces of oxtail in other versions tend to lose texture and flavour.

Scotch Broth

Cooking time: 2 to 2½ hours
Serves 4 to 6

Sometimes called Barley Broth, this is one of the best-known Scottish recipes and makes splendid cold-weather food. Instead of using lamb, you could substitute stewing beef.

Metric/Imperial	Ingredients	American
50 g/2 oz	pearl barley	good ¼ cup
675 g/1½ lb	scrag end of lamb	1½ lb
1.5 litres/2½ pints	water	6¼ cups
to taste	salt and freshly ground black pepper	to taste
to taste	faggot of herbs*	to taste
450 g/1 lb	mixed root vegetables	1 lb
¼	small cabbage heart	¼
To garnish	chopped parsley	

* 'Faggot' is the Scottish word for bouquet garni. Tie a mixture of parsley, chives and thyme in cotton or in a muslin bag.

Blanch the barley as described on page 223 and strain it.

Remove any surplus fat from the meat and place in the saucepan with the water, barley, seasoning and herbs. Bring to the boil, remove any scum that forms on the surface, then lower the heat and simmer for 1¼ hours.

Lift the meat from the liquid, cut into small, neat pieces and return it to the pan. If very tender, leave the meat on one side and return it to the liquid when adding the cabbage.

Peel and dice the root vegetables, add to the liquid in the pan and cook steadily for 25 to 30 minutes. Shred the cabbage, add to the rest of the ingredients and cook for 5 to 10 minutes only. Remove the herbs and garnish the soup with parsley.

FREEZING: This soup freezes well.

Sour-Hot Soup
(Suan la T'ang)

Cooking time: 15 minutes plus time to make stock
Serves 4

This Chinese soup makes an excellent first course, but could also be served as a light main dish because of its high protein content.

Metric/Imperial	Ingredients	American
4	dried mushrooms	4
175 g/6 oz	lean pork fillet	¾ cup when chopped
25 g/1 oz	bean curd (tofu)	¼ cup when chopped
900 ml/1½ pints	beef stock (see page 14)	3¾ cups
1 tablespoon	brown malt or red wine vinegar	1¼ tablespoons
1 tablespoon	soy sauce	1¼ tablespoons
2 tablespoons	rice wine or dry sherry	2½ tablespoons
2 teaspoons	cornflour (cornstarch)	2 teaspoons
2 tablespoons	water	2½ tablespoons
to taste	salt and freshly ground black pepper	to taste

Soak the mushrooms as directed on the packet, then drain and thinly slice or chop them. Finely chop the meat by hand or in a food processor. Chop the bean curd into very small pieces.

Bring the stock to the boil, add the mushrooms and pork and simmer for 10 minutes. Put in the bean curd, vinegar, soy sauce and wine. Blend the cornflour with the cold water, stir into the soup and simmer for 5 minutes, stirring well until slightly thickened. Season to taste.

VARIATIONS

- The authentic Chinese recipe adds about ¼ teaspoon monosodium glutamate to the other ingredients. Many people do not like to use this, but it is obtainable from shops specializing in Chinese foods.
- Omit the cornflour (cornstarch) thickening and leave the meat in larger pieces.

FREEZING: This soup freezes well but it is advisable to add the wine when reheating, as much of the alcohol flavour is lost in freezing.

Chapter Seven

POULTRY AND GAME SOUPS

In this chapter you will find that many of the recipes are based upon chicken. This is because chicken soups are a great favourite and there are so many different flavours that can be added to the chicken to increase its versatility. Chicken has become one of our most economical protein foods, so chicken soups are far from being a luxury. If you want to ring the changes, many of these soups can be made with alternative ingredients, such as turkey, guinea fowl, quail or pheasant. Duck and goose are not as usual in a soup as chicken or turkey but one of my favourite soups, using duck, with goose as an alternative, is on page 256.

Farmed and wild venison are becoming better known as they are increasingly available from supermarkets and good butchers. You could use this meat to give a robust flavour in the Game Soup on page 258 or in some of the meat soups in Chapter 6.

Poultry and game soups can be cooked in the same ways as those based on meat (see pages 216 to 235). Modern chickens, however, are easily overcooked, so it is important to time cooking carefully. This is particularly true of Old-fashioned Chicken Soup (see page 237), where a whole bird is used.

LOWERING THE CALORIE CONTENT

Like other soups in this book, some of the chicken recipes contain cream, which is delicious but does add to the calorific content of a dish. To reduce this you can substitute low-fat yoghurt or fromage frais. Take care, though, not to boil the soup or it will curdle, just as it would with cream. Simmer gently and whisk well while the soup is heating.

GARNISHES FOR POULTRY AND GAME SOUPS

If you would like to change the garnishes recommended in the recipes, consider a good colour contrast. Soups based on chicken or turkey or game birds often are creamy in flavour, which is delicious, but inclined to look a little pallid. Herbs, browned nuts, particularly almonds, finely chopped or sliced vegetables or slices of lemon or orange add both colour and flavour to pale soups.

Game soups are generally brown, so a little cream or sprinkling of herbs would be an excellent garnish.

Crisp croûtons make a pleasant contrast in texture to the soft consistency of the soups.

Chicken Soup
Cooking time: 1¾ hours
Serves 6 to 8

The cooking timing for chicken soup has varied over the years. In the days when it was made with an elderly fowl who was past laying eggs, the bird would have been rather fatty and taken probably 3 hours to tenderize. Modern chickens are younger and leaner, and therefore quicker to cook, but they have less flavour. None the less, the soup still tastes good.

Metric/Imperial	Ingredients	American
1	chicken weighing about 1.8 kg/4 lb when trussed, without giblets	1
2.4 litres/4 pints	water	10 cups
to taste	salt and freshly ground black pepper	to taste
450 g/1 lb	mixed root vegetables, see method	1 lb
1	bouquet garni*	1
1 large	onion	1 large
3 or 4	cloves, optional	3 or 4
75 g/3 oz	long-grain rice	scant ½ cup

* Sprigs of parsley, thyme and rosemary tied with cotton or in muslin.

Put the chicken and water into a large saucepan and add seasoning. Peel and chop the vegetables: use small onions, carrots, turnip, swede (rutabaga) and celery. Put about a quarter of the vegetables, plus the bouquet garni, into the pan with the chicken. Peel the onion, press in the cloves and add to the pan. Bring to the boil, remove any scum and lower the heat so the liquid is simmering steadily. Cover the pan and cook for 1 hour or until the chicken is just tender. Remove the chicken and cut about half the flesh, or the amount required, into neat pieces. Save the remainder for another dish.

Boil the liquid in an open pan for 15 minutes or until reduced to 1.8 litres/3 pints (7½ cups). Strain, return to the saucepan and bring to the boil again. Add the remaining vegetables plus the rice and any extra seasoning required. Cook steadily for 15 minutes. Return the diced chicken to the soup and heat for 10 minutes.

VARIATIONS

● In summertime add fresh peas and/or young broad (fava) beans to the selection of vegetables.

● **CHICKEN AND DUMPLING SOUP**
Omit the rice and serve the soup with Herbed Dumplings (see page 309). These should be added 20 minutes before the end of the cooking time. The stock must be allowed to boil rapidly for the first 10 minutes after the dumplings are added.

● **CREAMY CHICKEN SOUP**
Follow the main method, but allow only 1.2 litres/2 pints (5 cups) of stock in which to cook the rice and vegetables and heat the chicken. In a separate pan melt 50 g/2 oz (¼ cup) butter or chicken fat, stir in 50 g/2 oz (½ cup) plain (all-purpose) flour, cook for 1 to 2 minutes, then add 450 ml/¾ pint (scant 2 cups) milk. Bring to the boil and cook steadily until thickened. Add 150 ml/¼ pint (⅔ cup) double (heavy) cream. Warm gently for 2 or 3 minutes. Whisk this hot sauce into the very hot soup just before serving. Taste and adjust the seasoning. Serve garnished with parsley.

FREEZING: This soup freezes well if the second batch of vegetables, rice and chicken are not overcooked.

Chicken and Watermelon Soup

Cooking time: 25 to 30 minutes plus time to make stock
Serves 4 to 6

This is an unusual mixture of chicken and fruit. As the ingredients suggest, it is based on an Oriental recipe.

Metric/Imperial	Ingredients	American
25 g/1 oz	dried mushrooms	¼ cup when chopped
150 ml/¼ pint	boiling water	⅔ cup
225 g/8 oz	chicken breast	½ lb
100 g/4 oz	lean pork	¼ lb
750 ml/1¼ pints	chicken stock (see page 14)	good 3 cups
to taste	salt and freshly ground black pepper	to taste
100 g/4 oz	shelled fresh or frozen peas	¾ cup
100 g/4 oz	canned bamboo shoots	¼ lb
350 g/12 oz	watermelon pulp, weight without skin and seeds	¾ lb

Chop the dried mushrooms into small pieces, cover with the boiling water and leave to soak for 1 hour. Cut the chicken and pork into neat pieces, discard the skin from the chicken.

Heat the stock, add the pork and mushrooms and bring to simmering point. Add a little seasoning, cover the pan and simmer for 10 minutes only. Put in the chicken and fresh peas, and simmer for a further 10 minutes. If using frozen peas, add them with the bamboo shoots.

Cut the bamboo shoots into matchstick pieces and dice the watermelon pulp. Do this on a plate, so no juice is wasted. If preferred, the fruit can be cut into small balls using a vegetable scoop.

Add the bamboo shoots and watermelon, plus any juice from the fruit, to the soup, simmer for a further 5 minutes, then add any extra seasoning required and serve.

VARIATIONS

- About 1 tablespoon (1¼ tablespoons) lemon or lime juice can be added with the watermelon.
- The stock can be flavoured with 1 to 2 teaspoons finely grated root ginger or ¼ to ½ teaspoon ground ginger.

FREEZING: **Do not freeze.**

Chicken Mulligatawny Soup 1

Cooking time: 1¼ hours plus time to make stock
Serves 4 to 6

This highly spiced Indian soup has been a favourite in Britain for over two centuries. Indeed, 19th-century cooks, including Mrs Beeton and Eliza Acton, extolled its virtues and gave recipes for it in their books.

There are many versions of the soup, even in Britain, but some of the most interesting are from India itself. The version below is from Madhur Jaffrey's *Indian Cookery* (BBC Books, 1982).

Metric/Imperial	Ingredients	American
175 g/6 oz	red lentils	¾ cup
1.2 litres/2 pints	chicken stock (see page 14)	5 cups
½ teaspoon	ground turmeric	½ teaspoon
1	potato, about 100 g/ 4 oz (¼ lb)	1
200 g/7 oz	chicken breast	scant ½ lb
to taste	salt and freshly ground black pepper	to taste
5	garlic cloves	5
1	3 cm/1¼ inch cube fresh ginger	1
4½ tablespoons	water	5¾ tablespoons
3 tablespoons	vegetable oil	3¾ tablespoons
1 teaspoon	ground cumin seeds	1 teaspoon

Metric/Imperial	Ingredients	American
1 teaspoon	coriander	1 teaspoon
¼ to ½ teaspoon	cayenne pepper	¼ to ½ teaspoon
250 ml/8 fl oz	water	1 cup
1 tablespoon	lemon juice, or to taste	1¼ tablespoons

Wash and pick over the lentils, then drain them. Put into a heavy, medium-sized pan with the chicken stock and turmeric and bring to the boil. Partially cover the pan (leave the lid slightly ajar) and simmer for 30 minutes.

While the soup simmers, peel the potato and cut into 1.25 cm/½ inch dice. When the soup has cooked for 30 minutes, add the potato. Cover the pan, leaving the lid ajar as before, and simmer for a further 30 minutes.

Remove all fat from the chicken breast. Cut the flesh into 1.25 cm/½ inch dice, sprinkle with salt and pepper and toss to mix.

Peel the garlic cloves and ginger, chop and place in a food processor or liquidizer with the 4½ tablespoons (5¾ tablespoons) water and make into a smooth paste. (This could be done with a pestle and mortar.)

When the soup is cooked, sieve or liquidize it. Transfer to a bowl, add more salt and stir well.

Rinse and wipe out the saucepan. Pour the oil into it and place over a medium heat. When the oil is hot, add the garlic-ginger paste, the cumin, coriander and cayenne and fry, stirring continuously, until the mixture is slightly browned and separates from the oil. Put in the chicken pieces, stir well and fry for another 2 to 3 minutes, or until the chicken is opaque.

Add the 250 ml/8 fl oz (1 cup) water and bring to the boil. Cover, lower the heat and simmer for 3 minutes, or until the chicken is cooked. Pour in the puréed soup and the lemon juice, stir and bring to a simmer. Taste the soup for seasoning; you may need to add a little more lemon juice. If too thick, thin it with a little chicken stock or water. Simmer the soup very gently for another 2 minutes and serve.

FREEZING: This soup freezes well.

Cock-a-Leekie

Cooking time: 1½ hours plus time to make stock, if using
Serves 4 to 6

This dish is frequently the basis for two meals, as only a small amount of
chicken is used in the soup, leaving the rest of the bird for another day. It is one
of Scotland's most famous soups.

Metric/Imperial	Ingredients	American
12 large	prunes, tenderized if possible	12 large
450 g/1 lb	leeks	1 lb
1.2 litres/2 pints	chicken stock (see page 14) or water	5 cups
1 small	chicken	1 small
to taste	sprigs of parsley and thyme	to taste
to taste	salt and freshly ground black pepper	to taste
To garnish	chopped parsley	

If not tenderized, soak the prunes in water overnight or for several hours.
For soft prunes, cook steadily in the soaking water until they reach the
texture you like. This process can be omitted if you like firmer prunes.

Cut the leeks into thin rings. Put the chicken stock or water into a
saucepan, then add the chicken, herbs and seasoning to taste. Cover the pan
and cook steadily for 1 hour, or until the chicken is tender. Lift the bird out
of the pan. Strain the stock, measure and, if necessary, boil rapidly in an
open pan until reduced to 900 ml/1½ pints (3¾ cups).

Add the leeks and prunes to the stock, cover the pan and cook for 20 or
30 minutes or until tender.

If adding only a little chicken to the soup, dice approximately 225 g/8 oz
(½ lb) breast meat and add to the pan. Heat the soup and garnish with
chopped parsley.

VARIATIONS

- Use beef stock instead of chicken stock or water to give a stronger-flavoured soup.
- To give a more pronounced vegetable flavour to the soup, add a few chopped leeks, an onion and a little diced bacon with the chicken and herbs, then strain. These ingredients are not served in the soup but they add an excellent flavour to the stock, particularly if you are using water.
- Instead of cooking a whole chicken, cook one chicken portion, or as many as required, to give a satisfying soup.

Curried Chicken Soup

Cooking time: 40 minutes plus time to make stock

Serves 4 to 6

This is a splendid soup in which to use up leftover chicken. The carcass could be used to make the stock. The amount of curry powder in the recipe gives a moderately hot flavour, which is beautifully balanced by the addition of cream.

Metric/Imperial	Ingredients	American
2 large	onions	2 large
1 medium	sweet apple	1 medium
50 g/2 oz	butter or chicken fat	¼ cup
1 tablespoon	curry paste or powder	1¼ tablespoons
1 tablespoon	cornflour (cornstarch)	1¼ tablespoons
900 ml/1½ pints	chicken stock (see page 14)	3¾ cups
1 tablespoon	lemon juice	1¼ tablespoons
to taste	salt and freshly ground black pepper	to taste
225 g/8 oz	cooked chicken	½ lb
150 ml/¼ pint	milk	⅔ cup
150 ml/¼ pint	single (light) cream	⅔ cup
2	egg yolks	2
To garnish	watercress	
	diced red pepper or diced cooked bacon or ham	

Peel and finely chop the onions and apple. Heat the butter or chicken fat and gently fry the onions and apple for 5 minutes. Add the curry paste or powder and cornflower, mix well and cook for 1 to 2 minutes. Add the stock and lemon juice and bring to the boil. Season lightly, then lower the heat, cover the pan and simmer for 20 minutes. Dice the cooked chicken, add to the stock, then sieve or liquidize to give a smooth mixture.

Return to the pan and add the milk. Blend the cream and egg yolks together, whisk into the hot, but not boiling, soup and cook gently for 5 to 10 minutes. Adjust the seasoning and serve topped with the garnish.

VARIATIONS

- For a slightly thicker soup, add 1 or 2 peeled and diced potatoes to the onions and apple, or increase the amount of chicken to 350 g/ 12 oz (¾ lb).
- Use cooked turkey instead of chicken.

FREEZING: The puréed mixture freezes well. Add the milk, cream and egg yolks only when reheating the soup.

Indonesian Chicken Soup (Soto Ajam)

Cooking time: 45 minutes plus time to make stock
Serves 4 to 6

A pleasant mixture of European and Far Eastern influences, this soup requires a strongly flavoured chicken stock.

Metric/Imperial	Ingredients	American
2 medium	onions	2 medium
2	garlic cloves	2
2 small	leeks	2 small
2 small	potatoes, preferably new	2 small
225 to 350 g/8 to 12 oz	chicken breast or leg meat, boned weight	½ to ¾ lb
1 tablespoon	sunflower oil	1¼ tablespoons
1.5 litres/2½ pints	chicken stock (see page 14)	6¼ cups
1 to 2 teaspoons	grated root ginger	1 to 2 teaspoons
to taste	salt and freshly ground black pepper	to taste
2	eggs	2
4 tablespoons	chopped canned bamboo shoots	5 tablespoons
6 tablespoons	chopped canned water chestnuts	7½ tablespoons

Peel and finely chop the onions and garlic. Slice the leeks thinly, including a little of the tender green stalks. Scrape the potatoes and cut into thin matchsticks. Remove the skin from the chicken and dice the meat.

Heat the oil in a pan, add the onions and garlic and cook gently for 10 minutes, or until nearly tender. Stir well so they do not colour. Pour in the stock, add the ginger and bring to the boil. Season lightly, then cover the pan, lower the heat and simmer for 15 minutes. Add the chicken, potatoes and leeks and continue simmering for a further 15 minutes.

Hard-boil, shell and chop the eggs while the soup is cooking. Add to the pan with the bamboo shoots and water chestnuts. Continue cooking for a further 5 minutes. Taste the soup, adjust the seasoning and serve.

VARIATION

• Add 2 teaspoons light soy sauce towards the end of the cooking period.

FREEZING: **Do not freeze.**

Lorraine Soup

Cooking time: 20 minutes plus time to make stock
Serves 4 to 6

Often known as La Reine Soup, this dish dates back to the 16th century and reflects the culinary links between France and Scotland in the days of Mary Queen of Scots. It is undoubtedly my favourite chicken soup; I love the subtle thickening given to the stock by almonds. The chicken stock must be very well flavoured – almost like a Chicken Consommé (see page 71).

Metric/Imperial	Ingredients	American
2	eggs	2
50 g/2 oz	almonds	generous ½ cup
225 g/8 oz	cooked chicken breast	½ lb
900 ml/1½ pints	chicken stock or consommé (see pages 14 and 71)	3¾ cups
25 g/1 oz	soft breadcrumbs	½ cup
150 ml/¼ pint	single (light) cream	⅔ cup
to taste	salt and freshly ground black pepper	to taste
To garnish	chopped parsley	

Hard-boil the eggs, shell them and remove the yolks. Chop the yolks and whites separately. Reserve whites for garnish. Blanch and finely chop the almonds, unless you plan to liquidize or process the soup, in which case they can be left whole. Cut the cooked chicken into very small dice.

To prepare the soup by hand, put the egg yolks, almonds and chicken breast into a bowl, add a little chicken stock, then pound the mixture until smooth. Alternatively, liquidize or process the ingredients with some of the stock to a smooth purée.

Pour the remaining chicken into a saucepan, add the chicken purée with the breadcrumbs, cream and seasoning. Heat thoroughly but do not allow the soup to boil. Garnish each portion with the chopped egg whites and parsley.

FREEZING: **Do not freeze.**

Queen Soup
(Dronning Suppe)

Cooking time: 20 minutes plus time to make stock
Serves 4

Egg yolks and cream give this Norwegian soup a lovely rich taste, but take care not to overheat it or the mixture will curdle. The traditional garnish is small Chicken Balls (see page 302), but the quick tip offers an alternative to these.

Metric/Imperial	Ingredients	American
1.2 litres/2 pints	chicken stock (see page 14)	5 cups
3	egg yolks	3
150 ml/¼ pint	single (light) cream	⅔ cup
3 tablespoons	dry sherry	3¾ tablespoons
to taste	salt and freshly ground white pepper	to taste
To garnish	Chicken Balls (see page 302)	

In this recipe it is important that the stock is free from any fat; page 12 explains how to clarify stock. Put the egg yolks, cream and sherry into a really large bowl and place over a pan of hot, but not boiling, water. Whisk briskly until the mixture thickens.

Heat the stock to simmering point, then gradually whisk into the egg yolk mixture. Season to taste and serve topped with the chicken balls.

VARIATIONS

● Instead of cream, use ordinary or skimmed milk.

● VEGETARIAN QUEEN SOUP

Use vegetable stock and garnish the soup with very small diced, cooked carrots and grated cheese.

FREEZING: This soup is better freshly made as it is inclined to separate during freezing. Defrosted chicken stock could be used.

QUICK TIP *Garnish the creamy soup with finely diced chicken breast or diced cooked ham instead of chicken balls. Heat the stock on full power, then whisk into the thickened egg mixture. If not sufficiently hot, return to the microwave for 1 to 2 minutes on a low setting, whisking every ½ minute. Stand for 1 to 2 minutes before serving.*

Royal Soup (Sopa Real)

Cooking time: 15 minutes plus time to make stock
Serves 4

This quickly made and interesting Spanish soup needs a really well-flavoured chicken stock. The eggs and other ingredients are not heated, so the soup must be very hot.

Metric/Imperial	Ingredients	American
2	eggs	2
100 g/4 oz	cooked ham	¼ lb
100 g/4 oz	cooked chicken breast, weight without bone and skin	¼ lb
1 slice	bread	1 slice
1.2 litres/2 pints	chicken stock (see page 114)	5 cups
to taste	salt and freshly ground white pepper	to taste
1 wineglass	dry sherry, or to taste	1 wineglass

Make sure the soup bowls are thoroughly warmed. Hard-boil, shell and chop the eggs; dice the ham and chicken, and cut the bread into small neat pieces. Divide all these ingredients between the bowls. Heat the stock, taste and adjust the seasoning, then stir in the sherry and warm for 1 minute. Pour over the cold ingredients and serve immediately.

VARIATION

● Heat 1 tablespoon (1¼ tablespoons) olive oil in a frying pan, fry the diced bread until crisp, add the chopped eggs, diced ham and chicken. Fry in the oil for a few minutes, then place in the bowls. Add the heated stock and sherry.

FREEZING: **Do not freeze.**

Spiced Chicken Soup

Cooking time: 40 minutes plus time to make stock
Serves 4 to 6

This soup makes an excellent light main course or a good first course before a salad lunch or dinner. I suggest using leg meat but you can substitute breast if preferred.

Metric/Imperial	Ingredients	American
2 medium	onions	2 medium
1	chicken leg portion, weighing about 350 g/12 oz (¾ lb)	1
75 g/3 oz	chicken fat or butter	⅜ cup
25 g/1 oz	plain (all-purpose) flour	¼ cup
1 tablespoon	curry powder, or to taste	1¼ tablespoons
1.2 litres/2 pints	chicken stock (see page 14)	5 cups
25 g/1 oz	long-grain rice	2 tablespoons
to taste	salt and freshly ground black pepper	to taste

Metric/Imperial	Ingredients	American
25 g/1 oz	sultanas (seedless white raisins	3 tablespoons
2 small	dessert apples	2 small
1 tablespoon	lemon juice	1¼ tablespoons

Peel and finely chop the onions. Remove the chicken flesh from the bone(s) and cut into very small dice. Heat 50 g/2 oz (¼ cup) of the fat in a saucepan, add the onions and chicken and fry gently for 10 minutes. Stir during this time so the food does not brown. Stir in the flour and curry powder, continue stirring over a very low heat for about 2 minutes, then add the stock. The chicken bone(s) can be added if you want to increase the flavour. Bring to the boil, put in the rice and stir well. Add seasoning to taste. Lower the heat, cover the pan and simmer for 25 minutes. Remove the bones if these were added. Add the sultanas towards the end of the cooking time and adjust the seasoning.

While the soup is cooking, peel, core and thinly slice the apples and toss in the lemon juice. Heat the remaining chicken fat or butter in a frying pan and cook the apples steadily until just tender but unbroken. Ladle the soup into the bowls, add the apples and serve.

FREEZING: This soup freezes well, but it is advisable to freeze the cooked apples separately and add them to the soup only when reheating. Simmer for 2 to 3 minutes in the soup to make sure the apples are hot.

Thai Lemon and Coriander Soup

Cooking time: 15 minutes plus time to make stock
Serves 4 to 6

I have based this recipe on one I found in a delightful small book entitled *Herbs* by Marilyn Bright (Appletree Press, 1995). Although I love a curry flavour, I found the original amount of 2 tablespoons (2¼ tablespoons) hot curry paste rather overwhelmed the delicious taste of lemon and coriander, so I have reduced this. To emphasize the lemon in the soup, I have added a little chopped lemon grass to the original recipe.

Metric/Imperial	Ingredients	American
1	uncooked chicken breast	1
1	red chilli pepper	1
1 or 2 stems	lemon grass	1 or 2 stems
small bunch	coriander leaves	small bunch
900 ml/1½ pints	chicken stock (see page 14)	3¾ cups
1 tablespoon	hot curry paste, or to taste	1¼ tablespoons
2 tablespoons	lemon juice, or to taste	2½ tablespoons
to taste	salt	to taste

Skin the chicken and cut the flesh into thin shreds. Slit the pepper, remove the seeds and thinly slice the pod. (Wash your hands after doing this because chilli juice can sting sensitive skin and be very painful, especially near your eyes.)

Chop the lemon grass and coriander leaves finely. Put the stock and curry paste into a saucepan, heat until the paste has dissolved, then add the chicken, lemon juice and lemon grass. Bring just to the boil, lower the heat and cover the pan. Simmer for 8 minutes or until the chicken is tender.

Add the chilli pepper and coriander, heat for 2 to 3 minutes only, then add salt to taste. It is unlikely you will need to add any pepper. Serve hot.

FREEZING: Do not freeze.

Turkey and Chestnut Soup

Cooking time: 40 minutes
Serves 4 to 6

The combination of turkey and chestnuts is a traditional one, and extremely good too. The recipe below uses uncooked turkey, but it is also possible to use cooked poultry. The turkey carcass can be used to make stock.

Metric/Imperial	Ingredients	American
350 g/12 oz	chestnuts	¾ lb
2 medium	onions	2 medium
¼	celery heart	¼
350 g/12 oz	uncooked turkey portion	¾ lb
25 g/1 oz	turkey fat or butter	2 tablespoons
1.2 litres/2 pints	chicken or turkey stock (see pages 14 and 15)	5 cups
1 tablespoon	chopped parsley	1¼ tablespoons
1 teaspoon	chopped thyme or ½ teaspoon dried thyme	1 teaspoon
to taste	salt and freshly ground black pepper	to taste

Slit the chestnuts in a cross at the rounded end. Place into a little boiling water and cook for 10 minutes. Cool sufficiently to handle, then remove the outer shells and brown skins.

Peel and chop the onions and dice the celery. Cut the turkey flesh into small dice. Heat the fat or butter and cook the onions and turkey for 10 minutes, or until golden in colour, stirring often.

Add the stock, chestnuts, herbs and seasoning. Simmer for 25 to 30 minutes, then serve.

VARIATIONS
• If using cooked turkey, add rather more vegetables, such as sliced carrots and a little diced celeriac, to give the soup more flavour. Add the diced cooked turkey towards the end of the cooking time.

- **PURÉED TURKEY AND CHESTNUT SOUP**

Cook the soup as instructed above. Take out a few chestnuts and a little turkey for garnish, then sieve or liquidize the soup. Reheat and top with crème fraîche or soured cream, chopped chestnuts and turkey.

- **TURKEY GIBLET SOUP**

Cook turkey giblets with 1.8 litres/3 pints (7½ cups) of water and about 225 g/8 oz (½ lb) mixed diced vegetables. When tender, strain the stock. Pour 900 ml/1½ pints (3¾ cups) of the stock into a saucepan, add 350 g/ 12 oz (¾ lb) neatly diced vegetables and cook until the vegetables are tender. Add a little of the diced liver from the giblets to the soup and stir in 300 ml/½ pint (1¼ cups) single (light) cream. Heat gently and top with chopped parsley.

The remainder of the stock can be frozen or used to make gravy.

- **AFTER-CHRISTMAS SOUP**

Remove any cooked turkey clinging to the carcass and set aside. Use the carcass to make turkey stock (see page 15). Liquidize the amount of stock required with any suitable leftover vegetables, the reserved turkey flesh and any leftover stuffing. Heat and serve.

FREEZING: The Turkey and Chestnut Soup freezes well, as does the turkey stock.

Chicken Mulligatawny Soup 2

Cooking time: 1¾ hours
Serves 6

The following recipe comes from Australia, where it appears in *The Early Settler's Book of Household Lore* (Raphael Arts Pty Ltd, 1977), originally published in 1809. Most of the measurements in the recipe are those I have added, since the original instructions are somewhat vague. If using the suggested quantity of curry powder, use a mild variety.

Although this is a very satisfying soup, the original recipe states that it should be served with a dish of cooked rice 'if you can get it' – an indication that rice was something of a luxury in early 19th-century Australia.

Metric/Imperial	Ingredients	American
4 medium	onions	4 medium
1 small head	garlic	1 small head
50 g/2 oz	butter	¼ cup
1 small	chicken	1 small
3 tablespoons	curry powder, or to taste	3¾ tablespoons
2 tablespoons	plain (all-purpose) flour	2½ tablespoons
1 tablespoon	lemon juice	1¼ tablespoons
to taste	salt and cayenne pepper	to taste
600 ml/1 pint	water	2½ cups
600 ml/1 pint	chicken stock, see method	2½ cups

Peel and chop the onions and garlic. Heat the butter in a saucepan and gently cook the onions and garlic until light brown. Cut all the flesh from the chicken. Make stock from the carcass by simmering it in a covered pan of water. Meanwhile, cut the chicken flesh into small pieces.

Blend the curry powder and flour with the onions and garlic. Add the chicken, mix well, then add the lemon juice, a little salt and cayenne pepper and the water. Cover the pan and simmer for 30 minutes. Add the chicken stock, cover the pan tightly, simmer for 1 hour, then serve.

The original recipe makes no mention of sieving the soup, but you can sieve or liquidize it if you wish. This will produce a thick purée, in which case you will need to add more stock to give the desired consistency.

VARIATIONS
- A cold version of Mulligatawny Soup appears on page 286.
- A meat version of Mulligatawny Soup appears on page 229.

FREEZING: This soup freezes well, but the texture is better if the chicken is only lightly cooked, especially if you serve the soup without sieving or liquidizing it.

Duck Soup

Cooking time: 15 minutes plus time to cook the duck and make the stock
Serves 4 to 6

This recipe, inspired by Peking Duck, arose from an experiment I made one day when I had part of a cooked duck left over. The skin of the bird must be very crisp and the duck flesh free from fat. The duck stock, made from the carcass, must be full of flavour and fat-free. The pancakes served with this soup are not the true Chinese kind but they are an excellent alternative.

Metric/Imperial	Ingredients	American
1.2 litres/2 pints	duck stock (see page 16)	5 cups
2	garlic cloves	2
½ small	cucumber	½ small
225 g/8 oz	cooked duck	½ lb
5 tablespoons	sliced spring onions (scallions)	6 tablespoons
2 tablespoons	rice wine or dry sherry	2½ tablespoons
1 tablespoon	soy sauce, or to taste	1¼ tablespoons
to taste	salt and freshly ground black pepper	to taste
To garnish	1 or 2 pancakes (see page 97)	
	crisp duck skin, see Note	

Heat the duck stock. Peel, but do not chop, the garlic cloves, add to the stock and simmer for 5 minutes. Peel the cucumber and cut the pulp into matchstick-sized pieces. Finely dice the duck flesh. Add the cucumber, duck and spring onions to the stock and simmer for 5 minutes.

Gradually pour in the rice wine or sherry and soy sauce, tasting the soup as you do so. Heat for a few minutes, then add any seasoning required. Remove the garlic cloves. Cut the pancake(s) and duck skin into narrow shreds and add to the soup immediately before serving.

Note: If the duck skin is not as crisp as you would wish, heat it for a few seconds in a microwave or under a grill.

VARIATIONS
- For an even better soup, use the recipe for Duck Consommé (see page 71) instead of the stock. Add or 2 teaspoons of sugar to the soup if you wish.

FREEZING: The soup does not freeze well, but the stock or consommé can be frozen.

• DUCK BROTH
Lightly roast a small duck and save about 450 g/1 lb of the flesh. Use the remaining duck, plus the bones and giblets, to make a very well-flavoured stock. Boil briskly to reduce to 1.2 litres/2 pints (5 cups). Strain, allow to cool and remove all the fat.

Return the stock to the pan with 2 medium, finely diced onions, 2 medium skinned, deseeded tomatoes, several tablespoons finely diced celery and a small sprig of sage. Simmer for 10 minutes.

Add 225 g/8 oz (½ lb) diced potatoes and continue cooking for 15 minutes. Remove the sage and add the finely diced duck with 2 tablespoons (2½ tablespoons) port or Madeira wine. Simmer until the duck is hot, then serve.

FREEZING: The broth does not freeze well, but the stock can be frozen.

Game Soup 1

Cooking time: 40 minutes plus time to make stock
Serves 4

Although a little diced meat from the game can be added to the soup towards the end of the cooking time, this soup is still delicious without meat provided you use a really strong game stock. This can be made from the carcass of game birds or the bones of hare or venison (see page 15).

Metric/Imperial	Ingredients	American
2 medium	onions	2 medium
2 medium	carrots	2 medium
½ small	turnip	½ small
2	celery sticks	2
50 g/2 oz	game dripping or butter	¼ cup
25 g/1 oz	plain (all-purpose) flour	¼ cup
750 ml/1¼ pints	game stock (see page 15)	good 3 cups
1	bouquet garni*	1
150 ml/¼ pint	port or red wine	⅔ cup
1 tablespoon	redcurrant, rowan or apple jelly, or to taste	1¼ tablespoons
to taste	salt and freshly ground black pepper	to taste
about 100 g/4 oz	cooked game, if available	about ¼ lb
To garnish	chopped parsley	

* Use sprigs of tarragon, rosemary and parsley tied together with cotton.

Peel and finely dice the onions, carrots and turnip. Cut the celery into very thin slices. Heat the game dripping or butter and cook the vegetables gently for 10 minutes, stirring well so that they do not discolour. Stir in the flour, then pour in the game stock. Bring to the boil, stirring constantly. Add the bouquet garni, port or red wine, jelly and seasoning to taste. Simmer over a low heat until the jelly has dissolved. Check the flavouring: you may find you need to add a little more jelly. Cover the pan and simmer for 15 minutes. Finely dice the cooked game and add towards the end of this time.

Remove the bouquet garni and serve the soup topped with chopped parsley.

VARIATIONS

- Sieve or liquidize the cooked soup, including any cooked game it contains. If you find the soup is a little thick at this stage, add some more game stock to give a flowing consistency. Reheat and top with parsley and croûtons (see page 305).

- **CREAMED GAME SOUP**

Use only 600 ml/1 pint (2½ cups) stock with 100 g/4 oz (¼ lb) mushrooms. Cook these with the other ingredients. Sieve or liquidize the soup, including any cooked game added, return to the pan with 300 ml/½ pint (1¼ cups) single (light) cream and reheat gently. Garnish with chopped parsley and chopped tarragon, whipped cream and croûtons (see page 305).

FREEZING: This soup freezes very well, but it is better to omit the wine and add this when the soup is reheated.

Game Soup 2

Cooking time: see method
Serves 4 to 6

The flavour of this soup depends upon the particular type of game used. Whatever you choose, always taste game soup critically, for a little sweetening in the form of redcurrant, apple or cranberry jelly often greatly improves the flavour. After this recipe you will find specific hints to add an individual flavour to the particular game being used.

Metric/Imperial	Ingredients	American
1 large	grouse or pheasant or small rabbit	1 large
2 medium	onions	2 medium
2 medium	carrots	2 medium
¼	celery heart	¼
50 g/2 oz	butter	¼ cup
1.8 litres/3 pints	water	7½ cups
1	bouquet garni*	1
1 teaspoon	juniper berries	1 teaspoon
to taste	salt and freshly ground black pepper	to taste
300 ml/½ pint	red wine	1¼ cups

* Use a sprig of thyme, a sprig of parsley and 1 blade of mace tied in muslin.

Cut the grouse, pheasant or rabbit into joints. If using game birds, the giblets can also be cooked to give a stronger flavoured soup. If using rabbit, the offal can also be included. Wash the giblets or offal in plenty of cold water to which a few drops of vinegar have been added.

Peel and chop the onions and carrots; dice the celery. Heat the butter and add the game birds or rabbit. Cook steadily for 10 to 15 minutes, or until golden brown. Add the onions after 10 minutes' cooking. Pour the water into the pan, then add the carrots, celery, bouquet garni, juniper berries and a little seasoning. Bring to the boil, remove any scum that comes to the top of the liquid. Cover the pan, lower the heat and simmer gently until the bird or rabbit is tender. If these are young, the cooking time will be 1 to 1¼ hours; if older and tougher, allow 1¾ to 2 hours.

Strain and reserve the stock, then remove the vegetables and the bird or rabbit. Take the flesh off the bones if you wish, mix with the giblets or offal. Sieve, process or liquidize the meat and vegetables with a little of the stock. Return the purée to the pan with the red wine and enough stock to make a good, creamy consistency. Add extra seasoning if required and reheat. If the flavour of the soup is a little bitter, stir in 1 or 2 tablespoons (1¼ or 2½ tablespoons) redcurrant, apple or cranberry jelly and heat until dissolved.

Many garnishes, including croûtons or dumplings (see pages 305 and 306), can be added to this soup.

VARIATIONS
- Use 3 to 4 quails or other small game birds instead of the game suggested.
- Add 2 tablespoons (2½ tablespoons) glacé cherries or raisins to the soup and heat for a few minutes.

• CREAMY GAME SOUP
Omit the giblets or offal in making the basic soup. Save a little cooked breast from the game birds or rabbit, dice neatly and put on one side for garnish. Sieve or liquidize the soup as above, then return to the pan with 300 ml/½ pint (1¼ cups) double (heavy) cream instead of the red wine. Heat gently, then stir in a little dry sherry just before serving. Top with the diced game.

• HARE SOUP
Follow the main recipe, but use just the legs of a hare: the back (saddle) can be roasted for a main course.

Use the blood of the hare as part of the 1.8 litres/3 pints (7½ cups) of liquid. Cook as per main recipe but allow 2 hours or until the legs are tender. Remove all the flesh, dice a little for garnish and sieve or liquidize the rest with the vegetables.

Return the purée to the saucepan with enough stock to give the desired consistency. Flavour the soup with port rather than red wine, and add several tablespoons redcurrant or crabapple jelly to give a faintly sweet taste.

Garnish the soup with Forcemeat Balls (see page 311) and the diced hare.

• VENISON SOUP
Use 550 g/1¼ lb stewing venison in the main recipe. Add several bacon rashers (slices) and simmer until the venison is tender. Sieve or liquidize all the meat with the vegetables and bacon. Return to the pan with the

strained stock and a little port or Madeira wine. Reheat and flavour with a small amount of French or English mustard and any extra seasoning required.

You may like to add 1 to 2 tablespoons (1¼ to 2½ tablespoons) redcurrant jelly. Garnish with Herb Dumplings (see page 309).

FREEZING: Game soups freeze well, but add any alcohol or cream only when reheating.

Chapter Eight

FRUIT SOUPS

People sometimes express surprise at my enthusiasm for fruit soups as they are not traditional British fare. In fact, you are far more likely to encounter them in Scandinavia or Germany. It was my sister, who lives in Norway, who first introduced me to fruit soup, and since then I have experimented with many different varieties of fruit and been delighted with the results.

If you have any doubt as to the suitability of fruit for soups, consider tomatoes: although we treat them as a vegetable, they are just as much a fruit as apples, bananas and strawberries – all of which form the basis of very pleasant soups. It is, of course, essential to choose the fruits and their accompanying ingredients with care so that the mixture does not taste like a runny dessert. In some recipes I have used chicken stock, which gives a delicate savoury taste. Vegetarians could easily substitute a mellow vegetable stock. A savoury flavour is also achieved in some recipes by combining fruit and vegetables, e.g. Orange and Carrot Soup (see page 274).

Take care not to make fruit soups too sweet: they should be refreshing and stimulate the palate for the rest of the meal.

Nuts are a fruit too, and you will find two recipes based on them in this chapter. The Almond Soup (see page 263) is a good basic recipe which lends itself to many variations. Before serving nut soup, do ask your guests if they can tolerate nuts in order to avoid any allergic reactions.

USING FRUIT JUICE

If the recipe ingredients include fruit juice, this can be obtained in two ways. Rub ripe fruit through a hair or nylon sieve, or liquidize it, then strain through a jelly bag or fine muslin to obtain the juice. If the fruit is not very ripe, cook it lightly with a little, if any, water, then rub it through the sieve or liquidize it and strain as before.

Modern electric mixers have attachments to extract juice from fruit, so if you have this appliance, do make use of it.

GARNISHING FRUIT SOUPS

Herbs, such as mint, rosemary or thyme, make a pleasing garnish and one which adds a little flavour too.

Nuts may also be used, but some of the prettiest decorations on colourful fruit soups are flowers. Use edible ones like rose petals, apple and cherry blossom, borage flowers and primroses. Never use flowers from bulbs with food.

Almond Soup
(Sopa de Almendras)

Cooking time: 20 minutes plus time to make stock
Serves 4 to 6

A soup based on almonds is made in both Spain and Portugal; it has a delicate flavour and is ideal for a light first course.

Metric/Imperial	Ingredients	American
150 g/5 oz	almonds	1 cup
25 g/1 oz	butter	2 tablespoons
25 g/1 oz	plain (all-purpose) flour	¼ cup
600 ml/1 pint	chicken stock (see page 14)	2½ cups
300 ml/½ pint	milk	1¼ cups
¼ teaspoon	ground cinnamon or grated nutmeg	¼ teaspoon
pinch	allspice	pinch
to taste	salt and freshly ground white pepper	to taste
5 tablespoons	dry white wine	6¼ tablespoons

Blanch (skin) the almonds, reserve a few whole ones or slivered almonds (strips) for garnish, then chop the remainder very finely. Heat the butter in a saucepan, stir in the flour, then gradually add the chicken stock and milk. Stir as the liquid comes to the boil and thickens slightly, then add the chopped almonds and cook gently for 5 minutes. Stir in the spices and seasoning. Make sure the soup is no longer boiling, then whisk in the wine. Heat gently, garnish with the reserved almonds and serve.

FREEZING: **Do not freeze.**

QUICK TIP *Buy ready-chopped almonds or use 100 g/4 oz (1 cup) ground almonds instead of whole nuts. In this case, garnish the soup with paprika.*

Apple Soup

Cooking time: 35 to 40 minutes plus time to make stock
Serves 4 to 6

Refreshing apple soups are among the most suitable fruit mixtures to serve at the start of a meal. Apples are a splendid partner to other fruits as they can give a slight 'bite' to fruits that are too bland to serve by themselves. Choose cooking apples with a sharp flavour and add any of the numerous flavourings on page 265.

The use of white stock gives a slight savoury flavour to the soup, but this can be changed as you will see under variations. The stock must be free from any fat.

Metric/Imperial	Ingredients	American
450 g/1 lb	cooking apples, prepared weight	1 lb
1 medium	onion	1 medium
25 g/1 oz	butter	2 tablespoons
1 tablespoon	cornflour (cornstarch)	1¼ tablespoons
900 ml/1½ pints	white stock (see page 15)	3¾ cups
1 tablespoon	lemon juice, or to taste	1¼ tablespoons
to taste	salt and freshly ground black pepper	to taste
1 tablespoon	soft brown sugar, or to taste	1¼ tablespoons
150 ml/¼ pint	double (heavy) cream	⅔ cup
To garnish	1 or 2 red-skinned eating apples	

Peel and core the cooking apples, then cut into dice or slices. Peel and chop the onion. Heat the butter in a pan, mix in the cornflour and stir over a low heat for 2 minutes. Add the stock and lemon juice. Whisk or stir as the liquid comes to the boil. Add the apples and onion with a little seasoning and the sugar. Lower the heat, cover the pan and simmer for 20 minutes. Sieve or liquidize the soup.

If serving hot, return the soup to the saucepan and reheat, but do not allow to boil. Whisk in the cream, then adjust the seasoning and sweetness of the soup. Serve garnished with finely diced unpeeled eating apples and/ or croûtons (see page 305).

If serving cold, allow the soup to become completely cold. Whisk in the cream, taste and adjust the seasoning and sweetness. Garnish with the apple and serve with semi-sweet biscuits.

VARIATIONS

● Instead of stock, use half white wine or dry cider and half water.

● **CURRIED APPLE SOUP**
Add ½ teaspoon ground cinnamon and ¼ teaspoon ground cloves to the main recipe.

● **GINGER APPLE SOUP**
Add 1 teaspoon grated root ginger to the soup and omit the lemon juice.

● **SPICED APPLE SOUP**
Add ½ to 1 teaspoon ground cinnamon and ¼ to ½ teaspoon ground cloves to the ingredients in the main recipe. The lemon can be retained or omitted.

● **APPLE AND APRICOT SOUP**
Omit the onion in the main recipe. Use 350 g/12 oz (¾ lb) apples (weight when peeled and cored) and 225 g/8 oz (½ lb) halved fresh apricots. Use water, or half water and half white wine, instead of stock.

● **APPLE AND ELDERBERRY SOUP**
Use 350 g/12 oz (¾ lb) apples (weight when peeled and cored) and 100 g/ 4 oz (¼ lb) elderberries in the main recipe. The white stock blends well with this mixture of fruits, but you can also use water or three-quarters water and a quarter red wine.

The main recipe is delicious flavoured with a spray of elderflowers. Cook these with the apples and liquid but remove them before sieving or liquidizing the soup.

● **APPLE AND MELON SOUP**

Follow the main recipe, but omit the onion and use water or half water and half white wine instead of stock. Use 225 g/8 oz (½ lb) apples (weight when peeled and cored) and 350 g/12 oz (¾ lb) diced melon. You may like to increase the amount of lemon juice slightly or flavour this soup with a little ground ginger or grated root ginger.

● **APPLE AND ORANGE SOUP**

Use 350 g/12 oz (¾ lb) apples (weight when peeled and cored) plus 1 tablespoon (1¼ tablespoons) finely grated orange zest. Add the zest to the liquid when cooking the soup. Sieve or liquidize the pulp of 2 large oranges with the apple mixture. Garnish with orange segments.

Alternatively, sieve the flesh of 2 large oranges with the cooked apples.

FREEZING: All these soups freeze well, but do not add the cream until reheating the soup, or until it has defrosted if serving cold.

Apricot and Apple Soup

Cooking time: 25 minutes
Serves 4 to 6

This is an interesting combination of flavours which produces a most refreshing cold soup, although it can be served hot (see variations).

Metric/Imperial	Ingredients	American
350 g/12 oz	fresh apricots, prepared weight	¾ lb
225 g/8 oz	cooking apples, prepared weight	½ lb
1 tablespoon	lemon juice	1¼ tablespoons
600 ml/1 pint	water	2½ cups
to taste	sugar	to taste
To garnish	1 dessert apple soured cream	

Halve the apricots and remove the stones. Peel, core and thinly slice the apples. Put the two fruits into a saucepan with the lemon juice and water. Cover the pan and simmer steadily until the fruit is tender. Remove a few

Fruit Soups • 267

apricot halves and thinly slice these for garnish. Add sugar to taste to the fruit mixture. Sieve or liquidize and chill well.

Dice the apple finely and add to the soup with the sliced apricots. Top with the soured cream.

VARIATIONS

- The recipe on page 266 produces a soup that has a fairly thick consistency, although this will vary with the juiciness of the fruits. The amount of liquid can be increased but it is better to add this after sieving or liquidizing the mixture.
- If the soup is to be served hot, it tastes better with a stronger flavoured liquid. Use fat-free chicken stock (see page 14) or half white wine or cider and half water instead of all water.

• CREAMY APRICOT AND APPLE SOUP

Follow the main recipe but use only 450 ml/¾ pint (scant 2 cups) water in which to cook the fruits. Liquidize the soup with 300 ml/½ pint (1¼ cups) single (light) cream or soured cream. These proportions can also be used with the variations that follow.

If serving hot, heat the ingredients with great care so that the soup does not curdle. Never allow it to boil.

• CURRIED APRICOT AND APPLE SOUP

Add 1 teaspoon curry paste to the ingredients in the main recipe or the variations below.

• APRICOT SOUP

Follow the main recipe, but use 450 g/1 lb apricots (weight when stoned) and omit the apples.

This soup has more flavour if 450 ml/¾ pint (scant 2 cups) of water is mixed with 150 ml/¼ pint (⅔ cup) white wine.

• APRICOT AND ORANGE SOUP

Omit the apples in the main recipe and use the pulp of 3 large oranges instead. These should be free from any pips, skin or pith.

Garnish the soup with the soured cream and fine shreds of orange peel.

FREEZING: All these soups freeze well, but do not freeze the garnish.

Avocado Soup 2

Cooking time: 10 minutes plus time to make stock
Serves 4 to 6

Avocados have long been popular as a first course, but little known as a soup. Their distinctive flavour makes them an ideal fruit for this purpose. The chicken stock must be free of fat (see page 12). Take care if using chicken stock cubes as their flavour must not overpower the fruit.

Metric/Imperial	Ingredients	American
2 tablespoons	lemon juice	2½ tablespoons
2 large	ripe avocados	2 large
450 ml/¾ pint	chicken stock (see page 14)	scant 2 cups
150 ml/¼ pint	single (light) cream	⅔ cup
150 ml/¼ pint	yoghurt	⅔ cup
to taste	salt and freshly ground black pepper	to taste
few drops	Tabasco sauce	few drops
few drops	soy sauce (optional)	few drops
To garnish	finely chopped tomato	

Put the lemon juice into a basin. Halve the avocados, remove the skin and stones, and mash the pulp with the lemon juice. Sieve the mixture and mix with the stock. (This may be done in a liquidizer or food processor.)

Bring the soup to boiling point, remove from the heat and whisk in the cream and yoghurt. Heat gently without boiling, then add the seasoning and two sauces.

Garnish with the tomato and serve at once.

VARIATIONS
- To serve cold, add the cold stock, cream, yoghurt and flavouring to the mashed avocados. Chill and garnish just before serving.

● AVOCADO PRAWN SOUP

Use either fish stock or delicately flavoured chicken stock in the main recipe. Add about 100 g/4 oz (⅔ cup) small or finely chopped prawns (shrimp) to the soup with the cream and yoghurt.

Flaked white crabmeat could be used instead of prawns.

FREEZING: **Do not freeze.**

Mexican Banana Soup (Sopa de Platano)

Cooking time: 25 minutes plus time to make stock
Serves 4 to 6

Knowing my fondness for bananas, a friend told me about an interesting soup based on this fruit that she had tasted in Mexico. Her description was vague but inspired me to experiment, and this is the result. I cannot claim it is a classic Mexican recipe, but it tastes good. One thing my friend stressed was that the bananas must be very firm, certainly not over-ripe.

Metric/Imperial	Ingredients	American
1 large	green pepper	1 large
1 medium	onion	1 medium
4 medium	tomatoes	4 medium
1 tablespoon	olive oil	1¼ tablespoons
1 litre/1¾ pints	chicken stock (see page 14)	scant 4½ cups
225 g/8 oz	bananas, weight when peeled	½ lb
2 tablespoons	lemon juice, or to taste	2½ tablespoons
few drops	Tabasco sauce, or to taste	few drops
to taste	salt and freshly ground white pepper	to taste
To garnish	whipped cream	

Halve the pepper lengthwise and remove the core and seeds. Place rounded side uppermost, under a preheated grill until the skin becomes black (see page 152). Peel, then finely dice the flesh. Peel and finely dice the onion. Skin, halve and deseed the tomatoes, then chop the pulp into small neat pieces.

Heat the olive oil in a pan, add the onion and cook gently for 5 minutes. Add the stock and bring to the boil. Mash the bananas with the lemon juice until perfectly smooth. Stir into the stock and heat well. Add the diced pepper, tomatoes, Tabasco and a little seasoning. Simmer for 10 minutes. Serve the soup hot or cold topped with a little whipped cream.

VARIATION

● Add 1 teaspoon curry paste or powder to the soup instead of the Tabasco sauce.

FREEZING: **Do not freeze.**

Chestnut Cream Soup

Cooking time: 40 minutes plus time to make stock
Serves 4 to 6

There are many ways of using chestnuts in a soup. This particular recipe gives a rich, creamy mixture.

Metric/Imperial	Ingredients	American
450 g/1 lb	chestnuts	1 lb
2 medium	onions	2 medium
50 g/2 oz	butter	¼ cup
900 ml/1½ pints	chicken stock (see page 14)	3¾ cups
to taste	salt and freshly ground black pepper	to taste
150 ml/¼ pint	milk	⅔ cup
150 ml/¼ pint	single (light) cream	⅔ cup
2 tablespoons	dry sherry	2½ tablespoons
To garnish	paprika chopped parsley croûtons (see page 305)	

Wash the chestnuts and cut a cross into the rounded end. Put into water, boil for 8 to 10 minutes, then strain. Remove the outer shells and brown skins when sufficiently cool to handle.

Peel and roughly chop the onions. Heat the butter, add the onions and cook for 5 minutes. Add the chicken stock and chestnuts with a little seasoning, cover the pan and simmer for 15 minutes. Sieve or liquidize the mixture and return to the pan with the milk and cream. Bring to simmering point and cook for 10 minutes. Whisk the sherry into the hot, but not boiling, soup, simmer for 1 minute only, then garnish and serve.

VARIATION

- For a richer soup, use 300 ml/½ pint (1¼ cups) single (light) cream and omit the milk.

FREEZING: This soup freezes well, but do not add cream or sherry until the soup is being reheated.

QUICK TIP *Use 350 g/12 oz (¾ lb) canned unsweetened chestnut purée instead of fresh chestnuts. Simmer the onions in the stock for 10 minutes, then sieve or liquidize the mixture for an absolutely smooth soup (this is not essential). Add the chestnut purée, milk and cream. Season to taste and heat well, then whisk in the sherry as above.*

Norwegian Fruit Soup (Frugt Suppe)

Cooking time: 30 minutes or 1 hour
Serves 4 to 6

This is one of the most interesting hot fruit soups. The juice can be made from any fruit, but those with a sharp flavour, such as cooking apples, oranges or grapefruit, dark plums or berry fruits, are the nicest because they make a good contrast to the oats and prunes. Details of making fruit juice appear on page 262.

Metric/Imperial	Ingredients	American
100 g/4 oz	dried prunes	¼ lb
900 ml/1½ pints or 1.2 litres/2 pints	water, see method	3¾ cups or 5 cups
50 g/2 oz	rolled oats	good ½ cup
450 ml/¾ pint	unsweetened fruit juice	scant 2 cups
2 tablespoons	caster sugar	2½ tablespoons

If using tenderized prunes, place them in 900 ml/1½ pints (3¾ cups) of water and simmer for 20 minutes. If using non-tenderized prunes, place them in 1.2 litres/2 pints (5 cups) of water, soak overnight, then simmer for about 50 minutes.

Lift the prunes from the liquid, remove the stones, then return the fruit to the liquid. Place the pan over the heat, add the rolled oats and stir as the soup comes to the boil. Cook for 5 minutes, stirring briskly until thickened. Add the fruit juice and sugar, stir until the sugar has dissolved, then heat for a few minutes only and serve.

FREEZING: This soup freezes well. Do not overcook the oats, as they continue cooking when the soup is reheated.

Orange Soup

Cooking time: 15 minutes plus time to make stock
Serves 4

This rather unusual and very simple soup is equally good served hot or well chilled. A fat-free chicken stock is essential for this recipe.

Metric/Imperial	Ingredients	American
1 medium	onion	1 medium
450 ml/¾ pint	chicken stock (see page 14)	scant 2 cups
½ teaspoon	ground cinnamon, optional	½ teaspoon
450 ml/¾ pint	orange juice	scant 2 cups
150 ml/¼ pint	dry white wine	⅔ cup
to taste	salt and freshly ground black pepper	to taste
To garnish	1 orange	

Peel and finely chop the onion. Place in a saucepan with the stock and cinnamon, then cover and simmer for 10 to 15 minutes, or until the onion is very soft.

If serving hot, strain the stock and return to the pan. Add the orange juice and wine, together with any seasoning required, and bring just to boiling point. Meanwhile, cut away the skin and pith from the orange and chop the pulp into neat pieces, free from skin and pips. Add to the soup just before serving.

If serving cold, strain the stock, allow it to become completely cold, then mix with the orange juice and wine. Garnish as above.

VARIATIONS

- Pare the rind from 2 large oranges, avoiding the bitter white pith. Squeeze the juice from the fruit. Increase the amount of stock to 600 ml/1 pint (2½ cups). Simmer the rind in the stock with the onion for 15 minutes, then strain and blend with the juice of the oranges.
- To make a vegetarian soup use water or vegetable stock instead of chicken stock.

● **ORANGE AND MINT SOUP**

Add a sprig of mint to the stock instead of cinnamon. Garnish the soup with orange pieces and a little finely chopped mint.

● **ORANGE AND TOMATO SOUP 1**

Use tomato juice instead of chicken stock in the main recipe.

● **ORANGE AND YOGHURT SOUP**

Follow the main recipe or either of the variations, but blend 150 ml/¼ pint (⅔ cup) yoghurt with the mixture just before adding the white wine.

DO NOT FREEZE: This soup is better freshly made, but frozen orange juice could be used.

Orange and Carrot Soup

Cooking time: 15 minutes
Serves 4

This soup, and the variations that follow, are based on a mixture of fruit and vegetables. Use young tender carrots and grate or dice them finely to shorten the cooking time.

Metric/Imperial	Ingredients	American
350 g/12 oz	carrots, peeled weight	¾ lb
1 medium	onion	1 medium
600 ml/1 pint	water	2½ cups
to taste	salt and freshly ground white pepper	to taste
1 tablespoon	finely grated orange rind	1¼ tablespoons
300 ml/½ pint	orange juice	1¼ cups
To garnish	orange segments yoghurt watercress or mint leaves	

Peel and grate or dice the carrots; peel and finely chop the onion. Bring the water to the boil, add the carrots and onion with a very little seasoning and the orange rind. Cover the pan and cook steadily for 10 minutes or until the vegetables are tender. Sieve or liquidize the ingredients.

If serving hot, return the ingredients to the pan, add the orange juice and heat quickly. Adjust the seasoning and serve garnished with very small pieces of orange segment, a little yoghurt and watercress leaves.

If serving cold, allow the carrot mixture to become completely cold, then add the chilled orange juice. Season to taste and garnish as above, using mint instead of watercress leaves. Chill well before serving.

VARIATIONS
- To give a stronger flavour to the soup use fat-free chicken stock (see page 14) or add a small sprig of thyme or lemon thyme when cooking the carrots.

- **CITRUS CARROT SOUP**

Follow the main recipe, but use only 1 teaspoon grated orange rind with 2 teaspoons grated lemon rind. Use 2 tablespoons (2½ tablespoons) lemon juice and only 250 ml/8 fl oz (1 cup) orange juice.

Serve hot or cold and garnish as above.

- **MELON AND CARROT SOUP**

Use only 225 g/8 oz (½ lb) carrots and the pulp of a medium-sized melon. Cook the carrots and onion with the same amount of water as in the main recipe. Sieve or liquidize the mixture with most of the melon, then add 2 tablespoons (2½ tablespoons) lemon juice and 150 ml/¼ pint (⅔ cup) dry white wine or orange juice, or a mixture of the two.

Serve hot or cold garnished with small, neat pieces of melon and watercress or mint leaves, but no yoghurt.

FREEZING: The vegetable purée can be frozen without the orange juice, so this is added freshly, when the carrot mixture has defrosted. The purée may separate during freezing, so whisk well or liquidize again before using.

QUICK TIP *These soups can be cooked on full power in a microwave. As the cooking time is short, the amount of liquid need not be reduced.*

Strawberry Soup

No cooking
Serves 4 to 6

Strawberries may seem an unlikely basis for a soup, but the flavour is excellent. The fruit should be ripe, but not over-ripe, and a minimal amount of sugar is added.

If you have access to wild strawberries, do use them as they have an especially delicious taste.

Metric/Imperial	Ingredients	American
450 g/1 lb	strawberries	1 lb
900 ml/1½ pints	milk	3¾ cups
to taste	sugar	to taste
To garnish	small strawberries or lemon slices	

Hull the fruit, then sieve it, mix with the cold milk and add sugar to taste. Alternatively, liquidize or process the fruit with the milk, then add the sugar. Chill well before serving. Float small strawberries or lemon slices on the soup just before serving. Serve with plain biscuits or crackers.

VARIATIONS

• Use half milk and half white wine or cider.

• **FROSTED STRAWBERRY SOUP**
Pour the mixture into freezing trays or a suitable container. Freeze lightly, then stir well and return to the freezer. Always remove from the freezer about 15 minutes before serving.

FREEZING: It is better to freeze the strawberry purée alone and mix it with the milk after defrosting.

Summer Berry Soup

Cooking time: 30 minutes
Serves 4 to 6

In the past many savoury soups were thickened with tapioca or sago, which are unfashionable products these days. The sago in this Danish recipe goes well with the lovely mixture of summer fruits, but you can use rice if you prefer.

Metric/Imperial	Ingredients	American
450 g/1 lb	mixed berry fruits, see method	1 lb
600 ml/1 pint	water	2½ cups
600 ml/1 pint	rosé wine	2½ cups
50g/2 oz	caster sugar, or to taste	¼ cup
2 tablespoons	lemon juice, or to taste	2½ tablespoons
50 g/2 oz	sago	⅓ cup

Prepare a selection of raspberries, strawberries and loganberries with a few redcurrants or blackcurrants.

Bring the water and wine to the boil, add the sugar and lemon juice, then tip in the sago. Stir well and simmer for 15 to 20 minutes, or until the sago is almost cooked. Add the fruits and continue cooking for 5 minutes or until the fruits are softened but still a good shape. Chill well before serving.

VARIATION
• Use long-grain rice instead of sago.

DO NOT FREEZE

Chapter Nine

COLD SOUPS

There is something very inviting about hot soup, particularly on a cold day. People smile in anticipation of its warming effect and comforting flavour. Mention cold soups, however, and the reaction is rather different. People may express polite interest, but rarely enthusiasm.

If you are among the sceptics, I hope the recipes in this chapter will change your mind. Cold soups are not just for hot weather, although they are very appropriate at that time; they can be served throughout the year and are invaluable to busy cooks as they can be prepared well in advance.

Cold soups must have a really good flavour or they risk being insipid. Think of colourful Spanish Gazpacho and its exciting combination of ingredients, or cool Vichyssoise with its delicate flavour. Both are captivating dishes, whatever the weather.

Consommés, although delicious hot, are wonderfully refreshing cold, or even jellied and lightly frosted. Suggestions for making and serving these appear on pages 294 to 295.

The consistency of cold soups is important. In those that are equally good hot or cold, it may be necessary to adapt the consistency slightly. It may be perfect when the soup is hot but if it has been thickened by making a purée or adding flour, soups become slightly thicker when cold. You may therefore have to add a little extra stock, milk or wine. Taste and judge what is the best ingredient to incorporate into the soup.

Just as it is important to serve a hot soup really hot, it is equally important to ensure that cold soups are served really cold in well-chilled containers.

Chilled Cucumber and Cheese Soup

No cooking
Serves 4 to 6

The ingredients for this soup are similar to those in Cucumber and Mint Soup (see page 281) except the amount of mint is reduced and some cheese is used instead. Delicately flavoured cheese is best for this cold soup. A recipe for a hot version appears on page 119.

Metric/Imperial	Ingredients	American
½ large	cucumber	½ large
100 g/4 oz	soft cream cheese	¼ lb
1 teaspoon	chopped mint	1 teaspoon
300 ml/½ pint	milk	1¼ cups
450 ml/¾ pint	yoghurt	scant 2 cups
to taste	salt and freshly ground white pepper	to taste
to taste	little English or French mustard	to taste
To garnish	chopped parsley or chervil	
	chopped chives	

Remove most of the peel from the cucumber, but retain about 5 cm/2 inches to give a delicate green colour to the soup. Slice the cucumber, place in a liquidizer or food processor with the rest of the ingredients and purée until smooth. Chill and serve garnished in chilled soup cups.

VARIATIONS
- For a stronger taste, increase the amount of cheese to 225 g/8 oz (½ lb).
- Camembert cheese is an excellent alternative to cream cheese.

- **CHILLED CELERY AND CHEESE SOUP**
The mint can be omitted from the main recipe. Use the heart from a medium-sized head of celery instead of cucumber. Chop and use raw, or

steam until just tender, then leave until cold. Liquidize with the other ingredients. Garnish with a few celery leaves and finely chopped chives.

- Use 225 g/8 oz (½ lb) diced celeriac (weight when peeled) instead of celery.

- **CHILLED COURGETTE SOUP**
Omit the mint in the main recipe. Use 350 g/12 oz (¾ lb) young courgettes (zucchini) instead of cucumber. Cut away the tough ends of the washed courgettes but do not peel. Use raw, or slice and steam until just tender, then leave until cold.

    A stronger flavoured cheese is required with courgettes. Use grated Cheddar or Gruyère cheese, or crumbled Stilton and liquidize with the other ingredients. Garnish with small pieces of tomato and chopped chives.

- **CHILLED FENNEL AND CHEESE SOUP**
Omit the mint in the first recipe. Use 1 good-sized fennel bulb or 2 smaller ones instead of cucumber, together with the cream cheese and the other ingredients. Liquidize until smooth, then chill. Garnish with chopped fennel leaves.

    Fennel has a very distinct flavour, and a creamy goat's cheese makes a good partner to the vegetable.

FREEZING: **Do not freeze any of these recipes.**

Cucumber and Mint Soup

No cooking
Serves 4

This recipe, and the variations that follow, give wonderful cold soups which are light and refreshing. Retain about 5 cm/2 inches of the cucumber skin to give a delicate colour to the soup. If you use too much, the soup tends to taste slightly bitter. Use low-fat yoghurt to lower the calorie content of this recipe.

Metric/Imperial	Ingredients	American
½ large	cucumber	½ large
3 teaspoons	chopped mint	3 teaspoons
300 ml/½ pint	milk	1¼ cups
450 ml/¾ pint	yoghurt	scant 2 cups
to taste	salt and freshly ground white pepper	to taste
To garnish	mint leaves finely chopped chives	

Peel most of the cucumber (see introduction above). Cut into slices and place in a liquidizer or food processor with the other ingredients. Purée until perfectly smooth, then chill well. Garnish and serve.

VARIATIONS

- To give slightly more flavour to the soup add about 6 spring onions (scallions).
- For a richer taste, use single (light) cream instead of milk.

- **CELERY AND MINT SOUP**
Use the heart from a medium-sized head of celery instead of the cucumber. Chop the stalks and reserve a few tender celery leaves for garnish. The celery can be used raw, or steamed until just tender, then left until cold. Liquidize with the other ingredients given above, including most of the mint. Garnish with mint leaves and celery leaves rather than chives.

Another version of this cold soup can be made without the mint. Add several spring onions (scallions) and chopped chives to the other ingredients. Garnish with a little cream, rings of spring onion and chopped chives.

Use 225 g/8 oz (½ lb) diced celeriac (weight when peeled) instead of celery.

• **CHILLED COURGETTE SOUP**

Use 350 g/12 oz (¾ lb) small young courgettes (zucchini) instead of cucumber. Cut the tough ends from the washed vegetables but do not peel. Use raw, or slice and steam until just tender, then leave until cold. Liquidize with the other ingredients. Garnish with chopped chives.

Mint can be used to flavour the soup, or substitute 2 tablespoons (2½ tablespoons) finely chopped spring onions (scallions) plus 3 teaspoons chopped parsley or chervil, 1 teaspoon chopped tarragon and 3 teaspoons chopped chives. If using the mixed herbs, save a few to garnish the soup.

• **CHILLED FENNEL SOUP**

Use 1 good-sized fennel bulb or 2 smaller ones instead of the cucumber. Omit the mint leaves and use chopped fennel leaves instead. Slice the fennel and liquidize with the other ingredients in the main recipe. Garnish with browned flaked almonds or chopped fennel leaves.

FREEZING: **Do not freeze any of these soups.**

Gazpacho

No cooking
Serves 4 to 6

This famous Spanish soup is delicious throughout the year, but is at its best when the tomatoes are beautifully fresh. Like many classic recipes, there are several versions, and each area of Spain feels that its version is the best. The recipe below is one I have used for many years, and includes some of the variations I have enjoyed. It contains less olive oil than many versions, but do use best quality extra virgin olive oil nonetheless.

Metric/Imperial	Ingredients	American
900 ml/1½ pints	water	3¾ cups
675 g/1½ lb	ripe tomatoes	1½ lb
1 medium	cucumber	1 medium
2 medium	Spanish or red onions	2 medium
2	garlic cloves	2
2 tablespoons	extra virgin olive oil	2½ tablespoons
1 tablespoon	lemon juice, or to taste	1¼ tablespoons
to taste	salt and freshly ground black pepper	to taste
To top the soup	½ small cucumber	
	2 small Spanish or red onions	
	1 small red pepper	
	1 small green pepper	
	100 g/4 oz (¼ lb) bread	

Chill the water until required. If you intend sieving the soup, you can use the tomatoes whole. If using a liquidizer or food processor and you want a completely smooth soup, it is advisable to skin, halve and deseed (concass) the tomatoes, then chop the pulp. Peel the cucumber, onions and garlic and chop into small pieces.

Sieve all these ingredients, pound until smooth, or liquidize or process until smooth. Gradually blend in the olive oil, lemon juice and seasoning, then add sufficient chilled water to make a flowing consistency. The soup should not be too thick, for the rest of the ingredients add bulk. Pour into a tureen or glass bowl and refrigerate until required.

Meanwhile, peel and finely dice the cucumber and onions. Deseed and dice the peppers. Trim the crusts from the bread and cut the crumb into neat dice. These ingredients can be placed in small bowls around the tureen, or sprinkled on top of the soup immediately before serving.

VARIATIONS

- The onions chosen have a fairly mild flavour but spring onions (scallions) could be substituted.
- To emphasize the tomato flavour add 2 tablespoons (2½ tablespoons) tomato purée (paste).
- Chicken or veal stock, absolutely free from fat (see pages 14 and 15), could be used instead of water.
- Instead of diced bread, top the soup with crisp croûtons (see page 305).
- Add ½ to 1 teaspoon cumin powder and/or a few drops of Tabasco sauce to the other ingredients.
- Sieve or liquidize ½ a green and ½ a red pepper with the rest of the ingredients.
- A less classic version of this soup includes a ripe avocado sieved or liquidized with the other ingredients.

- **MALAGA GAZPACHO**

Simmer 1 chopped onion and 2 chopped garlic cloves in 1.2 litres/2 pints (5 cups) good white stock (see page 15) for 30 minutes. Strain the stock and cool. Mix with 450 g/1 lb peeled, seeded and chopped tomatoes, 1 peeled and finely diced small cucumber, 1 diced red pepper, 1 diced green pepper and 5 tablespoons (6¼ tablespoons) cooked rice. A small amount of finely chopped spring onions (scallions) could also be added. Season well and flavour with lemon juice. Olive oil is not necessary in this soup, but a little could be incorporated. Chill very well before serving. No topping ingredients are added to this soup.

FREEZING: The puréed tomatoes and other ingredients can be frozen, but the topping ingredients in the classic soup should be freshly prepared so that they keep their firm texture. The Malaga Gazpacho should not be frozen.

QUICK TIP *Prepare the cucumber and onions as in the main recipe, then pound, sieve or liquidize and blend with enough tomato juice to make a flowing consistency. Gradually add a little lemon juice and seasoning, plus a little olive oil, if you wish. Some of the ingredients suggested in the variations would improve this particular version of gazpacho.*

Guacamole Soup

No cooking
Serves 4

This soup, based on the famous Mexican dip, contains avocados, garlic, tomatoes and peppers to make a piquant and refreshing cold soup. If the ingredients are liquidized, the peppers and onions need not be diced very finely, except those used for garnish. If pounded or sieved, it is easier to obtain a smooth mixture if the ingredients are cut into very small pieces. If soya milk is used, this becomes a strictly vegetarian soup.

Metric/Imperial	Ingredients	American
3 or 4	garlic cloves	3 or 4
½	red pepper	½
½	green pepper	½
2 large	tomatoes	2 large
2 tablespoons	lemon juice	2½ tablespoons
2 large	ripe avocados	2 large
3 tablespoons	chopped spring onions (scallions)	4 tablespoons
750 ml/1¼ pints	milk or soya milk (see page 29)	good 3 cups
few drops	Tabasco sauce	few drops
to taste	salt and freshly ground black pepper	to taste

Peel and chop the garlic cloves; deseed and dice the peppers; skin, deseed and chop the tomatoes. Put the lemon juice into a bowl, then halve the avocados, remove the stones and scoop the flesh into the lemon juice to prevent discoloration. Sieve, pound or liquidize the garlic, half the peppers, the tomatoes, avocados and lemon juice and half the spring onions. Gradually mix in the milk, Tabasco sauce and seasoning.

Chill well. Serve topped with the remaining peppers and spring onions.

DO NOT FREEZE

Cold Mulligatawny Soup

Cooking time: as specific recipe, see below
Serves 4 to 6

This is one of my favourite cold soups. The hot spicy flavour is lessened slightly by adding cream or yoghurt, and the colourful garnish makes it look most inviting.

Metric/Imperial	Ingredients	American
	as Mulligatawny Soups (see pages 229 and 253)	
300 ml/½ pint	single or double (light or heavy) cream or yoghurt	1½ cups
To garnish	1 red pepper	
	1 green pepper	
	1 yellow pepper	

Prepare either of the soups and allow to become completely cold. Sieve or liquidize the soup and mix with the cream or yoghurt. Chill well.

Deseed the peppers and cut into very small pieces. Sprinkle a little on each portion of soup immediately before serving and place the remainder in a dish so everyone can add more if wanted.

FREEZING: This soup freezes well, but add the cream or yoghurt only when defrosted.

Russian Cucumber Soup (Okrochka)

Cooking time: 10 minutes plus time to make stock
Serves 4 to 6

This is a sustaining cold soup, which would be ideal for a light meal in summertime. The mixture of two different stocks may sound troublesome but they and the wine make a good alternative to the *kvass* (a drink produced from fermented rye bread) which would be used in Russia. If using stock cubes, be sparing with them so that their flavour does not overpower the other ingredients.

Metric/Imperial	Ingredients	American
300 ml/½ pint	chicken stock (see page 14)	1¼ cups
300 ml/½ pint	beef stock (see page 14)	1¼ cups
300 ml/½ pint	white wine	1¼ cups
1 small	bunch mint	1 small
2	eggs	2
1 medium	cucumber	1 medium
2 small	pickled gherkins	2 small
225 g/8 oz	cooked chicken	½ lb
1 teaspoon	French mustard	1 teaspoon
to taste	salt and freshly ground black pepper	to taste
150 ml/¼ pint	yoghurt or soured cream	⅔ cup
4 tablespoons	sliced spring onions (scallions)	5 tablespoons
To garnish	chopped dill	

Chill the two stocks well, then mix with the white wine and add the mint. Place in the refrigerator. Hard-boil, shell and chop the eggs. Peel the cucumber and cut into 6 mm/¼ inch dice. Thinly slice the gherkins. Cut the chicken into small, neat pieces. Blend the mustard and a little seasoning with the yoghurt.

Remove the mint from the stock, gently mix all the ingredients together and chill well. Garnish with the dill just before serving.

VARIATION
- Diced cooked meat could be used instead of chicken; try salted silverside or brisket of beef.

FREEZING: **Do not freeze.**

COLD TOMATO SOUPS

The Tomato Soup recipe on page 162 and the Lentil and Tomato Soup variation on page 176 may both be served cold as well as hot. The other variations on pages 160 to 164 are excellent as hot soups but less successful when cold.

Tomato and Apple Soup

Cooking time: 30 minutes
Serves 4 to 6

Choose a really good cooking apple with a pronounced bite for this soup.

Metric/Imperial	Ingredients	American
450 g/1 lb	tomatoes	1 lb
450 g/1 lb	cooking apples, prepared weight	1 lb
1 medium	onion	1 medium
1	garlic clove	1
450 ml/¾ pint	water	scant 2 cups
150 ml/¼ pint	white wine or dry cider	⅔ cup
to taste	salt and freshly ground black pepper	to taste
2 teaspoons	caster sugar, or to taste	to taste
150 ml/¼ pint	single (light) cream	⅔ cup
To garnish	mint or parsley leaves and croûtons (see page 305)	

Skin, seed and chop the tomatoes if you plan to liquidize the soup, but not if you intend to sieve it. Peel, core and slice the apples. Peel the onion and garlic but leave whole. Put the tomatoes, apples, onion and garlic into a pan with the water and wine or cider. Add a very little seasoning and the sugar. Bring to boiling point, lower the heat, then cover the pan and simmer for 20 minutes.

Remove the onion and garlic, which will have imparted a delicate taste to the mixture, then sieve or liquidize the soup. Cool, then add the cream and any extra seasoning or sugar required. Chill and serve topped with the garnish.

VARIATIONS

- Although fresh tomatoes, especially the plum variety, are best in this soup, you can substitute 350 g/12 oz (¾ lb) canned tomatoes or Italian pomodori.
- Slimmers can omit the cream in the recipe and use low-fat yoghurt instead.

• TOMATO AND APRICOT SOUP
Substitute 450 g/1 lb ripe apricots for the apples in the main recipe. Halve and stone the fruit. Add 1 tablespoon (1¼ tablespoons) lemon juice to sharpen the taste of the soup. Follow the main recipe. Garnish with crème fraîche or fromage frais and lemon slices.

When fresh apricots are not available, use 350 g/12 oz (¾ lb) canned apricots in natural juice. Use the juice from the can plus enough water to give 450 ml/¾ pint (scant 2 cups).

Tenderized dried apricots can also be used. Simmer 175 g/6 oz (1½ cups) sliced apricots in 300 ml/½ pint (1½ cups) water until soft; most of this liquid will evaporate. Add to the tomatoes and other ingredients in the main recipe and cook as directed.

• TOMATO AND BEETROOT SOUP
Follow the main recipe, but add 1 small peeled and diced, cooked beetroot to the other ingredients. Garnish with soured cream or yoghurt and chopped chives. The amount of apples can be reduced to 350 g/12 oz (¾ lb).

• TOMATO AND CARROT SOUP
Omit the apples in the main recipe and add 450 g/1 lb young carrots instead. Peel and slice thinly or grate them so that they cook in the same time as the tomatoes. In this variation the onion and garlic can be peeled and chopped, then sieved or liquidized with the other ingredients.

A sprig of chervil and one of rosemary can be added to the other ingredients, but these should be removed before sieving or liquidizing the soup. Garnish with cream or curd cheese plus chopped chives and chervil.

● **TOMATO AND CUCUMBER SOUP**

Substitute 1 large cucumber for the apples in the main recipe. Remove all the peel from the cucumber and cut the flesh into slices. Peel and chop the onion and garlic and add good-sized sprigs of parsley and one of mint to the other ingredients. The sugar can be omitted. Retain the onion and garlic, but remove the herbs before sieving or liquidizing the soup. Top with whipped cream and mint leaves.

This soup can be pleasurably spiced by adding a good pinch of chilli powder or a few drops of Tabasco sauce.

● **TOMATO AND FENNEL SOUP**

Omit the apples in the main recipe and substitute 1 large or 2 medium heads of fennel, weighing about 350 g/12 oz (¾ lb) in total. Cut off the leaves, chop finely and put most of them on one side to garnish the soup. Thinly slice the fennel bulb(s), add to the tomatoes and continue as before. In this variation the onion and garlic can be peeled and chopped, then sieved or liquidized with the rest of the ingredients.

Garnish with soured cream and the chopped fennel leaves.

● **TOMATO AND ORANGE SOUP 2**

Omit the apples in the recipe on page 288 and use 3 large oranges instead. Cut the peel from 1 orange into short, fine shreds the size of matchsticks, and set aside for garnish. Grate sufficient zest to give 1 tablespoon (1¼ tablespoons).

Cut away the peel and pith from the oranges and divide into segments; do this over a basin so no juice is wasted. The segments should be free from skin and pips. Peel the onion and garlic and leave whole. Put the 450 g/1 lb chopped tomatoes, orange segments, grated orange zest plus any orange juice into a saucepan with the onion and garlic. Add 450 ml/¾ pint (scant 2 cups) water, but omit the white wine or cider in the main recipe. Season the ingredients and add 2 teaspoons sugar.

Cook as the main recipe, then remove the onion and garlic and sieve or liquidize the ingredients. Add the cream and chill.

While the soup is cooking, soak the shredded orange rind in water to soften, then drain and use as a garnish on the soup.

FREEZING: All these soups freeze well, but do so without adding the cream. Whisk this into the ingredients when these are defrosted.

Vichyssoise

Cooking time: 20 to 25 minutes plus time to make stock
Serves 4 to 6

This is one of the best known and most delicious cold soups. In order to preserve the fine flavour, it is essential not to overcook the vegetables. Old rather than new potatoes give a better texture to the soup.

Metric/Imperial	Ingredients	American
8 medium	leeks	8 medium
2 medium	potatoes	2 medium
50 g/2 oz	butter	¼ cup
750 ml/1¼ pints	chicken stock (see page 14)	good 3 cups
to taste	salt and freshly ground white pepper	to taste
150 ml/¼ pint	dry white wine	⅔ cup
150 ml/¼ pint	double (heavy) or whipping cream	⅔ cup
To garnish	chopped chives	

Wash and thinly slice the leeks. Peel and dice the potatoes. Heat the butter in a saucepan, add the vegetables and stir for 4 minutes without browning. Pour in the stock, add seasoning and bring to the boil. Lower the heat, cover the pan and simmer gently for 15 to 20 minutes. Allow to become completely cold, then sieve or liquidize with the wine and cream. Chill very well and serve garnished with the chives.

VARIATIONS
- For a vegetarian soup use water or vegetable stock.
- Omit the wine and use 150 ml/¼ pint (⅔ cup) extra stock with a squeeze of lemon juice, or use milk without lemon juice.

- **APPLE VICHYSSOISE**
Omit half the leeks and use a large peeled and diced cooking apple instead.

- **CHICKEN AND COCONUT VICHYSSOISE**
Use only 5 medium-sized leeks and 1 potato. Make certain the chicken stock has a strong flavour. Add 100 g/4 oz (¼ lb) cooked, skinned chicken breast

and 50 g/2 oz (¼ cup) creamed coconut to the other ingredients. Melt the coconut and heat the chicken in the stock just before the vegetables are cooked. Sieve or liquidize and garnish with chopped chives.

● **CUCUMBER VICHYSSOISE**
Omit the leeks and use half a large peeled and diced cucumber instead. A better flavour is given to the soup if several finely chopped spring onions (scullions) are added.

You can use 4 leeks in the main recipe and add just half a peeled and diced large cucumber. Garnish with chives as before.

● **GREEN PEA VICHYSSOISE**
Use only 6 leeks and 1 potato in the main recipe, and add 100 g/4 oz (¾ cup) shelled peas plus a sprig of mint half way through the cooking period. Remove the mint before sieving or liquidizing the soup. Garnish with chives as before.

● **PRAWN VICHYSSOISE**
Use fish stock (see page 16) instead of chicken stock. Add 100 g/4 oz (¼ lb) peeled prawns (shrimps) to the other ingredients when the vegetables are almost cooked. Garnish with whole prawns.

White crabmeat makes an excellent alternative to the prawns.

● **CREAM OF LEEK SOUP (POTAGE CRÈME DE POIREAUX)**
This classic hot French soup uses much the same ingredients as Vichyssoise, but substitute milk for the wine and add 1 medium, finely chopped onion. Cook the soup as above, then sieve or liquidize the ingredients. Reheat, whisk in the cream and heat gently for another few minutes. Garnish as before.

● **WELSH GREEN MILK SOUP**
This is a traditional recipe which uses somewhat similar ingredients to Vichyssoise. It is generally served hot. Use only 4 leeks and 2 small potatoes plus 2 small onions. Dice the onions, leeks and potatoes finely and neatly, as this soup is not sieved or liquidized. Simmer in 450 ml/¾ pint (scant 2 cups) lamb or mutton stock (see page 15) until tender. Meanwhile, make 600 ml/1 pint (2½ cups) White Sauce (see page 28). Gradually mix the vegetables and stock into the sauce, then add a few tablespoons single (light) cream and season to taste. Garnish with chopped parsley.

FREEZING: All the versions of Vichyssoise freeze well, except the last soup, which tends to lose texture when frozen. Whisk or liquidize the soups after defrosting to make sure they are velvety smooth.

 This is an ideal soup for cooking in the microwave.

Watercress Bortsch

Cooking time: to make stock
Serves 4

This is a delicious cold soup. Make it with cooked baby beetroot for a really sweet taste and tender texture.

Metric/Imperial	Ingredients	American
225 g/8 oz	cooked beetroot (beets)	½ lb
1 medium bunch	watercress	1 medium bunch
600 ml/1 pint	beef or chicken stock (see page 14)	2½ cups
300 ml/½ pint	soured cream or yoghurt	1¼ cups
1 tablespoon	lemon juice or white wine vinegar	1¼ tablespoons
to taste	salt and freshly ground white pepper	to taste
To garnish	chopped chives	

Peel and finely dice or coarsely grate the beetroot. Discard the watercress stalks and chop the leaves finely. Whisk or liquidize the cold stock with the soured cream or yoghurt to make a smooth mixture. Add the beetroot, watercress, lemon juice or vinegar and seasoning to taste. Chill well and garnish with the chopped chives just before serving.

DO NOT FREEZE

JELLIED SOUPS

The recipes that follow should be set lightly and not be sufficiently firm to turn out.

Powdered gelatine, which appears in all these recipes, is easy to use: simply sprinkle it on to the cold liquid, allow it to stand for a short time to soften, then dissolve over a pan of hot water or in the microwave. Do not stir the gelatine while it is standing or early in the process of dissolving; doing so tends to move the undissolved powder to the edges of the bowl, where it will harden. Stir briskly when the gelatine appears dissolved to check that the liquid is quite clear, then blend with the remaining ingredients in the recipe.

if you buy gelatine in bulk rather than in sachets (envelopes), use 1 level tablespoon (1¼ level tablespoons) instead of 1 sachet.

Serving Jellied Consommés

- Spoon into chilled soup cups and allow to set lightly. Garnish with small pieces of tomato, cucumber, hard-boiled eggs or chopped herbs, slices of lemon or orange, crème fraîche, mayonnaise or cream cheese. If using two consommés, allow one consommé to set lightly, then spoon over the second one.
- Set in a basin, then whisk until frothy. Spoon into soup cups and garnish.
- Allow to set in a shallow dish, then cut into squares with a sharp knife dipped in hot water. Two kinds of consommé look attractive served this way.

Jellied Consommés

Cooking time: as recipes
Serve as recipes

Metric/Imperial	Ingredients	American
	selected	
	consommé(s)	
	gelatine, as required,	
	see method	

Make one or two consommés. It is interesting to use two flavours rather than just one, e.g. Beef or Chicken with Tomato Consommé (pages 73, 71 and 80).

If the consommé shows no sign of natural setting, allow 11 g/0.4 oz (1 sachet) to each 750 ml/1½ pints (3¾ cups).

If there are signs of light setting, allow 11 g/0.4 oz (1 sachet) to 1.2 litres/2 pints (5 cups).

If the consommé is almost sufficiently stiff, allow 1 teaspoon gelatine to each 750 ml/1½ pints (3¾ cups).

Soften the gelatine in a little cold consommé, allow to stand for 3 minutes, then dissolve over a pan of hot water or in the microwave. Blend with the remaining warm consommé, then add any extra seasoning and flavouring such as sherry or brandy.

FREEZING: Always allow the jelly to set before freezing.

Jellied Gazpacho

No cooking
Serves 6 to 8

This jellied form of Gazpacho (see page 283) makes a very refreshing start to a summer meal. If you have a juice extractor, it would be far nicer to use fresh tomato juice than bottled or canned.

Metric/Imperial	Ingredients	American
900 ml/1½ pints	bottled or canned tomato juice	3¾ cups
2 sachets (22 g/0.8 oz)	gelatine (see page 294)	3 envelopes
1 tablespoon	lemon juice, or to taste	1¼ tablespoons
to taste	salt and freshly ground black pepper	to taste
1 bunch	spring onions (scallions)	1 bunch
1	green pepper	1
½ medium	cucumber	½ medium
2 medium	tomatoes	2 medium

Pour 4 tablespoons (5 tablespoons) of the cold tomato juice into a bowl. Sprinkle the gelatine on top and allow to stand for 3 minutes. Place the bowl over a pan of very hot water or heat in the microwave until the gelatine has completely dissolved. Add to the rest of the tomato juice with the lemon juice and a little seasoning. Put on one side until the mixture becomes like a thick syrup.

Trim and slice the white bulbs of the spring onions; deseed the pepper and chop the pulp into very small dice. Skin half the cucumber and cut the pulp into matchstick pieces; dice the remainder. Skin, halve and deseed the tomatoes, then dice the pulp.

Stir half the chopped spring onions, half the diced pepper, the matchstick pieces of cucumber and half the diced tomatoes into the jelly. Spoon into 6 to 8 glasses or bowls. Leave until lightly set. Top each portion with the reminder of the vegetables. Chill well before serving.

DO NOT FREEZE

ICED SOUPS

A surprising number of soups can be iced, rather than served cold or hot. Take care that they are lightly frozen rather than firm. It is generally wise to bring them out of the freezer about 15 minutes before serving: spoon into the chilled containers and stand these in the refrigerator.

Serving Iced Soups

- Serve in tall chilled sundae rather than soup bowls. Make them look more colourful by adding a rim of finely chopped parsley. Simply brush the rim of the empty container with a little unwhisked egg white, then invert over a bed of chopped parsley: this will adhere to the rim. Chill until ready to add the iced soup.
- Garnishes for iced soups should be well chilled but not iced, unless specified in the recipe.

Iced Cucumber Soup

No cooking
Serves 4 to 6

This is a wonderfully refreshing soup. The chopped herbs add a pale green colour to the mixture, so the cucumber skin, which can taste rather bitter when the soup is iced, can be discarded.

Metric/Imperial	Ingredients	American
1 large	cucumber	1 large
600 ml/1 pint	yoghurt, see Note	2½ cups
1 tablespoon	lemon juice	1¼ tablespoons
3 tablespoons	finely chopped chives	3¾ tablespoons
2 teaspoons	chopped mint	2 teaspoons
1 tablespoon	chopped chervil or parsley	1¼ tablespoons
to taste	salt and freshly ground white pepper	to taste
To garnish	yoghurt mixed chopped herbs	

Peel and slice the cucumber, then sieve or liquidize until smooth. Mix with all the other ingredients. Spoon into a suitable container and freeze slightly. Stir to redistribute the herbs through the cucumber mixture (they may have sunk to the bottom). Freeze again lightly, then serve in chilled bowls, topped with the yoghurt and herbs.

VARIATION
• Slimmers can use low-fat yoghurt or fromage frais.

Note: This soup will not keep well in the freezer for more than 48 hours if low-fat yoghurt or fromage frais is used. Full-cream yoghurt is necessary for longer storage up to one month.

Iced Orange Soup

Cooking time: 10 minutes
Serves 4 to 6

Despite the large quantity of oranges, this soup has a distinctly savoury taste. It can be kept in the freezer for up to 3 months and is ideal for slimmers.

Metric/Imperial	Ingredients	American
4	very large oranges	4
or 6	moderately large oranges	or 6
450 ml/¾ pint	water	scant 2 cups
½	chicken stock cube	½
3 tablespoons	chopped spring onions (scallions)	3¾ tablespoons
2 or 3 drops	Tabasco sauce	2 or 3 drops
1 small	sprig thyme or lemon thyme	1 small
To garnish	orange and lemon slices	

Pare enough zest from the oranges to give 3 level tablespoons (3¾ tablespoons); do not use any bitter white pith. Place in a saucepan with the water, bring to the boil, then lower the heat and simmer for 7 minutes. Do not cover the saucepan; the liquid should evaporate to leave barely 300 ml/½ pint (1¼ cups) of orange-flavoured stock. Remove the zest, then dissolve the stock cube in the hot liquid.

Halve the oranges, scoop out all the flesh and add to the liquid with the other ingredients. Sieve or liquidize the soup. When completely cold, pour into a suitable container and freeze lightly (see page 296). Spoon into serving bowls and garnish with the orange and lemon slices.

Chapter Ten

GARNISHES AND ACCOMPANIMENTS TO SOUPS

The garnishes added to soup should give instant eye-appeal, so choose them carefully to add contrast in colour and texture. Suggestions about suitable garnishes appear at the end of recipes in this book.

The dumplings included in this chapter can also be called a garnish because, besides adding extra food value, they also look very inviting. In addition to the well-known suet variety, this chapter also includes dumplings based on bread and potatoes, which are deliciously light.

In my opinion, nothing is nicer with soup than delicious home-made bread or rolls. If you have never attempted baking your own bread, I hope you will consider changing your mind. It is not hard to make and modern, dried fast-acting yeasts make it a quick and easy process. Do ensure that you use strong (hard) flour, as it is specially milled for this purpose: it helps the dough to rise better and gives a better texture. Once you have tried the basic bread recipe, I'm sure you'll want to try some of the interesting variations, including milk bread, oatmeal bread and French bread.

As a change from bread, why not serve scones or American-style muffins with soup? Both are easy to make and can be flavoured in various ways (see pages 325 and 328).

Crisp toppings, such as croûtons and Melba toast, are familiar accompaniments to soup, but there are many others. Some of my favourites include Bruschetta and Crostini, which are flavoured with garlic and olive oil.

TOPPINGS FOR BREAD AND ROLLS

To give a good shine to the loaves and rolls, mix the yolk of an egg with a little milk or water and brush over the dough before the final proving.

For a moist topping, brush the dough with a little olive oil before the final proving.

Glaze the dough as described above, then sprinkle with rolled oats, wheat flakes, celery seeds, poppy seeds or sesame seeds.

RECIPE MEASUREMENTS

Throughout this book all the recipe ingredients have been carefully measured to give the result that I find most palatable. In most cases you can 'customize' the soups to *your* taste with a little extra butter or herbs. In this chapter, however, it is advisable to follow the recipes exactly, as baking requires a precise balance of ingredients.

Note that the metric conversion of 4 oz, usually given as 100 g, is sometimes converted to 115 g in this chapter, and that 3 oz (usually 75 g) is converted to 85 g. This is intentional and designed to give the best result wherever this occurs.

Spoon measures should always be level, particularly when adding raising agents such as baking powder: too generous a measure can make scones or muffins taste very unpleasant.

Parmesan Cheese Balls (Parmesanboller)

Cooking time: 10 or 3 minutes
Serves 4

Although Parmesan cheese is generally used for these balls, other mature and relatively dry-textured cheeses could be substituted. The soup looks very attractive if quail's eggs are used, and their smaller size makes them easier to eat with a soup spoon.

Metric/Imperial	Ingredients	American
2	hen's eggs	2
	or	
6	quail's eggs	6
25 g/1 oz	butter	2 tablespoons
3 tablespoons	finely grated Parmesan cheese	3¾ tablespoons
to taste	salt and freshly ground white pepper	to taste

Hard-boil and shell the eggs; hen's eggs take just 10 minutes in boiling water, while quail's eggs take 3 minutes. Halve the eggs lengthwise, remove the yolks and mash them. Blend the butter, cheese and seasoning with the egg yolks and form the mixture into very small balls. Place these in the egg whites and float on the soup just before serving.

FREEZING: The Cheese Balls freeze reasonably well if the mashed yolks are well blended with the other ingredients. Do not freeze the egg whites or whole hard-boiled eggs: they become rubbery.

Chicken Balls (Honsekjott Boller)

Cooking time: 8 to 10 minutes
Serves 4 to 8, depending upon the recipe

A speciality of Norwegian cuisine, these chicken balls are an excellent garnish for chicken and other soups. It is important to use uncooked chicken to give the maximum flavour to the mixture.

Metric/Imperial	Ingredients	American
225 g/8 oz	uncooked chicken breast, weight without skin and bone	½ lb
2	egg yolks or	2
1	egg	1
75 g/3 oz	butter, chicken fat or margarine	⅜ cup
2 tablespoons	double (heavy) cream, or amount needed, see method	2½ tablespoons
to taste	salt and freshly ground black pepper	to taste

Finely mince or process the chicken breast. Add the egg yolks or egg, the unmelted butter or other fat and mix very well. Stir in the cream, using a little extra if the chicken flesh is very lean. Season to taste and form into balls about the size of a small olive with the help of a teaspoon.

Fill a deep frying pan with water, bring to the boil and add a little salt. Drop in the balls, cook for 8 to 10 minutes and drain well.

VARIATIONS
- Use breast of turkey instead of chicken.
- Use breast of quail, pheasant or other birds instead of chicken. Game balls are excellent on game soups (see pages 258–261) or Game Consommé (see page 72).

- For a less rich flavour, substitute fromage frais or low-fat yoghurt for the cream.

FREEZING: Place the uncooked or cooked balls on a flat tray, freeze until hard, then pack. There is no need to defrost the mixture before cooking or heating. If uncooked, simmer as directed in the main recipe, or poach for about 12 minutes in the very hot soup. If cooked, poach for 3 or 4 minutes only.

QUICK TIP *Mix all the ingredients in a food processor; take care not to over-process or the ingredients will become too sticky.*

Norwegian Fish Balls (Fiskebollar)

Cooking time: 10 to 12 minutes
Serves 6 to 8, depending upon the recipe

These fish balls, often served as a main course in a creamy sauce, are also a great favourite in Norway. They make an excellent garnish to fish soups, including the Fish Soup and Fish Consommé on pages 209 and 71.

Metric/Imperial	Ingredients	American
450 g/1 lb	white fish, see method, weight when skinned and boned	1 lb
1 tablespoon	cornflour (cornstarch) or potato flour (fécula)	1¼ tablespoons
1 teaspoon	salt, see method	1 teaspoon
15 g/½ oz	butter	1 tablespoon
to taste	freshly ground white pepper	to taste
pinch	ground or grated nutmeg	pinch
1 tablespoon	cream or milk, see method	1¼ tablespoons
To coat and cook the balls		
2 tablespoons	plain (all-purpose) flour	2½ tablespoons
1.2 litres/2 pints	water	5 cups

One of the best fish for this recipe is fresh haddock, but whiting or cod or plaice can be used instead. Finely mince or process the fish, but do not over-process, or it becomes too sticky. Blend with the cornflour or potato flour and the salt. Soften the butter slightly and stir into the fish mixture with the rest of the ingredients, slowly adding enough cream or milk to bind the mixture together. With floured fingers, form the mixture into small balls, about the size of an olive.

Heat the water, add a very little salt and gently poach the fish balls for 10 to 12 minutes. Drain well.

VARIATION

● **SALMON BALLS**

Use fresh salmon instead of white fish. This variation adds colour as well as flavour to a soup.

FREEZING: The quantities in the recipe produce a generous number of fish balls – too many for one meal; but in view of the time it takes to make them, it is worth preparing the whole amount and freezing any surplus uncooked. They tend to lose flavour if cooked before freezing.

Freeze until firm, then pack. Cook in water from frozen.

Croûtons

Cooking time: 5 to 6 minutes
Serves 4 to 6

The quantities below will make enough for 4 to 6 servings. Since croûtons store or freeze very well, it is worth making a large batch.

White bread makes more attractive-looking croûtons, but those made from brown or wholemeal bread have a very good flavour. If anxious to avoid fried foods, bake or toast the croûtons instead, see below.

Metric/Imperial	Ingredients	American
2 large	slices of bread	2 large
For frying		
40 g/1½ oz	butter	3 tablespoons
1 tablespoon	sunflower or olive oil	1¼ tablespoons

Trim off the crusts and cut the crumb into 6 mm/¼ inch dice. Heat the butter and oil in a frying pan, add the diced bread and fry steadily, turning frequently, until golden brown on all sides. Drain on kitchen paper and use immediately, or cool and freeze (see below).

VARIATIONS

● **DEEP-FRIED CROÛTONS**

Heat the oil in a deep fryer to 190°C/375°F. Put the diced bread into a fine-meshed frying basket and cook for 2 minutes or until crisp and golden brown. Drain on kitchen paper and serve immediately or freeze (see below).

• BAKED CROÛTONS 1

Dice the bread and place on ungreased baking trays. Preheat the oven to 180°C/350°F/gas mark 4 and bake the bread for about 12 minutes, or until crisp and golden in colour. If more convenient, cook for about 30 minutes at 150°C/300°F/gas mark 2. There is no need to drain these croûtons. If really dry and crisp, they can be stored in tins or airtight jars.

• BAKED CROÛTONS 2

Toss the diced bread in 1 tablespoon oil or melted butter, then place on baking trays and bake in the oven preheated to 180°C/350°F/gas mark 4. Drain on kitchen paper and serve immediately or freeze (see below).

• TOASTED CROÛTONS

Toast the slices of bread until brown and crisp then cut into small dice. These toasted croûtons are better freshly made.

• GARLIC CROÛTONS

Follow the main recipe or the first variation but add 1 or 2 crushed garlic cloves to the butter and oil.

Another way to incorporate a garlic flavour is to toss the cooked croûtons in a very little garlic salt before serving.

FREEZING: Put the croûtons on flat plates or trays and freeze until firm. Pack and use within 3 months.

Cheese Croûtons

Cooking time: 25 to 30 minutes
Serves 8 to 10

These make an excellent garnish on a variety of soups, especially vegetable soups. It is advisable to use Parmesan cheese because it sticks to the buttered bread better than any other cheese, and its strong flavour means that only a small amount is necessary.

Metric/Imperial	Ingredients	American
5 large	slices of bread, about 1.25 to 2 cm/½ to ¾ inch thick	5 large
75 g/3 oz	butter	⅜ cup
50 g/2 oz	Parmesan cheese, see method	½ cup

Trim off the crusts, then cut the crumb into 1.25 to 2 cm/½ to ¾ inch squares. Melt the butter and finely grate the cheese. Carefully turn the bread in the melted butter, then roll in the grated cheese. If you want a really thick coating, use at least 50 per cent more cheese.

Preheat the baking trays and the oven to 150°C/300°F/gas mark 2. This ensures that the croûtons do not stick to the trays. Arrange the croûtons in a single layer on the trays and bake until golden. Allow to cool.

FREEZING: Open-freeze the croûtons on flat trays, then pack into bags or boxes. (Open-freezing ensures they do not stick together.)

Suet Dumplings

Cooking time: 10 to 15 minutes
Makes 8 to 12

A traditional feature of British cooking, suet dumplings are served with stews and boiled meats. Those added to soups must be much smaller, but the same golden rules apply.

Make sure the mixture is sufficiently moist. If it is the correct consistency, you must form the mixture into small balls with floured fingers. If you can roll the dough into balls without flour, the mixture is too dry, so add a few more drops of water.

Always cook dumplings in rapidly boiling liquid. If it will spoil the soup to boil it, cook the dumplings separately in stock or salted water. They can stay in the hot liquid until ready to serve.

It is now possible to obtain vegetarian suet, so the following recipe is suitable for non-meat eaters.

Metric/Imperial	Ingredients	American
100 g/4 oz	self-raising flour or plain (all-purpose) flour sifted with 1 teaspoon baking powder	1 cup
good pinch	salt	good pinch
50 g/2 oz	shredded suet	¼ cup
to bind	water, see method	to bind

Make sure the stock or water in which the dumplings are to be cooked is boiling.

Sift the flour and salt into a basin, mix in the suet, then gradually add sufficient cold water to make a soft rolling consistency. This will be about 1½ tablespoons (1¾ tablespoons) of water, but makes of flour vary in the amount of moisture they absorb, so add it gradually. Roll into balls with floured fingers. Drop into the boiling liquid and cook until well risen.

VARIATIONS
• Use butter, margarine, beef dripping or chicken fat instead of suet. Rub the fat into the flour, then add the liquid.
• Use half wholemeal (wholewheat) and half white flour.

- **HERB DUMPLINGS**

Follow the main recipe or the variations above, but add 2 tablespoons (2½ tablespoons) finely chopped herbs to the flour.

- **CHEESE DUMPLINGS**

Use only half the amount of suet or other fat suggested and add 2 tablespoons (2½ tablespoons) finely grated Cheddar, Lancashire or other good cooking cheese.

- **TOMATO DUMPLINGS**

Instead of using water, mix the dough with tomato juice or fresh tomato purée made by rubbing chopped tomatoes through a sieve.

FREEZING: The dumplings can be frozen with the soup but not separately.

Sponge Dumplings

Cooking time: 10 to 15 minutes including cooking basic mixture
Makes about 18

This recipe, given to me by an American friend, makes delicious dumplings which have the light consistency of a sponge. They must be cooked in only simmering liquid, so are ideal therefore to cook in the soup itself.

Metric/Imperial	Ingredients	American
5 tablespoons	milk	6 tablespoons
50 g/2 oz	butter	¼ cup
75 g/3 oz	flour	¾ cup
good pinch	salt	good pinch
2	eggs	2

Pour the milk into a saucepan, add the butter and heat for 1 or 2 minutes until the butter has melted. Remove from the heat. Sift the flour and salt; separate the eggs. Add the flour to the pan, stir well, then add the unwhisked egg whites and stir again. Return the pan to a very low heat and cook gently, stirring all the time, until the mixture is thick and comes cleanly away from the sides of the pan. Remove from the heat again, beat the egg yolks and gradually incorporate into the flour mixture.

Check that the soup is simmering gently – it must not be boiling briskly. Drop small spoonfuls of the mixture into the soup and cook for 5 minutes or until well risen and firm.

Liver Dumplings

Cooking time: 12 minutes
Makes 16

Take care not to overcook these dumplings as this will make the liver dry and tough. Serve them on clear soups, poultry soups and vegetable soups.

Metric/Imperial	Ingredients	American
100 g/4 oz	calves' or lamb's liver	¼ lb
25 g/1 oz	butter	2 tablespoons
2 tablespoons	very finely chopped shallot or onion	2½ tablespoons
2 tablespoons	very fine, soft breadcrumbs	2½ tablespoons
50 g/2 oz	self-raising flour or plain (all-purpose) flour sifted with ½ teaspoon baking powder	½ cup
1	egg yolk	1
to taste	salt and freshly ground black pepper	to taste

Finely mince, process or very finely chop the liver; do not over-process, as this makes the meat sticky. Heat the butter, add the shallot or onion and cook for 5 minutes. Mix in the remaining ingredients. Allow to become cold, then form into 16 small balls. If you damp your fingers you will find this helps this process, but if the mixture seems too soft, chill it for a short time, then roll into balls with floured fingers.

These dumplings can be cooked in the soup, in stock (chicken stock is ideal) or in boiling salted water. Make sure the liquid has reached boiling point when adding the dumplings, then lower the heat so the liquid simmers steadily throughout the cooking period. If using liquid, remove from the liquid with a perforated spoon and add to the hot soup.

FREEZING: Open-freeze the cooked dumplings on a flat tray, then pack. Heat for 1 to 2 minutes only in the hot soup.

Forcemeat Balls

Cooking time: 10 to 15 minutes
Makes about 24

These crisp, herb-flavoured balls are generally served with roast poultry or game dishes, but are also excellent in soups, particularly those based on chicken, turkey or game.

Metric/Imperial	Ingredients	American
50 g/2 oz	butter	¼ cup
100 g/4 oz	soft breadcrumbs	2 cups
1½ tablespoons	finely chopped parsley	2 tablespoons
1 teaspoon	finely chopped thyme or ½ teaspoon dried thyme	1 teaspoon
1 teaspoon	finely chopped lemon zest	1 teaspoon
2 teaspoons	lemon juice	2 teaspoons
1	egg yolk	1
to taste	salt and freshly ground black pepper	to taste

Melt the butter, then mix with the other ingredients. If the mixture is a little soft, chill it for a time. Preheat the oven to 200°C/400°F/gas mark 6.

Grease a flat baking tray or line this with baking parchment. Place the balls on the tray and bake for 15 minutes or until crisp and golden on the outside. Add to the soup immediately before serving.

VARIATIONS
- Use shredded suet instead of butter; vegetarian suet is now obtainable.
- Omit the lemon zest and juice. Use 2 teaspoons finely grated orange zest and 2 tablespoons (2½ tablespoons) orange juice. This variation goes well with Duck Consommé (see page 71).

FREEZING: Forcemeat balls freeze well; warm in the oven or microwave without defrosting.

Melba Toast

The orthodox way of making Melba toast is to toast slices of bread on both sides, then split them horizontally to give ultra-thin slices. The untoasted sides are then toasted until crisp and brown.

I find this process somewhat dangerous, even with a good sharp knife and a steady hand. My preferred method is to cut wafer-thin slices of bread and bake them on baking trays in the oven preheated to 180°C/350°F/gas mark 4. After about 10 minutes the slices are really crisp and brown. Serve with butter.

Flavoured Toast

Fingers of savoury toast combine well with many soups. The toast must be freshly made, then spread with butter and topping and served at once.

● ANCHOVY TOAST

Spread the hot toast with a little butter and some anchovy paste.

Instead of anchovy paste, use canned anchovies in oil. Drain and chop the fish and blend with a little unsalted butter. Spread on the bread, cut into fingers and top with chopped parsley.

Cooked fresh anchovies can be used in the same way as the canned variety. Serve with fish soups.

● BRAINS ON TOAST

Wash the (calf's) brain and dry well on kitchen paper. Coat in seasoned flour, then fry in a little hot butter, flavoured with a few drops of vinegar or lemon juice, for 7 to 8 minutes. Place on fingers of hot buttered toast and garnish with cayenne pepper.

Serve with Mock Turtle Soup (see page 88) or meat soups.

● CHEESE ON TOAST

Spread hot toast with a little butter, then add thin slices of Cheddar, Gruyère or other good cooking cheese. Put under a preheated grill for just a few minutes until the cheese melts, then cut into neat fingers.

Herb-flavoured cream cheese can be used instead of sliced cheese, but do not heat this: simply spread on hot toast.

Serve particularly with vegetable soups.

● **PÂTÉ ON TOAST**

Soft liver pâté or fish pâté can be spread neatly on hot, buttered toast, then garnished with small pieces of lemon, orange or tomato. If the pâté is firm, cut in slices to fit the toast.

Tapenade, an anchovy and olive spread from Provence, and similar mixtures, such as Gentleman's Relish, make good toppings on hot toast. They can also be used on fingers of bread and butter.

Bruschetta (Grilled Italian Bread)

Cooking time: a few minutes

This is a simple but delicious Italian delicacy, in which bread is grilled and flavoured with garlic and olive oil.

Metric/Imperial	Ingredients	American
1	Italian loaf	1
1	garlic clove	1
several tablespoons	extra virgin olive oil	several tablespoons

Slice and toast the bread, or prepare it in the oven, as described in Melba Toast (see page 312). Peel the garlic clove, cut across the middle, then rub the cut ends over the hot bread. Drizzle with olive oil and eat at once.

VARIATIONS

● The toasted or oven-baked crisp bread can be topped with the ingredients suggested on page 312. I also like to use finely chopped mixed peppers fried in a little olive oil as a topping. Ricotta cheese is an excellent topping, by itself or under the cooked peppers.

● **Crostini:** is another name given to these slices of toast. Crostini can be flavoured with garlic and oil too or topped with various savoury ingredients.

FREEZING: **Do not freeze.**

Cheese Straws

Cooking time: 7 to 8 minutes
Makes about 30

Cheese straws are the perfect accompaniment to clear soups, particularly consommés. The first recipe is for a rich biscuit, which is very fragile and must be handled carefully. The second recipe still has a good cheese flavour but is much less delicate in texture.

Metric/Imperial	Ingredients	American
115 g/4 oz	plain (all-purpose) flour	1 cup
pinch	salt and dry mustard powder	pinch
shake	freshly ground black pepper	shake
85 g/3 oz	butter	⅜ cup
85 g/3 oz	Parmesan cheese	¾ cup when grated
1	egg yolk	1
To glaze	1 egg white	

Sift the flour with the seasonings, then rub in the butter very carefully with the tips of your fingers: do not overhandle or the mixture will become sticky. Grate the cheese very finely, add to the flour mixture and bind with the egg yolk. If the mixture seems too soft to roll out, cover and chill in the refrigerator for at least 30 minutes.

Meanwhile, preheat the oven to 220°C/425°F/gas mark 7 (200°C/400°F/gas mark 6 if your oven is fan-heated or rather fierce). Thoroughly grease two baking sheets or line with baking parchment.

Roll out the dough on a lightly floured surface until just over 6 mm/¼ inch thick. Cut into fingers 6 mm/¼ inch wide and 6.5 to 7.5 cm/2½ to 3 inches long. Place on the baking sheets and brush with the unbeaten egg white. Bake for 7 to 8 minutes, or until pale golden. Allow to cool on the baking sheets, then store in an airtight tin.

VARIATION

● **ECONOMICAL CHEESE STRAWS**
Use only 50 g/2 oz (¼ cup) butter or margarine and 50 g/2 oz (½ cup) grated Parmesan cheese. You will need a few drops of milk as well as the egg yolk to bind the biscuit dough. Bake as above, using the lower oven setting.

FREEZING: **Do not freeze.**

Oatmeal Biscuits

Cooking time: 15 minutes
Makes about 20

These lightly sweetened biscuits are excellent with fruit soups or cold soups. You will find the dough easier to mix with hot, rather than cold, water.

Metric/Imperial	Ingredients	American
225 g/8 oz	self-raising flour or plain (all-purpose) flour sifted with 2 teaspoons baking powder	2 cups
½ teaspoon	salt	½ teaspoon
115 g/4 oz	butter or margarine	½ cup
225 g/8 oz	medium oatmeal	1⅓ cups
2 tablespoons	golden (corn) syrup	2½ tablespoons
5 tablespoons	hot water, or as required	6¼ tablespoons

Preheat the oven to 160°C/325°F/gas mark 3. Thoroughly grease two baking sheets or line with baking parchment.

Sift the flour, or flour and baking powder, with the salt. Rub in the butter or margarine, add the oatmeal, then the syrup; stir well. Gradually pour a little of the hot water on to the ingredients; then stir briskly with a flat-bladed knife. Continue like this until the mixture binds together.

Turn the dough on to a lightly floured surface and roll firmly until about 6 mm/¼ inch thick. Cut into rounds or triangles and place on the baking sheets. Cook for 15 minutes, or until quite firm. Allow to cool on the baking sheets.

Store in an airtight tin, away from other biscuits, which soften an oatmeal mixture like this.

VARIATION

● OATCAKES

Omit the golden (corn) syrup from the main recipe, then bake as before. These traditional Scottish biscuits are generally cut into triangles.

FREEZING: **Do not freeze.**

Macaroons

Cooking time: 15 to 20 minutes
Makes 18 to 24

Small macaroon biscuits are a usual accompaniment to fruit soups in Scandinavia and Germany. The recipe below uses ground almonds, but you can substitute ground unblanched almonds or hazelnuts for a less sweet taste. For slightly sticky textured macaroons put a dish of water in the oven while they are baking.

Metric/Imperial	Ingredients	American
2	egg whites from small eggs	2
few drops	almond or ratafia essence	few drops
175 g/6 oz	caster sugar	¾ cup
150 g/5 oz	ground almonds	1¼ cups
about 1 teaspoon	rice flour or cornflour (cornstarch)	about 1 teaspoon
few sheets	rice paper, optional	few sheets
To decorate	blanched and flaked (slivered) almonds	

Preheat the oven to 180°C/350°F/gas mark 4, or 160°C/325°F/gas mark 3 if you have a fan oven. Whisk the egg whites until just frothy, add the essence, sugar and ground almonds and blend well. The mixture should be stiff enough to roll into 18 to 24 balls. If slightly sticky, add the rice flour or cornflour. Place the rice paper, if using, on the baking sheets, or grease and flour them or line with baking parchment.

Arrange the macaroons, allowing plenty of space between them, as they flatten and spread during cooking. Top each biscuit with a flaked (slivered) blanched almond and bake until golden. Lift off the sheets, or cut round the rice paper and allow to cool.

FREEZING: Macaroons do not keep well, except when frozen. Use within 3 months.

Home-made White Bread

Cooking time: 45 minutes
Makes 1 loaf and about 10 rolls

Nothing is better with soup than freshly baked bread, and this simple recipe really couldn't be easier. One sachet (envelope) of quick-acting yeast is generally correct for the amount of flour used below, but do check the instructions on the packet. The quantities below are sufficient to make a good-sized loaf and some rolls.

Metric/Imperial	Ingredients	American
675 g/1½ lb	strong (hard) flour	6 cups
1 teaspoon	salt	1 teaspoon
1 sachet	quick-acting dried yeast	1 envelope
40 g/1½ oz	butter or margarine, optional	3 tablespoons
450 ml/¾ pint	warm water	scant 2 cups

Sift the flour and salt into a large mixing bowl, add the yeast, then rub in the butter or margarine. It is not essential to use any fat but it does improve the flavour of the bread.

Blend with the warm water. (If you measure out half very hot water and half cold water, you will achieve just the right temperature.) Mix the dough, then turn out of the bowl on to a floured surface and knead until smooth.

Test for readiness by pressing the dough with a floured finger – if the impression stays, you must continue kneading; if the impression comes out the dough is sufficiently kneaded.

Check your yeast sachet (envelope). If it instructs you to prove the dough (allow it to rise) before shaping it, return it to a clean bowl, cover and leave in a warm place for about 1½ hours, or until just double in bulk. When ready, transfer to a floured surface and 'knock back' (knead) the dough, testing it as described above. Never overknead a yeast dough.

In some cases the sachet simply instructs you to knead the dough, form it into the desired shape and allow it to prove (rise).

It is a good idea to use about two-thirds of the dough to make a loaf and the rest to make rolls.

For bread: Grease a 900 g/2 lb loaf tin. Shape the dough to fit the tin: the easiest way to do this is to press the dough out neatly until it is three times the width of the tin and the same length. Fold the dough in three and fit into the tin with the fold underneath, thus giving a perfect top to the bread. Leave to prove for about 30 to 35 minutes, or until almost doubled in size.

For rolls: Grease a flat baking sheet and place the rolls on this. Allow to prove for about 15 minutes or until nearly doubled in size.

Preheat the oven to 220°C/425°F/gas mark 7 while the bread and rolls are proving. It is essential that the oven is well heated. Bake the rolls for 12 to 15 minutes and the loaf of bread for 45 minutes. To test if cooked, turn the bread out of the tin and knock on the bottom of the loaf – it should sound hollow.

If you want to make only the loaf, use 450 g/1 lb (4 cups) flour with 300 ml/½ pint (1¼ cups) liquid. Use slightly less dried yeast (but check packet instructions) and reduce the salt very slightly.

If using fresh yeast allow exactly 15 g/½ oz (2 cakes).

VARIATIONS
- If using fresh yeast, allow 20 g/¾ oz (3 cakes) for the amount of flour. Cream the yeast, then add the warm water and a sprinkling of flour, as described in Grissini (see page 321).

• BROWN BREAD
Follow the main recipe, but use half strong (hard) white flour and half strong (hard) wholemeal (wholewheat) flour. You will need 1 to 2 extra tablespoons (1¼ to 2½ tablespoons) extra liquid to produce the right texture.

• WHOLEMEAL (WHOLEWHEAT) BREAD
Follow the main recipe, but use wholemeal (wholewheat) flour instead of white flour. You will need more liquid to give the right texture to the dough and you will find the bread and rolls take a few minutes longer to cook.

Wholemeal (wholewheat) bread looks attractive if topped with rolled oats.

• MILK BREAD

This is a soft bread and better made with white flour, as described on page 317. Follow the main recipe but use warm milk instead of water. Form into a loaf and rolls, and proceed as instructed on page 318.

• OATMEAL BREAD

Use the recipe for white, brown or wholemeal (wholewheat) bread. Omit 115 g/4 oz (¼ lb) of the flour and substitute the same amount of oatmeal or rolled oats. Top the loaf with rolled oats before the final proving.

• RYE BREAD

Follow the recipe for white, brown or wholemeal (wholewheat) bread, but use one-third rye flour and two-thirds white flour.

• TREACLE BREAD

This dark, richly flavoured bread is surprisingly good with soup, especially those based on green vegetables.

Follow the recipes for white, brown or wholemeal (wholewheat) bread, but add 2 tablespoons (2½ tablespoons) black treacle (molasses) to the flour before adding the liquid. This means you will have to use slightly less water to achieve the right consistency.

• FRUIT BREAD

This is a good accompaniment to fruit soups and cold soups. Use the recipe for white, brown or wholemeal (wholewheat) bread and add up to 150 g/5 oz (1 scant cup) mixed dried fruit.

Diced tenderized apricots give a delicious flavour to the bread.

FREEZING: All these breads freeze well. Use within 3 months for the best flavour.

• FRENCH BREAD

Good French bread depends upon having the right flour. As this is not readily available in the UK, you will get the best result if you allow 400 g/14 oz (3½ cups) flour and 50 g/2 oz (½ cup) cornflour (cornstarch) instead of 450 g/1 lb (4 cups) flour to make several loaves.

To give a light texture I find it essential to prove the dough twice, 'knocking it back' after the first proving. Form it into several long batons (baguettes). Make light diagonal slashes along the top surface, place on lightly greased baking sheets and allow to prove again until almost doubled in size. Bake for 25 to 30 minutes in a preheated oven set to 220°C/425°F/gas mark 7.

FREEZING: French bread freezes less well than most breads as the crust is inclined to break away. It happens less if the extreme ends of each loaf are removed.

Bran Loaf

Cooking time: 30 to 35 minutes
Makes 1 loaf

This loaf has an excellent flavour and texture, and combines particularly well with vegetable soups. Serve fingers of it with butter and cream cheese as toppings.

Metric/Imperial	Ingredients	American
350 g/12 oz	self-raising flour or plain (all-purpose) flour sifted with 3 teaspoons baking powder	3 cups
½ teaspoon	salt	½ teaspoon
115 g/4 oz	butter	½ cup
25 g/1 oz	bran	¼ cup
25 g/1 oz	sugar	2 tablespoons
225 ml/7½ fl oz	milk	scant 1 cup

Preheat the oven to 200°C/400°F/gas mark 6. Grease a flat baking sheet.

Sift the flour or flour and baking powder with the salt, rub in the butter, then add the bran, sugar and milk to bind. Turn out on to a lightly floured surface, knead lightly, then pat or roll out to form an 18 cm/7 inch round.

Place on the baking sheet and lightly mark into 8 portions. Bake for 30 to 35 minutes until firm and golden brown. Place on a wire rack to cool.

VARIATIONS

● **WHOLEMEAL BRAN LOAF**

Use half plain (all-purpose) white and half wholemeal (wholewheat) flour, plus a little extra milk to bind. This mixture of flours can be used in the variations below.

● **CHEESE AND HERB BRAN LOAF**

Omit the sugar in the main recipe, and sift a good shake of cayenne pepper and dry mustard powder with the flour. Rub in only 85 g/3 oz (⅜ cup) butter, then add 85 g/3 oz (¾ cup) finely grated cheese with 1 tablespoon (1¼ tablespoons) chopped parsley. Mix and bake as before.

● **FRUIT AND NUT BRAN LOAF**

Follow the main recipe, but add 50 g/2 oz (½ cup) chopped walnuts and 115 g/4 oz (good ¾ cup) raisins. Mix and bake as before.

FREEZING: All these breads freeze well. Use within 3 months.

Grissini

Cooking time: 30 minutes
Makes 30

Breadsticks are a feature of many restaurants, and a great Italian favourite. They make an excellent accompaniment to soups.

Metric/Imperial	Ingredients	American
15 g/½ oz	fresh yeast	½ cake
300 ml/½ pint	milk	1¼ cups
450 g/1 lb	strong (hard) flour	4 cups
1 teaspoon	salt	1 teaspoon
1 teaspoon	sugar	1 teaspoon
25 g/1 oz	butter or margarine	2 tablespoons
To glaze	little milk	

Cream the yeast in a basin, warm the milk until tepid (blood heat), pour over the yeast and sprinkle a little of the flour on top of the liquid. Leave for 10 minutes or until the surface is covered with bubbles. Sift the flour and salt into a mixing bowl, add the sugar, then rub in the butter or margarine. Add the yeast liquid and mix thoroughly.

Turn the dough on to a floured surface and knead until smooth. Return to a clean bowl, then cover and leave in a warm place for about 45 minutes to 1 hour, or until the dough has doubled in size. Knead again and cut into about 30 portions. Roll each piece until it measures about 25 to 30 cm/10 to 12 inches in length and is about the thickness of a woman's little finger.

Lightly grease baking sheets or cover them with baking parchment. Add the breadsticks and brush with a little milk. Leave to prove (rise) for 20 minutes.

Meanwhile, preheat the oven to 180°C/350°F/gas mark 4. Bake the sticks for 30 minutes.

VARIATION

- Use quick-acting dried yeast, mix into the dry ingredients and continue as instructed in White Bread (see page 317).

FREEZING: The sticks do not freeze well; the outer crust seems to break away. Store in an airtight tin, away from soft bread.

Garlic Bread

Cooking time: 10 to 15 minutes
Serves 4 to 6

This is one of the nicest accompaniments to hot soup and takes just a matter of minutes to prepare.

Metric/Imperial	Ingredients	American
1	long French loaf (baguette) (see page 319)	1
For the filling		
85 g/3 oz	butter	⅜ cup
2 to 3	garlic cloves, to taste	2 to 3
little	salt	little

Preheat the oven to 200°C/400°F/gas mark 6. Make several slits in the loaf at regular intervals, but do not cut right the way through.

Cream the butter. Peel and crush the garlic cloves. Blend the garlic with the butter, then insert in the slits in the loaf. Wrap in foil and place in the oven for 10 minutes. If you want a crustier finish, leave unwrapped and heat for 15 minutes.

VARIATIONS

- **ANCHOVY BREAD**

Blend the 85 g/3 oz (⅜ cup) butter with 1 teaspoon anchovy essence or several finely chopped anchovies. Insert into the loaf and bake as above.

- **GARLIC CHEESE BREAD**

Blend 50 g/2 oz (¼ cup) butter, 50 g/2 oz (½ cup) grated Gruyère or other cheese with the crushed garlic. Insert into the loaf and bake as above.

● **SAVOURY CREAM CHEESE BREAD**

Mix approximately 100 g/4 oz (½ cup) cream cheese with 1 tablespoon (1¼ tablespoons) chopped gherkins, 2 teaspoons chopped capers and 1 tablespoon (1¼ tablespoons) chopped parsley. Insert into the loaf and bake as on page 322.

● **TOMATO BUTTER**

Blend 85 g/3 oz (⅜ cup) butter with 1 to 2 tablespoons (1¼ to 2½ tablespoons) tomato purée (paste). Insert into the loaf and bake as above.

QUICK TIP *The filled bread can be heated for approximately 1½ minutes on defrost setting in the microwave. Using a higher setting makes the bread hard.*

FREEZING: All except the garlic filling freeze well. Do not freeze the filled and baked loaf.

Irish Soda Bread

Cooking time: 30 minutes
Makes 1 loaf

As this bread requires no yeast, it is quickly and easily made. Always ensure the oven is thoroughly preheated before baking the loaf.

Metric/Imperial	Ingredients	American
450 g/1 lb	plain (all-purpose) flour	4 cups
½ to 1 teaspoon	salt	½ to 1 teaspoon
½ teaspoon	bicarbonate of soda (baking soda)	½ teaspoon
1 teaspoon	cream of tartar	1 teaspoon
300 ml/½ pint	milk, preferably skimmed	1¼ cups

Preheat the oven to 220°C/425°F/gas mark 7 or to 200°C/400°F/gas mark 6 if fan-heated or rather fierce.

Sift the flour, salt, bicarbonate of soda and cream of tartar. Gradually add the milk to make a soft dough. Knead until smooth, then turn on to a lightly floured surface and form into a round loaf approximately 3.5 cm/

1½ inches thick. Mark into 4 or 6 'farls' (segments). Do not cut right through the loaf.

Place on an ungreased baking sheet and bake for 30 minutes or until golden and firm. Check towards the end of the baking time and lower the heat slightly if necessary.

This bread should be served soft, so wrap it in a cloth while still hot. Slice in the usual way.

VARIATIONS

- To make segments sufficiently small to serve individually, mark the loaf into 8 to 10 farls and pull them apart as required.
- Use buttermilk instead of ordinary milk and reduce the cream of tartar to ½ teaspoon.

- **WHOLEMEAL SODA BREAD**

Use wholemeal (wholewheat) flour instead of white, or use half and half of each. Follow the main recipe, but use a little more milk to form the right consistency.

FREEZING: These breads freeze well. Use within 3 months.

Sweet Muffins

Cooking time: 20 to 25 minutes
Makes about 18

The slightly sweet flavour of these muffins makes them a good accompaniment to fruit soups. All muffins should be freshly baked and preferably served while still warm. Do not overheat the mixture or the texture will be heavy.

Metric/Imperial	Ingredients	American
225 g/8 oz	self-raising flour or plain (all-purpose) flour sifted with 2 teaspoons baking powder	2 cups
good pinch	salt, or to taste	good pinch
50 g/2 oz	caster sugar, or to taste	¼ cup
2	eggs	2
50 g/2 oz	butter	¼ cup
175 ml/6 fl oz	milk	¾ cup

Preheat the oven to 200°C/400°F/gas mark 6, or 190°C/375°F/gas mark 5 if you have a fan oven. Thoroughly grease small patty tins or muffin pans.

Sift the flour, or flour and baking powder, with the salt. Add the sugar. Beat the eggs in a separate basin. Melt the butter. Mix the milk with the eggs, then add the melted butter. Stir gently but thoroughly into the dry ingredients.

Spoon into the prepared tins and bake until well risen and firm. Allow to cool in the tins for 5 minutes before removing.

VARIATIONS
- **For more economical muffins**, use only 25 g/1 oz (2 tablespoons) melted butter.

- FRUIT MUFFINS
Add 2 tablespoons (2½ tablespoons) chopped nuts and 3 tablespoons (3¾ tablespoons) dried fruit, such as raisins or finely chopped tenderized dried apricots, to the sifted flour mixture. Mix well, then add the egg mixture. Bake as above.

● **WHOLEMEAL MUFFINS**

Use half white and half wholemeal (wholewheat) flour, following the proportions in the main recipe, but add 1 tablespoon (1¼ tablespoons) extra milk as wholemeal flour absorbs more liquid.

The recipes on page 325 can also be made with this mixture of flours.

FREEZING: As muffins do not keep well, it is a good idea to freeze the surplus and reheat them for a very short time just before they are needed. Allow 2 or 3 minutes in a preheated oven set to 200°C/400°F/gas mark 6.

If using a microwave, warm 2 muffins for about 30 seconds on defrost. A larger number of muffins will take a little longer.

Bacon Muffins

Cooking time: 25 to 30 minutes
Makes about 18

These savoury muffins go well with many different kinds of soup.

Metric/Imperial	Ingredients	American
100 g/4 oz	bacon rashers, weight when derinded, cooked and chopped	¼ lb slices
225 g/8 oz	self-raising flour or plain (all-purpose) flour sifted with 2 teaspoons baking powder	2 cups
pinch	salt	pinch
to taste	freshly ground black pepper	to taste
25 g/1 oz	butter	2 tablespoons
2	eggs	2
150 ml/¼ pint	milk	⅔ cup

Preheat the oven to 200°C/400°F/gas mark 6, or 190°C/375°F/gas mark 5 if you have a fan oven. Grease small patty tins or muffin pans.

Derind the bacon and grill, or cook in the oven or microwave until crisp. Drain on kitchen paper, then chop finely; weigh to ensure you have the right amount. Allow to become completely cold.

Sift the flour, or flour and baking powder, with the salt and pepper. Melt the butter. Beat the eggs, add the milk and then the melted butter. Mix the bacon with the flour, then stir in the egg mixture.

Spoon into the prepared tins and bake until well risen and firm. Allow to cool in the tins for 5 minutes, then remove and serve.

VARIATION

● **CHEESE MUFFINS**
Follow the main recipe, but omit the bacon. Finely grate enough Cheddar or other firm cheese to give 75 g/3 oz (½ cup). Sift the flour, or flour and baking powder, with the salt, pepper and ¼ teaspoon dry mustard powder. Add the cheese and mix with the flour. Stir the egg mixture into the dry ingredients and bake as before.

FREEZING: See Sweet Muffins on page 326.

Herb Scones

Cooking time: 10 to 12 minutes
Makes 12 to 14

Freshly baked savoury scones make a good accompaniment to soups, particularly vegetable soups. As they freeze well, it is worth making a large batch at one time. The dough should be slightly sticky and the scones should be baked as quickly as possible after preparation.

Metric/Imperial	Ingredients	American
225 g/8 oz	self-raising flour or plain (all-purpose) flour sifted with 2 teaspoons baking powder	2 cups
pinch	salt and/or celery salt	pinch
40 g/1½ oz	butter or margarine	3 tablespoons
1 tablespoon	finely chopped parsley	1¼ tablespoons
1 tablespoon	finely chopped chives	1¼ tablespoons
150 ml/¼ pint	milk	⅔ cup
To glaze	1 egg or a little milk	

Preheat the oven to 220°C/425°F/gas mark 7.

Sift the flour, or flour and baking powder, with the salt(s). Rub in the butter or margarine, then add the herbs and enough milk to make a soft rolling consistency. Roll or pat out on a lightly floured board until just under 2 cm/¾ inch thick. Cut into rounds or triangles. Brush the tops with beaten egg or milk to give a pleasing shine.

Place on an ungreased baking sheet and bake for 10 to 12 minutes.

Test if cooked by pressing the side of one scone: it should feel firm. Transfer to a wire tray to cool. Cover with a teacloth to keep the outside of the scones soft.

VARIATIONS

- Vary the herbs, use a mixture of parsley, chives, tarragon and thyme to give a total of 2 tablespoons (2½ tablespoons).

- **CHEESE SCONES**

Use only 25 g/1 oz (2 tablespoons) butter or margarine in the main recipe. Omit the herbs. Sift a shake of freshly ground white or cayenne pepper and ½ teaspoon dry mustard powder with the flower and salt. Add 50 g/2 oz (½ cup) finely grated Cheddar, Cheshire, Gruyère or Lancashire cheese. Bind the mixture with milk as main recipe, or with a beaten egg and enough milk to make a soft rolling consistency.

Glaze the tops of the scones before baking with beaten egg or milk and cover with a little extra finely grated cheese.

These scones are better baked slightly more slowly, so preheat the oven to 200°C/400°F/gas mark 6 and allow 12 to 14 minutes' baking time.

- **CHEESE, DATE AND WALNUT SCONES**

Follow the recipe for Cheese Scones, but add 50 g/2 oz (good ¼ cup) finely chopped dates and 50 g/2 oz (½ cup) chopped walnuts to the flour.

- **OATMEAL SCONES**

Use any of the recipes above, but omit 50 g/2 oz (½ cup) flour and add the same amount of rolled (porridge) oats. You will need to add an extra ½ teaspoon baking powder, even with self-raising flour.

Brush the tops of the scones with a little milk and sprinkle with a light dusting of rolled oats before baking.

- **TOMATO SCONES**

Follow the main recipe, but use only 1 teaspoon of each of the herbs. Mix with tomato juice instead of milk, or dissolve 2 teaspoons tomato purée (paste) in the milk and use this.

FREEZING: All these scones freeze well. If reheating in a microwave, use the defrost setting.

Orange and Banana Bread

Cooking time: 1 to 1¼ hours
Makes 1 loaf

The combination of bananas with orange zest and juice makes a delicious loaf that keeps moist for several days. It is ideal to serve with fruit soups, but also makes a good accompaniment to chicken soups and certain vegetable soups.

Metric/Imperial	Ingredients	American
225 g/8 oz	self-raising flour or plain (all-purpose) flour sifted with 2 teaspoons baking powder	2 cups
pinch	salt	pinch
115 g/4 oz	butter or margarine	½ cup
85 g/3 oz	light brown sugar	⅜ cup
2 teaspoons	finely grated orange zest	2 teaspoons
85 g/3 oz	raisins	good ½ cup
1	egg	1
3 tablespoons	orange juice	3¾ tablespoons
2 medium	ripe bananas (approximately 350 g/12 oz before being peeled)	2 medium (approximately ¾ lb)

Preheat the oven to 180°C/350°F/gas mark 4, or 160°C/325°F/gas mark 3 if you have a fan oven. Grease and flour a 900 g/2 lb loaf tin.

Sift the flour, or flour and baking powder, with the salt into a mixing bowl. Rub in the butter or margarine, then add the sugar, orange zest and raisins.

Beat the egg, add the orange juice, then pour into the dry ingredients. Peel and mash the bananas until smooth; add to the flour mixture. Stir briskly until thoroughly combined, then spoon into the prepared tin and bake for 1 to 1¼ hours or until firm to the touch.

Cool in the tin for 10 minutes, then turn out on to a wire rack. When completely cold, wrap in foil or place in an airtight tin, away from other breads. Store in a cool place. Use within 4 days.

VARIATIONS

● LEMON AND BANANA LOAF

Follow the main recipe, but use 2 teaspoons finely grated lemon zest instead of orange zest. Substitute 1 tablespoon (1¼ tablespoons) lemon juice plus 2 tablespoons (2½ tablespoons) milk for the orange juice. Bake as before.

● WALNUT BANANA BREAD

Omit the orange or lemon zest and juice. Add 4 tablespoons (5 tablespoons) chopped walnuts to the ingredients and mix the loaf with 3 tablespoons (3¾ tablespoons) milk. Bake as before.

FREEZING: All these loaves freeze well. Use within 3 months.

PUT IT RIGHT

Q What can be done if a soup has been over-salted?

A Add a little cream or milk. If this makes the soup too thin, mix a little milk with flour or cornflour (cornstarch), as suggested on page 8, add to the soup and stir over the heat until thickened to the correct consistency.

An egg or eggs can also help to counteract saltiness. Beat the egg(s) with a little cold liquid, add several ladlesful of hot soup, tip into the pan and cook slowly, stirring or whisking all the time.

A combination of egg(s) and cream can work miracles in reducing a salty taste.

Another alternative is to add raw potato. If time permits, peel and dice the potato. If the soup is already cooked and time is short, peel and grate at least one good-sized potato, add to the other ingredients and cook for a time, then taste.

Yet another alternative is to add rice or pasta to the soup, as both of these will absorb some of the salt.

Q Are there any last-minute additions to improve the flavour of a soup?

A Yes, there are many, some of which are listed below.

Herbs: add a fairly generous amount of freshly chopped herbs (see pages 20 to 22) or dried herbs.

Spices: stir in ground spice (see pages 23 to 24).

Seasonings: add more salt and pepper. These condiments help to bring out the taste if used judiciously.

Add other seasonings, such as celery salt, garlic salt and mustard. (If using powdered mustard, mix it with a little water, wine or milk if adding to a ready-cooked soup.) Many excellent mustards are now available.

Sauces: soy sauce is extremely good in many soups, but add carefully so that it does not overwhelm the flavour and colour.

Worcestershire sauce is a good addition to fish, meat and poultry soups.

Tabasco sauce is made from hot peppers and adds a real kick to many dishes. Use only a few drops.

Flavourings: tomato ketchup, tomato purée (paste) or sun-dried tomatoes add instant flavour.

Lemon or orange juice adds a refreshing taste.

Sherry or other alcohol immediately gives more flavour.

Q What causes soup to curdle and how can it be rectified?

A Soups curdle when they have been overheated, particularly if they contain an acid ingredient such as wine or lemon juice plus eggs and/ or cream or milk. Always heat such mixtures with great care and do not allow to reach boiling point.

If soup has curdled, try one or more of the following techniques to rectify it.

- Whisk briskly with a hand whisk, preferably a balloon type.
- Liquidize the ingredients; this generally produces a smooth texture.
- Strain the soup through a sieve, but do not rub it through if you want to leave the curdled lumps behind.

After liquidizing, you will find that the soup appears somewhat thinner. Do not try to thicken it: just heat it *very gently* or, if suitable, serve as a cold soup.

Sieving also makes the soup considerably thinner; simply reheat it *very gently* and serve topped with whipped cream, cream cheese or thick yoghurt, or serve it cold.

QUICK SOUPS

Nowadays most of us seem to be short of time and are looking for tasty dishes that do not need prolonged cooking. Chapter Two is devoted to quickly made soups, but there are many others in the book that you might like to try. A complete list appears below.

With any soup you can save time by using stock cubes instead of fresh stock. You can also speed up the cooking time by using a microwave or pressure cooker (see page 6).

SOUPS MAKE A MEAL

Many soups contain enough satisfying ingredients to serve them as a satisfying main dish. If followed by a salad and fruit or a light dessert, you produce a well-balanced meal.

To make a soup more sustaining, try the following.

- Serve with good bread or other accompaniments (see pages 312 to 331).
- Add grated cheese, dumplings (see pages 308 to 310) or other satisfying garnishes (see pages 301 to 307).
- Most soups in this book serve 4 to 6 as a first course. If serving as a main dish, serve more generous portions.

The most suitable soups to serve as a main dish are listed below.

Soups	Pages
Soups made with Pulses – Chapter 4	169 to 179
Fish Soups – Chapter 5	180 to 213
Meat Soups – Chapter 6	214 to 235
Poultry and Game Soups – Chapter 7	236 to 261
Arbroath Smokie Broth	42 to 43
Crab Soups	185 to 189
Salmon and Ginger Soup	46
Seafood Bisques	16 and 47
Beef and Liver Soup	50
Beef, Potato and Mushroom Soup	51
Chicken Broth (increase the amount of chicken)	53
Oriental Chicken Soup (increase the amount of chicken)	54
Chicken and Bacon Chowder	56
Golden Cheddar Soup	60
Pasta and Cheese Soup	62
Chicken Quenelles	95 to 96
Beansprout Soup	103 to 104
Corn Chowder	114 to 115
Minestrone	131 to 132
Cheddar and Potato Chowder	167 to 168
Mussel Cream Soup	195 to 196

SOUPS FOR SLIMMERS

If you are slimming, or trying to keep your weight down, soups can form a useful part of your diet, as they can be both sustaining and filling. To make them suitable for well-balanced slimming diet:

Have smaller portions. Most recipes in this book make 4 to 6 servings, so allow yourself one-sixth of the total amount, unless serving the soups as a main dish.

- Where 50 g/2 oz (½ cup) of fat is specified in the recipe, reduce to 25 g/ 1 oz (2 tablespoons). This is quite feasible, particularly if cooking the soup in a microwave or non-stick pan.
- Use semi-skimmed milk where full-cream milk is specified.
- Substitute fromage frais or low-fat yoghurt for cream or full-fat yoghurt in the recipes. remember that all these ingredients must be heated carefully and not allowed to boil or the soup will curdle.

The following are the best soups for slimmers:

SOUPS FOR VEGETARIANS

Many soups in this book are suitable for vegetarians, or can be easily adapted for them.

- Replace chicken or other meat stocks with vegetable stock (see page 15), or use water and a vegetable stock cube or a little yeast extract.
- Be slightly more generous with ingredients such as onions, garlic and herbs to compensate for not having the relatively strong taste of a meat stock.
- Use a vegetarian cheese as a topping.
- Use vegetarian suet in the recipe for Dumplings (see pages 308 to 309).
- Margarine or a vegetable oil can replace the butter in recipes, and soya milk (see page 29) can replace ordinary milk.
- Use agar-agar wherever gelatine is specified; follow the directions on the packet.

The following recipes will be of particular interest to vegetarians:

INDEX